Management Education and the Rise of Uncertainty of Global Business

Management Education and the Rise of Uncertainty of Global Business

Edited by Eric Cornuel

OXFORD
UNIVERSITY PRESS

OXFORD
UNIVERSITY PRESS

Oxford University Press is a department of the University of Oxford.
It furthers the University's objective of excellence in research, scholarship,
and education by publishing worldwide. Oxford is a registered trade mark of
Oxford University Press in the UK and in certain other countries.

Published in the United States of America by Oxford University Press
198 Madison Avenue, New York, NY 10016, United States of America.

Library of Congress Cataloging-in-Publication Data
Names: Cornuel, Eric author
Title: Management education and the rise of uncertainty of
global business / Eric Cornuel.
Description: New York, NY : Oxford University Press, [2025] |
Includes bibliographical references and index.
Identifiers: LCCN 2025028900 (print) | LCCN 2025028901 (ebook) |
ISBN 9780197794449 hardback | ISBN 9780197794456 epub | ISBN 9780197794470
Subjects: LCSH: Management—Study and teaching |
Business | Business education
Classification: LCC HD30.4 .C68 2025 (print) | LCC HD30.4 (ebook) |
DDC 658.4/07124—dc23/eng/20250922
LC record available at https://lccn.loc.gov/2025028900
LC ebook record available at https://lccn.loc.gov/2025028901

DOI: 10.1093/9780197794470.001.0001

The manufacturer's authorized representative in the EU for product safety is
Oxford University Press España S.A. of Parque Empresarial San Fernando de Henares,
Avenida de Castilla, 2 – 28830 Madrid (www.oup.es/en or product.safety@oup.com).
OUP España S.A. also acts as importer into Spain of products made by the manufacturer.

CONTENTS

Contributors *vii*

Introduction: Management Education and the Rise of Uncertainty of Global Business *1*
Eric Cornuel

1. Educating for Uncertainty Management: The Meaning of History and the Principle of Complexity *6*
Eric Cornuel

2. The Changing Contours of Faculty Internationalization in European Business Schools: Strategic Implications and Opportunities for Business School Leaders *20*
Ansgar Richter and Wilfred Mijnhardt

3. Shaping Perspectives: The Impact of the Pandemic on the Evolution of Internationalization at Home in Higher Education Institutions *40*
Catherine Pereira-Villa

4. Locally Relevant, Globally Inspired: What 'Glocal' Means for a Business School *58*
Marion Debruyne

5. US MBA Programmes: Clearing the Runway for Global Business Leaders *66*
Isabelle Bajeux-Besnainou and Oliver Hahl

6. Navigating Change: The Impact of the COVID-19 Pandemic on the Internationalization Strategies of Business Schools *83*
Adriana Kudrnova Lovera, Rita Ribeiro and Sofia Salgado Pinto

7. Finding Strategic Balance: Protecting Global and Local Legitimacy within an Internationalization Agenda *108*
Robina Xavier

8. Creating Strong Innovation Ecosystems: How TUM Campus Heilbronn Is Driving Applied AI in Europe *121*
Gunther Friedl

9. Business Schools and a New Global World: Will They Never Walk Alone? *136*
Stefano Caselli

10. A Peregrination in China Europe Business Education: Revisiting Internationalization and Management at CEIBS *149*
Frank Bournois and Hong Wang

11. Overcoming Particularism: Universalistic Management Education and the Rise of Uncertainty *165*
Pierre Kletz

12. Inclusive Internationalization: Discovering the New World of Management Education *180*
Ian Fenwick

13. Academic Institutions and Peacebuilding *195*
EloÏc-Anil Peyrache

Index *214*

CONTRIBUTORS

Isabelle Bajeux-Besnainou, Dean and Richard P. Simmons Professor of Finance, Tepper School of Business, Carnegie Mellon University, United States

Frank Bournois, Vice President and Dean, CEIBS, China

Stefano Caselli, Dean, SDA Bocconi School of Management, Italy

Eric Cornuel, President, EFMD Global, Belgium

Marion Debruyne, Dean, Vlerick Business School, Belgium

Ian Fenwick, Director, Sasin School of Management, Chulalongkorn University, Thailand

Gunther Friedl, Dean, TUM School of Management, Technical University of Munich, Germany

Oliver Hahl, Associate Dean, Undergraduate Programs, Director of International Partnerships, and Associate Professor of Organization Theory, Strategy and Entrepreneurship, Tepper School of Business, Carnegie Mellon University, United States

Pierre Kletz, Professor, Ben-Gurion University of the Negev, Guilford Glazer Faculty of Business and Management, Israel

Adriana Kudrnova Lovera, Manager, EFMD Global, Belgium

Wilfred Mijnhardt, Policy Director General, Rotterdam School of Management Erasmus University, Netherlands

Catherine Pereira-Villa, Associate Professor and Dean, International School of Economic and Administrative Sciences, Universidad de La Sabana, Colombia

Eloïc-Anil Peyrache, Dean and General Director, HEC Paris, France

Rita Ribeiro, Assistant Professor, Católica Porto Business School, Universidade Católica Portuguesa, Portugal

Ansgar Richter, Vice President of Academic Affairs, Dean of Faculty Frankfurt School of Finance & Management, Germany

Sofia Salgado Pinto, Professor and Former Dean, Católica Porto Business School, Portugal

Hong Wang, President, CEIBS, China

Robina Xavier, Deputy Vice-Chancellor and Vice-President (Academic), QUT, Australia

INTRODUCTION
Management Education and the Rise of Uncertainty of Global Business

ERIC CORNUEL

Lionel Terray was one of the great mountaineers of the post-war period. He conquered, among many others, the summits of Jannu and Makalu in the Himalayas, and Chacraraju Este and Fitz Roy in South America; above all, he made numerous first ascents.

However, in his book *Les Conquérants de l'inutile* (*The Conquerors of the Useless)*, Terray (1961) maintained that his most important role was that of mountain guide in his home region of Savoie, assisting both amateur and experienced mountaineers on routes and summits commonly climbed in the Alps. He explained that although conquering world-famous summits was important, this supposed importance made him a 'conqueror of the useless'. He felt that his other mission was at least as important, which was to ensure that known and frequented mountain routes did not become dangerous and that they were always welcoming and practical, for use by all.

He maintained that conquering new peaks with a few other prominent mountaineers was a galvanizing goal, but that contributing to the ability of a greater number of people being able to climb the known peaks was more important. He added that the more common summits and routes can conceal formidable dangers and need to be constantly checked and their access improved. This potential danger may be different but is no less important than that faced by those attempting the most inaccessible summits.

He also insisted on the fact that while the most fabled peaks concern only a minority of explorers who assume the accepted risks, the most frequented

Eric Cornuel, *Management Education and the Rise of Uncertainty of Global Business*. In: *Management Education and the Rise of Uncertainty of Global Business*. Edited by: Eric Cornuel, Oxford University Press. DOI: 10.1093/9780197794470.003.0001 routes in the best-known regions can lead to disaster for a far greater number of people. Thus, as an elite mountaineer, he felt an enormous responsibility both for the maintenance and improvement of climbing routes and for the training of the many mountaineers less experienced than himself. Finally, he added that paths and places that are supposedly well known and that have been mastered by many in the past can often lead to inattentive and conformist behaviour by those tackling them in the present—whereas routes that are well-marked and maintained allow the mass of mountaineers to express their creativity in their approach to conquering a summit.

This clear-cut stance on the part of a post–World War II mountaineer resonates with the most pressing issues facing contemporary educators, especially in institutions such as business schools whose mission is to train elites.

It reminds us that in addition to the importance of opening up new avenues by undertaking avant-garde research, which may perhaps resemble 'a conquest of the useless', and by stimulating students to engage in innovative debate on unresolved questions, it is the responsibility of the educator to ensure that familiar issues, already widely debated, do not initiate conformism by dint of certain answers appearing to impose themselves in an obvious way.

Thus, we should not focus entirely on burning and emergent issues but also re-examine those that have already been extensively studied, both to prevent the introduction of false evidence as well as to check the imposition of conformism in the way these issues are approached. By revisiting these questions, creative answers to supposedly settled questions may arise.

The European Foundation for Management Development (EFMD) prides itself on being an innovative institution that conquers new roads and new heights: the creation of an evaluation system focused on the relationship between management education institutions and their territories; the training of deans, especially in institutions in the process of maturation, by their experienced peers constitutes a novel approach in the field of education. The recent launch of a research journal by a management education agency has been a challenging project but one that has fantastic potential to link academic research with the business world.

But a bit like Lionel Terray, the EFMD considers that it has a fundamental mission to readdress questions that have already been debated and which run the risk of getting mired in the conviction that their answers have been definitively established.

It is therefore with full knowledge of the facts that the EFMD has chosen to work on the theme of management education and the rise of uncertainty of global business, accepting the assertion that both the question of the relationship between management education and uncertainty, and that of the rise of uncertainty in global business, have already been widely examined. We were driven by the conviction that it is important to revisit the routes and to monitor the continuing relevance of the established approaches in this dynamic field.

In other words, it seemed to us that by adopting a comfortable conformism, current approaches to these issues would lose all relevance. It appeared to us that two major issues are in force, as detailed below.

A UNIVOCAL APPROACH TO UNCERTAINTY IN MANAGEMENT EDUCATION

In his book *The Great Transformation*, Karl Polanyi (1944) coined the term 'embeddedness' in economics and social science to indicate that in non-market societies economic activities are embedded in, and inseparable from, social institutions. He showed that liberal society had succeeded in disembedding economic activity from its social context; in market societies, economic activity had been rationalized and economic action 'disembedded' from society and capable of following its own distinct logic, paving the way for a scientific approach to the economy and a purely theoretical understanding of its evolution through the use of models.

This observation has multiple consequences that dissociate the field of economics from that of management. Indeed, it has been commonly accepted, since the work of Thomas S. Kuhn, that science progresses in a fundamentally discontinuous manner; that is, not by accumulation but by rupture (Kuhn 1962). The particular consequence of this thesis is to emphasise that paradigm shifts in science are long processes, even in situations of uncertainty.

On the other hand, management, even when taught in the best business schools, is by its very nature practical and technical, and therefore easily linked to the exchange of best practices between practitioners. In situations of uncertainty, and the dysfunctions it necessarily implies, a rhythm of change in practices is needed to test and then apply what works. Above all, the emergence of uncertainty leads to exchanges between actors who inform each other of ways to respond to the challenges posed by the consequences of uncertainty.

Thus, if management is much more reactive than economics to the challenges arising from uncertainty, there is also the supposition that uncertainty necessarily provides possibilities for improvement in management practices. This may explain why the claim that uncertainty is a source of opportunity has become received wisdom within the field of management education.

This largely dominant approach needs to be reconsidered. It too easily overlooks the fact that uncertainty can be a source of anxiety, discomfort, and indeterminacy. In addition, uncertainty gives rise to failure, something that is all too often neglected in management work, despite the fact that basic practice shows us that something that is accomplished without a hitch and implemented perfectly can become a source of failure simply because the person doing it has become aware of the risk involved. More prosaically, children who can ride a bicycle perfectly suddenly fall off when they think about the risk of falling off, or even just because they have looked down and seen themselves pedalling.

The contributions in this book seek to find a new balance regarding the uncertainty of global management, between both the opportunities and the difficulties it creates.

UNCERTAINTY ABOUT INSTITUTIONS AND THE ASSUMED PURSUIT OF GROWTH

Global business models are based both on a context of growth in the world economy and on the quest for growth within the companies in question, which is a source of profit. The models taught in business schools have long since moved beyond blissful optimism about growing companies in expanding economies. They have considered and taught the case of slowdowns in growth and economic recession, and also the cases of individual companies that are experiencing difficulties and moving away from growth. But they are largely devoted to ways of returning to growth, which is accepted as a conventional state of affairs.

This book, while offering analyses of the consequences of slowdowns in global business growth, also offers innovative analyses of the uncertainties induced by institutional change for global business lessons. Some of these works relate to the change induced by cyclical or structural crises (the COVID-19 pandemic, the reappearance of war in Europe, the emergence of political populism, the rise of protectionism, etc.) but others even go so far as to consider changes in social norms and the aspirations of company employees.

Finally, it should be stressed that to renew the reflection on the theme of management education and the rise of uncertainty of global business, this book is distinguished by the fact that all its contributors have developed a pertinent reflection on issues relating to management education and have long-term experience in this field as high-level leaders. They thus characterize the concept of the EFMD, which eschews tenuous and speculative approaches, in favour of a vibrant association between theory and practice—the only guarantee of delivering tangible impact in the sphere of management education.

REFERENCES

Kuhn, T. S. (1962). *The Structure of Scientific Revolutions*. Flammiron.

Polyani, K. (1944, 2nd ed. 2001). *The Great Transformation: The Political and Economic Origins of Our Time*. Beacon Press.

Terray, L. (1961). *The Conquerors of the Useless*. Gallimard.

1

Educating for Uncertainty Management

The Meaning of History and the Principle of Complexity

ERIC CORNUEL

Uncertainty is a disturbing notion for management education institutions because it emphasizes two of their most crucial missions: that of enabling students to form a clear representation of the future, sometimes characterized by the ambition to teach 'the meaning of history', and that of providing a holistic set of guidelines for students to orientate themselves, define their actions, and not be daunted by the rise of uncertainty.

This chapter is a reflection on renouncing this dual ambition. It is based on the abandonment of belief in the meaning of history and the recognition that the science of management cannot be an autonomous system for leadership. However, this is not tantamount to a renunciation of the possibility of educating students in the leadership and management of organizations. On the contrary, it proposes a reflection on the way in which management education can, through a multifaceted approach, seek to analyse the issue of complexity and how those in organizations can adapt and respond to this challenge, while also emphasizing the huge contribution of voluntarist approaches which take the view that nothing is written in stone when it comes to the development of companies, and everything is always to be developed (which amounts to maintaining that there is no meaning of history).

The response of management education to the rise of uncertainty in global business is an excellent example of how business schools need to undergo a process of change in order to move away from the kind of development that triumphant globalization brought into being, and to reinstate innovative approaches.

Eric Cornuel, *Educating for Uncertainty Management*. In: *Management Education and the Rise of Uncertainty of Global Business*. Edited by: Eric Cornuel, Oxford University Press. © Oxford University Press (2025).
DOI: 10.1093/9780197794470.003.0002

THE RISE OF UNCERTAINTY AS A TOTAL SOCIAL FACT

The title of this book, *Management Education and the Rise of Uncertainty of Global Business*, draws a parallel between a moral and professional imperative and a general trend: institutions and teachers in the management sphere need to prepare their students for developing a satisfactory career that makes a useful contribution to the institutions in which they will participate, in a context marked by rising uncertainty on a global scale.

However, a title such as *Management Education and the Rise of Uncertainty of Global Business* is problematic.

Indeed, the way it is formulated might seem to suggest that the rise in uncertainty is a phenomenon specific to global business. Insofar as nothing to do with business should be alien to the education provided in business schools, students should be taught how management can specifically respond to the rise of uncertainty. Therefore, management education would seek answers to the question of the rise of uncertainty within the specific corpus of management science.

But the rise of uncertainty does not only concern the sphere of business; it is a social phenomenon that needs to be examined, otherwise management science will become merely utilitarian and decontextualized. It is a question of recognizing that the rise of uncertainty is a total social fact with the scope to move an entire society in the sense of the concept coined by Marcel Mauss in his *Essay on the Gift* (Mauss, 2000). Management education must take a broad view and not limit itself to considering the rise of uncertainties solely within the management sphere.

Recent events allow us to back up our point: the COVID-19 crisis was a major crisis with implications for all sectors of society (e.g. health, economy, culture, tourism). We have shown elsewhere (Cornuel, 2022) how the generality of this event encouraged management science to step out of its comfort zone to tackle this phenomenon in a relevant way.

Moreover, the chain of consequences following the pandemic has shown us that uncertainty is on the rise in all areas, and so presenting students with answers to the rise of uncertainty in global business based purely on management science gives them an overly short-sighted vision preparing them poorly for their entry into social and corporate life.

The rise of uncertainty is a total social fact and cannot be accommodated by a fragmentary consideration that focuses on only one of its manifestations in a given sphere, namely business.

THE LIMITS OF A SCIENTIFIC APPROACH TO MANAGEMENT

The life of companies and their actors is profoundly impacted by the global evolution of societies, forcing changes and modifications in social behaviour both locally and globally. Management education institutions must include in their teaching the explicit statement that all social changes and crises are linked, and to try to make the connection in order to be able to reflect on uncertainty, which is its main characteristic. Thus, while the natural tendency would be to focus on the consequences of a crisis and the ways to deal with it, it is important to understand the genesis of uncertainty in the business sphere and on the systems that generate it, even if they are not directly related to management science.

For example, the COVID-19 crisis introduced uncertainty in the field of urban planning. For two centuries people had been converging towards cities; however, during and since the pandemic this flow has been reversed with people choosing to live and work away from major centres. There has also been a shift in the location of the manufacture of certain products, such as medicines and weapons, reverting to Western countries.

All this gives rise to great uncertainty that has nothing to do with the world of business administration, although with has necessary consequences for the business world. Therefore, it is important for management education institutions to enter spheres that would not be naturally associated with them in order to help understand and apprehend such uncertainties.

In the face of social uncertainty, Edgar Morin has shown the importance of constructing a global vision of society and of a return to humanism, an approach which is intrinsically linked to the progress of science but which does not elevate it to the rank of an end. He emphasizes that the rise of uncertainty must distance us from the conception of science 'as the repertoire of absolute truths, of irrefutable affirmations' (Morin, 1977; 1991; 1995; 2014).

Above all, there is no one-size-fits-all approach to the issue of rising uncertainty. Scientists put forward different and sometimes contradictory views regarding the measures to be taken at the level of society as a whole, as well as within discrete spheres of society—political, social, cultural, and more, with each sector having its own experts with their diverging, individual views. Management science is in exactly the same situation as the other social sciences—it cannot provide companies and business actors with specific and unambiguous recommendations.

The rise of uncertainty in business can be linked to that affecting other spheres of society, with the discussions between different sectors reinforcing the debate taught in management education. It is a question of acknowledging the complexity and turning away from the dogmatism induced by the adoption of a single specific response to a given field. Interdisciplinarity and the possible controversies which may arise are the best guarantees of appropriate responses. Thus, in the context of rising uncertainty, the theories, approaches, and methods of management taught in business schools should never be considered absolutes. Management science has nothing specific or original to offer regarding the question of uncertainty—not even on the question of uncertainty in management. Therefore, business schools have a duty to teach their students the relativity of the validity and reliability of the methods taught.

Management science has been built on the need for ever more certainties about the future, even if these are illusory or superficial. The mission of business schools was to teach their students certainties, so that in the workplace they could then profitably contribute to their companies. The big business schools conveyed the image that their graduates would become managers who were sure of themselves and quick to act, with the attitude that in the face of uncertainties it was best to accept and learn to live with them. To abandon the desire for established plans and overly confident convictions represents a major paradigm shift for management education. The idea that one would study in a business school to learn to doubt may seem strange and more likely in a faculty of philosophy, for example (where, among other things, Cartesian doubt is firmly established), or at a faculty of physical sciences (where the theory of relativity has moderated the more overly unequivocal tendencies).

FOR A TRANSDISCIPLINARY APPROACH TO UNCERTAINTY THROUGH EDUCATION MANAGEMENT

A title such as *Management Education and the Rise of Uncertainty of Global Business* carries another ambiguity that is important to remove: it should not propose the idea that management education has only recently started to face this type of challenge.

Indeed, organizations are subject to uncertainty due to their very act of functioning and inclusion in the social sphere. Developing a strategy and actions to deal with uncertainty is one of the fundamental missions of management. Thus, management education must train students the challenges this represents.

Far from being about a rise of uncertainty in the field of management from a zero level, the relevance of the questioning carried by the book's title is that the issue of uncertainty has risen beyond generally accepted standards, and now constitutes an imperative challenge deserving of specific consideration for which students must be prepared.

In such a situation, the message conveyed by the notion of complexity, as formalized by Edgar Morin, leads us to consider the question of whether this growing uncertainty comes from the specific functioning of companies or whether it is 'imported' into the business world from other social spheres, as fundamentally futile. Indeed, Morin's notion of complexity invites us to consider the matter from various perspectives and assumes that a subject such as this cannot be properly taken into account by a single system of analysis or paradigm but should be studied in all its causes, drivers, and consequences within the social field.

The mission or duty of management education in such a case is to awaken students to an understanding of complexity, and its causes and consequences, as a multidisciplinary phenomenon. This will lead to strengthening the teaching of the humanities as part of the business school curriculum. The general approach, proposed by Edgar Morin, consists in 'breaking with research, or the thesis that encloses its object. The slightest subject, even a seemingly tiny one, can only be known in and through its context' (Lecompte, 2018).[1]

Obviously, this approach represents a challenge in terms of management education.

Indeed, Morin insists on the fact that 'complex is that which cannot be summed up in a key word, that which cannot be reduced to a law, nor can it be reduced to a simple idea. Complexity is a problem word, not a solution word' (Morin, 2014). However, teaching in business schools often aspires to teaching simple ideas, which should allow future managers to make decisions and take action. In addition, the claim to the scientificity of the teachings leads to the search for the teaching of general laws which will prepare future managers to make coherent and rational actions. Agreeing to face a problem through the notion of complexity should not lead to abandoning this ambition but should allow managers to propose local and specific solutions, which may not necessarily be valid in all circumstances. This perspective is particularly appropriate when faced with uncertainty, the modalities of which can be understood through expressions such as an 'uncertain context' or 'an uncertain world'. These expressions remind us that uncertainty not only affects the precise place in which a manager acts but also impacts everywhere around him.

This approach is justified by the belief that 'any big or important problem is invisible from a closed discipline and requires a transdisciplinary approach' (Lecompte, 2018). This quotation shows that Edgar Morin does not claim to use a complex thinking approach, as well as the transdisciplinary approach that it implies, for all types of problems, but only when the subject studied acquires a certain importance either by its frequency or by its impact. He gives a particularly demonstrative illustration of this: 'I remember a thesis devoted to ministerial attachés, which described how they proceeded to identify urgent files. At first, they used a U stamp, which became TU [*trés urgent*], for "very urgent", then TTU [*trés trés urgent*], and so on. Put in context, the anecdote opened up a very interesting reflection on the increased chronometric pressure in our civilization' (Lecompte, 2018). Just as in this example, urgency is initially a problem for managers that can only be dealt with by management, and its intensification makes it a complex object. Uncertainty cannot be dealt with by management sciences alone but must be addressed in a transdisciplinary manner.

PRINCIPLES FOR EDUCATION IN MANAGING UNCERTAINTY THROUGH COMPLEXITY

Complex thinking does not lead to disembodied and ethereal approaches. It is essential to present its principles and guidelines and how they apply in terms of management education and the lessons it generates.

The Dialogic Principle

The refusal to consider that knowledge is compartmentalized and that fields are dissociated when they should be linked leads to teachings that combine the science of management with disparate elements from other scientific disciplines, interwoven in the same course.

It leads to the adoption of the 'dialogical' principle, which is driven by the idea that themes can be both complementary and antagonistic: 'The term dialogic means that two logics, two principles, are united without their duality being lost in this unity: hence the idea of uni-duality' (Morin, 1990, 276). Edgar Morin's classic example of the dialogic principle concerns European culture, a unity formed by the complementary antagonism of two competing cultures, one Judeo-Christian and the other Greco-Roman: 'Together, they form a complex unity, European culture, but in which their duality remains intact' (Morin, 1990, 276).

In the field of management education, this dialogical principle is perfectly embodied in the teaching of economics and finance, relating to the maximization of production and profit, on the one hand, with, on the other hand, those related to sustainability and corporate responsibility, which refer to the preservation of nature and resources through self-control. These two a priori antagonistic perspectives are found in the approach to social impact finance, defended, in particular, by Ronald Cohen (2007): dialogism is expressed by the fact that the principle of making a profit as well as that of preserving the environment and market conditions are two antagonistic but consubstantial principles for the functioning of the liberal economy. If, in later times, it is possible to understand and analyse companies using only the prism of microeconomics and management science, the increasing complexity of their functioning and the multiplication of interactions with other social spheres make it necessary to view them through complex thinking.

Refusal to Give Up in the Face of a Contradiction

It is now often peddled in management science that the whole is more than the sum of its parts. Lessons on systems and all interactionist approaches, but also seminars on decision-making as well as activities related to, for example, group dynamics have spread this idea, which is a matter of complex thinking. But it can also show that the whole is sometimes less than the sum of its parts, as Edgar Morin reminds us: 'In some organisations, we see that the system can inhibit qualities specific to its elements'. This state of affairs, which football fans have long since accepted (think of all teams made up of superstars but whose results are collectively mediocre), should be taught in business schools. From a theoretical point of view, Morin refers to the Greek philosopher Heraclitus to assert that 'when one arrives at a contradiction, this is not necessarily a sign of error, but it is a sign that we have touched on a fundamental problem. I believe that these contradictions must therefore, be affirmed, acknowledged and not evaded' (Lecompte, 2018). This statement has a more general scope in management sciences than in science or even in the social sciences. Indeed, in these two fields, this consideration is essentially a matter of research methodology; the primary purpose of management is to interact with people in organizations, and it focuses first and foremost on the real world. Thus, being faced with a contradiction should not be seen as a reason to give up but, on the contrary, to focus on solving a problem that it is rational to assume is important. As such, this type of approach has a firm place in the teaching of business schools (its scope in market finance and human resources is, for example, notable), reminding us that management education institutions have a responsibility to inculcate a holistic world view.

Educating to Deal with Difficult Situations

When it comes to attitudinal training, introducing complexity has important consequences for teaching in business schools. Indeed, it makes it possible to move away from an approach that only teaches what should to be done in certain situations and how one should arrive at the right decision before implementing the necessary action. Although not calling into question the fact that the objective is to teach students the right thing to do, it also takes into account that the sequence 'identification of the problem—implementation of an appropriate and desirable response' (Lecompte, 2018) applies to the simplest situations. However, by definition, managers often have to deal with delicate and sometimes deteriorating situations and may constantly run the risk of failure; their actions are implemented in situations marked by complexity. This is why teaching complexity makes it possible to integrate the study of ambiguous and difficult situations in which future managers may find themselves. It is not limited to teaching the right or wrong thing to do when things are going well, but to better understand the environments in which failure can occur in the hope that future managers will be able to steer their organizations away from it.

A report to UNESCO has examined the list of topics to be included in curricula from this perspective (Morin, 1999, 141). The questions addressed make a lot of sense for management education:

1. The blindness of knowledge: error and illusion;
2. The principles of relevant knowledge;
3. Teaching about the human condition;
4. Teaching Earth identity;
5. Dealing with uncertainty;
6. Teaching comprehension;
7. The ethics of the human race.

Educate to Evaluate Ongoing Processes and Stop Them If Necessary

Contemporary science has shown us that forecasting and planning must be relative with an element of fluidity. It is important to teach students that they should not expect to carefully orchestrate a sequence of events and expect them to be executed according to plan. However, this should not lead to the fear of embarking on erroneous projects which may be doomed to failure. We must ask ourselves certain questions that Edgar Morin rightly linked explicitly to globalization: 'Is the path we are going towards the right one? Isn't it dangerous? Do we have the ability to change it? . . . Such questions arise for me in relation to globalisation' (Lecompte, 2018). These questions show an alternative to the forecast-planning-execution sequence and also create the possibility of considering going back in the course of a process that has begun or even cancelling it along the way. They show that the path towards globalization should not be taken without the possibility of reversing or changing our choices. Thus, the rise of uncertainties implies that we can re-examine our choices or take a step backwards, which has enormous consequences in terms of management education.

THE CHANGE IN BUSINESS SCHOOLS BROUGHT ABOUT BY THE UNCERTAINTY OF GLOBAL BUSINESS

Understanding uncertainty as a total social fact existing beyond the business sector does not exempt the leaders of management education institutions from forging an image of future business.

Indeed, one of the most important responsibilities of business school leaders is to assess future trends in business and management education in order to prepare both the institutions they run and, crucially, through them, their students. To call for a transdisciplinary and complex approach to this process is not to accept a dilution of responsibility for this fundamental work. In this process, attention is paid to the apparently major underlying trends while also considering the phenomena of rapid transformation that can lead to erratic changes in this environment.

The globalization of business has undergone an evolution that would have been considered impossible 30 years ago, at a time when Francis Fukuyama (1992) was referring to the notion of the end of history in the 1990s. Complex thinking makes it possible to analyse the rise of uncertainty in global business, which puts it in parallel with many elements external to the business sphere: international relations that have become strained, such as the return of war in Europe, an increasingly unstable situation in the Middle East, intense tension in the South China Sea, and the re-emergence of inflation and economic protectionism. These changes have led us out of a period in which uncertainty had greatly diminished (a period of the 'end of history') and into a rise in uncertainty. It has caused a systemic change within business schools. Therefore, questions about how business schools are responding to this rise in uncertainty are relevant.

The internationalization of business schools has steadily evolved during the past 30 years; recently, however, this movement has become a phenomenon with developments that are difficult to predict. Business schools had forged a paradigm in terms of internationalization determined by the development of global business. It is now marked by uncertainty, making it necessary to analyse how business schools are responding to this new situation determined by social changes on a global scale.

Internationalization as a Fundamental Trend in Management Education

Over the past 30 years, internationalization has been seen as a determining factor in many areas of business school activity, complementing the progress of globalizations. It was manifested through greater diversity in classes thanks to the increased mobility of students; the development of international campuses and partnerships with foreign institutions; internships and consultancy projects in an international business environment; recruitment of international professors; and international research collaboration.

The Questioning of Internationalization During the COVID-19 Pandemic

The COVID-19 pandemic put an end to a 30-year trend in the internationalization of business schools—travel restrictions making it difficult for international students and faculty to travel to other countries. This has resulted in a decrease in the number of international students and has limited opportunities for international collaboration and exchange; partnerships between schools in different countries for study abroad and exchange programmes have been discontinued; and schools had to rapidly adopt and develop distance learning techniques, having consequences in all areas of pedagogy and didactics, most notably in the very different way of dealing with the diversity of students at a distance compared to face-to-face.

While the COVID-19 crisis has largely affected the internationalization process of business schools, a relevant question is whether this should be considered as a necessary parenthesis for the duration of the pandemic or whether, now the pandemic is over, the previous nature of internationalization will re-emerge.

New Trends in the Internationalization of Business Schools

It seems that the internationalization of business schools, which stalled in the period immediately after the pandemic, is now re-emerging but in often novel ways, of which we give some examples below:

- **Real-world issues:** Business schools are placing more emphasis on global issues such as sustainability, social responsibility, and entrepreneurship. This reflects a growing awareness of the importance of these issues in the global trade landscape.
- **Digital innovation:** Business schools are exploring new ways to use technology to improve the student experience and facilitate global collaboration. This includes the use of virtual reality and other immersive technologies, as well as social media and other digital platforms to connect students and teachers internationally.
- **Online and hybrid education:** Despite the end of the pandemic, online education has not diminished, and many business schools now offer online or hybrid programmes that can be accessed from anywhere in the world.
- **A focus on emerging markets:** Business schools are increasingly focusing on emerging markets, such as China, India, and Southeast Asia, which are experiencing rapid economic growth and have become major players in global business.

MANAGEMENT EDUCATION AND DETERMINISTIC APPROACHES

The world of academic research, like that of university teaching, sees a succession of concepts, approaches and practices which, once dominant, fall into disuse at a given moment.

The notion of the 'meaning of history' provides an excellent example of this phenomenon characterizing the movement of ideas and practices. Indeed, the conviction that objective causes determine developments in the political, economic, and social sectors was a dominant conception in the twentieth century, in particular during the period from the end of World War II to the 1990s.

Its origins go back a long way, with its foundation in the philosophy of the Enlightenment. As early as 1784, Kant stated 'the history of the human race as a whole can be regarded as the realization of a hidden plan of nature to bring about an internally—and for this purpose also externally—perfect political constitution' (Kant 1991).

Adherence to the notion of the meaning of history reached its most successful form in the following century in the work of Hegel, for whom history is guided by universal reason, which constitutes both the true driving force of history and its finality. History must be conceived as the progress of reason: 'universal history has developed rationally' (Hegel, 1953).

He thus paved the way for paradigms that sought the most essential determinants of historical evolution. This deterministic approach was pre-eminent at the end of World War II until the 1990s, in various conceptually advanced forms (structuralism, Marxism, Durkheimian and Bourdieusian approaches, etc.) leading to research approaches and methodologies and in practice, modes of education and teaching—the meaning of history was imposed independently of the conscious will of the actors.

In this context, paradigms which focused on freedom and the potential for change of actors vis-à-vis social systems were both in the minority and often viewed with condescension. This gives considerable importance to the radical reversal that took place in the last decade of the twentieth century, during which paradigms based on liberal, individualistic, and anti-deterministic approaches, supported by hitherto marginalized authors such as Karl Popper, Raymond Aron, and Leo Strauss, triumphed.

With hindsight it is easy to trace paradigmatic questioning, the reversals of theoretical perspectives, the changes in practices that crossed many academic fields, so profound has been the resulting upheaval.

The academic field of management, both in its research component and in its teaching, has been much less affected than most other academic fields by the abandonment of problems revolving around the search for long-term determinants of the organization of society. This is due to the fact that management and business administration had largely abstracted themselves from deterministic approaches even when they were dominant—issues of liberalism and 'anti-determinism' remained prevalent.

Indeed, management and business administration were too closely linked to questions of leadership, approaches to methodological individualism, and a tropism marked by economic liberalism, to refer to deterministic issues. It was much less a question of getting rid of determinism for management and business administration than for other fields, since it had hardly entered them, and has thus been spared the shock of the return of liberalism and methodological individualism affecting many other academic fields.

This state of affairs seemed to confirm the way in which business schools defined themselves. Indeed, business schools claim their pragmatism: it is a question of meeting the needs of companies and students instigated by the state of markets and society. When it came to management education, there seemed to be a consensus that the future is not determined or written anywhere. The expression 'rising uncertainty' is tautological; in a liberal and competitive economy uncertainty is necessarily inherent in the life of companies. In reality, the expression 'rising uncertainty' is improperly used in management, and it should more appropriately be called the 'rise of perils'.

CONCLUSION

The question of whether a pivot has occurred and whether we are at an inflection point in the internationalization of business schools is not just an academic question.

Indeed, it leads us to question, from a renewed perspective, the unanimity that has reigned in the world of management education for the last 30 years, calling into question the assumption that the world of business schools and management faculties is immune to the influence of the doctrine of the meaning of history. In many respects, it may seem that the world of management education has adhered to a dual determinism which is now being called into question. The assertion that companies were caught up in an endless and necessarily positive movement of internationalization, and therefore business schools had to accompany this process by internationalizing as quickly, and on as large a scale as possible, in order to fulfil their mission and establish themselves as institutions.

This is a crucial issue that goes far beyond being an academic one. Indeed, if we accept that their raison d'être is to prepare their students to make a career in business alongside providing companies with the management skills they need, it is reasonable to argue that they must be pragmatic and constantly attentive to changes in the economic world.

However, if the world of educational management has abandoned this attitude in the face of the phenomenon of internationalization, this calls for extreme caution with regard to new trends which are now appearing to dominate strategy, such as the need to define a vision, involvement in achieving a 'third mission', and taking into account the elements of the ERS. This attitude is also reflected in the fact that the management of the education sector has become more and more aware of the importance of the third mission. It calls for constant vigilance on the part of business schools, to be sure that these developments are indeed a response adapted to a given economic, social, and business situation and not a belief in the fact that they constitute a means of conforming to the meaning and direction of history.

NOTE

1. All translations in the text are done by the author.

REFERENCES

Cohen, R. (2007). *The Second Bounce of the Ball: Turning Risk into Opportunity*. Weidefeld & Nicolson.

Cornuel, E. (2022). *Business School Leadership and Crisis Exit Planning*. Cambridge University Press.
Fukuyama, F. (1989). 'The End of History'. *The National Interest*, 16 (Summer), 3–18.
Fukuyama, F. (1992). *The End of History and the Last Man*. Free Press.
Hegel, G. W. (1953). *Reason In History*. Bobbs-Merrill Company.
Kant, I. (1991). 'Idea for a Universal History with a Cosmopolitan Purpose'. In H. S. Reiss, ed., *Kant: Cambridge Texts in the History of Political Thought* (2nd ed.). Cambridge University Press, 41–53.
Lecompte, F. (2018). 'Edgar Morin ou l'éloge de la pensée complexe'. *Carnet de Science La Revue du CNRS*. Issue 4, Spring/Summer. https://lejournal.cnrs.fr/articles/edgar-morin-ou-leloge-de-la-pensee-complexe.
Mauss, M. (2000). *The Gift: Forms and Functions of Exchange in Archaic Societies*. Norton.
Morin, E. (1977). *La méthode 1, La nature de la nature*. Le Seuil.
Morin, E. (1990). *Science avec conscience*. Le Seuil.
Morin, E. (1991). *La méthode 4, Les idées*. Le Seuil.
Morin, E. (1995). *La méthode 5, Humanité de l'humanité*. Le Seuil.
Morin, E. (1999). *Les sept savoirs nécessaires à l'éducation du future*. UNESCO.
Morin, E. (2014). *Introduction a la pensée complexe*. Poche.

2

The Changing Contours of Faculty Internationalization in European Business Schools

Strategic Implications and Opportunities for Business School Leaders

ANSGAR RICHTER AND WILFRED MIJNHARDT

INTRODUCTION

Over the past 30 to 40 years, the academic labour market for faculty at leading business schools (B-schools) has become an increasingly international and competitive ecosystem (Baruch, 2013). Several factors have contributed to this development. First, changing student demographics and increasing mobility have meant that many B-schools have far more international student bodies than used to be the case. B-schools, in turn, have looked for faculty members who reflect the diversity of their students. Second, in an increasingly global research context, faculty with exposure to and experience in the global research environment—such as those with PhDs or other forms of research training from international institutions—have an advantage over those with more localized backgrounds (Finkelstein & Jones, 2019). More broadly speaking, the globalization of B-schools is a corollary to the increasing globalization of business, with companies operating across borders and cultures. International executives—and students aspiring to such roles—expect their teachers and mentors to serve as role models in terms of international experience. Following Engwall (2023), we define internationalization as the intentional process of integrating an international, intercultural, or global dimension into the purposes, functions, and delivery of post-secondary education, in order to

Ansgar Richter and Wilfred Mijnhardt, *The Changing Contours of Faculty Internationalization in European Business Schools*. In: *Management Education and the Rise of Uncertainty of Global Business*. Edited by: Eric Cornuel, Oxford University Press. © Oxford University Press (2025). DOI: 10.1093/9780197794470.003.0003 achieve intended academic, socio-cultural, economic, and/or political goals (Engwall, 2023, 204).

Many observers of the B-school world have welcomed this internationalization. The arguments underpinning this view include the conviction that international faculty bring new perspectives and insights to the classroom, which can help students to develop a broader understanding of global business. In this view, international faculty tend to be better able to prepare students for the globalized workforce than those with less international experience. Furthermore, internationalization is an important dimension of overall faculty diversity. Internationalization may be conducive to a more inclusive and welcoming classroom experience, where students can learn about different perspectives and ways of thinking. Faculty internationalization may help to break down stereotypes and prejudices and promote understanding and respect for different cultures. The internationalization of faculty has co-evolved together with the internationalization of other dimensions of business school development, in particular in terms of programme design and student demographics (see the contributions in Çaliokoĝlu et al., 2023 and in Fumasoli et al., 2015). Thus, faculty internationalization can be a powerful tool for promoting *interculturalization* in business schools.

However, in recent years, there has been a counter-development against the trend towards the increasing internationalization of B-school faculty (Trapczyński, 2016; Ding, 2022). There are a range of factors that have limited, decelerated or cast doubt on the belief that faculty internationalization would continue to rise. Among these factors are both external and internal ones. In terms of the former, in many countries there is growing scepticism against international students; and some countries have introduced rules that make recruitment of both international students and international staff more difficult, or the atmosphere for them less welcoming, than used to be the case. The COVID-19 pandemic in 2020–2021 created distinct pressures on international faculty members (Buckner et al., 2022) which have also led to a return of some foreign faculty members to their home countries. At the same time, internal factors are at play, too. Many B-schools have begun to pursue strategies that emphasize regional, entrepreneurial, and corporate engagement among faculty, and have integrated mechanisms to foster these activities in their recruitment, promotion, and retention policies. Though it may not have been the motivation of these new rules to reduce the attractiveness or feasibility for foreign faculty to pursue a career in a location outside their home countries, it may have been their unintended consequence. International faculty—in particular younger ones who have not built up the requisite connections, or who may not even speak the language of the host country—are often at a disadvantage in providing these more engagement-oriented activities, as compared to domestic staff. The same may hold with respect to more administrative and managerial activities, which may be harder to do for international faculty members than for domestic ones. Whereas in the past their very foreignness may have been an advantage for international faculty members in recruitment and promotion decisions, the liabilities associated with this foreignness (Zaheer, 1995) have begun to weigh more heavily.

Against the background of these conflicting trends, we address two questions in this chapter: First, what is the future of faculty internationalization in European B-schools? Will faculty internationalization continue to grow further in the years to come, or is the trend reversing? Indications are that the latter is the more likely outcome, as much as we would like to believe otherwise. At the same time, the barriers to faculty internationalization create incentives and opportunities for B-schools to develop focused, more convincing approaches in this area.

Second, amidst the emergence of new faculty models that reflect new priorities among B-schools, we discuss which strategies they can deploy in managing (i.e. attracting and recruiting, retaining and developing) international faculty, in order to ease the potential tensions between the dual objectives of engagement and faculty internationalization. We believe that B-school leaders should acknowledge these tensions rather than wishing them away. With good strategizing and a clear focus on the qualitative rationales underlying faculty engagement and faculty internationalization objectives, the tensions between these two objectives can be managed and even be turned into complementarities. Our focus is in particular on the implications for the management of international early-career and pre-tenure faculty.

DRIVERS OF FACULTY INTERNATIONALIZATION IN EUROPEAN AND GLOBAL BUSINESS SCHOOLS

Despite significant differences across geographies, academic disciplines, and types of institutions, there is evidence of a clear—if slow—long-term trend towards greater faculty internationalization in higher education institutions (HEIs) in Europe. An analysis of the European Tertiary Registration Register, covering nearly 3,500 higher education institutions across up to 40 European countries, reveals that the proportion of foreign academic staff has grown steadily from 10.6% in 2011 to 12.2% in 2020 (Lepori et al., 2023). However, the data indicate that there are significant variations in faculty internationalization among European countries. This disparity likely reflects differences in the differential importance of national markets for HEIs, national policies, institutional strategies, and the overall attractiveness of academic careers in various European nations.

Faculty internationalization in B-schools, particularly those that have earned specific reputational markers (inclusion in rankings; accreditation with leading international organizations), tends to exceed the average found at HEIs in general by a considerable margin. For the purpose of this chapter, we conducted a detailed analysis of data from the *Financial Times* Master's in Management (MiM) ranking from 2015 to 2023. The following graph (Figure 2.1) contains an overview of the average international faculty ratio per region represented in the FT MiM ranking over the years 2015–2023.

This data reveals significant regional differences and trends in the internationalization of faculty in leading B-schools from 2015 to 2023. Europe and Australia show steady increases in international faculty, with Europe rising from 41.1% to 48.4% and Australia from 31% to 43%. North America maintains the highest overall percentage, fluctuating at around 50%–55%. Asia, starting lowest at 4.5%, saw a notable jump to 13.3% in 2017 and has since stabilized at around 12%–14%. These patterns reflect varying approaches to global academic recruitment and retention across regions, possibly influenced by factors such as immigration policies, funding for international collaboration, and efforts to enhance institutional prestige through diversity.

In the following, we focus on a subset of the schools included above, namely the 46 schools for which data was continuously available for each of the nine years. This list contains 43 schools from Europe and three schools from Asia-Pacific (China, Australia). The figure provides an overview of the

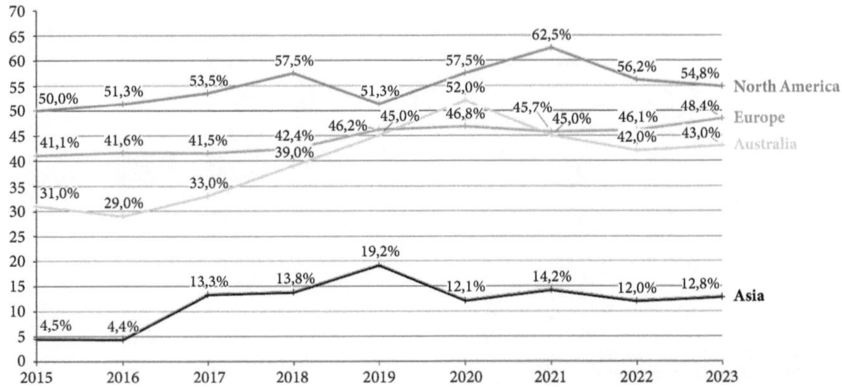

Figure 2.1: Average share of international faculty among all B-schools included in the FT MiM ranking, 2015–2023

average total faculty count as well as the average national and international faculty in the set of the 46 schools.

Overall, the analysis provided in Figure 2.2 shows that faculty internationalization in these 46 schools has increased year-on-year from 28.4% in 2015 to 33.5% in 2023, and these averages also represent the schools from continental Europe. Faculty internationalization is considerably stronger in the UK, where it has grown from 41.6% to 44.2% over the nine years, and weakest in the three schools from Asia-Pacific where it now stands at 16.4%. Faculty internationalization is particularly weak in the schools from China and India that have joined the MiM ranking in recent years (and are thus not included in Figure 2.2).

Focusing more specifically on the state of faculty internationalization in the 43 European schools included in Figure 2.2, two facets are particularly noteworthy:

First, there is *considerable heterogeneity* in terms of B-school faculty internationalization between different European countries. The country that clearly stands out in this respect is France, which also accounts for the largest number of schools (15) in the list. Not only does their share of international faculty members stand at 37.5% on average; they also have the largest share of faculty members from Asia-Pacific, from Africa and the Middle East, the US and Canada, and even from Latin America. The latter result is particularly noteworthy in that there are few obvious language-related or historical connections that would account for the higher share of faculty from Latin America in France (we were surprised to see that the share of faculty members from Latin America is higher in the French schools than it

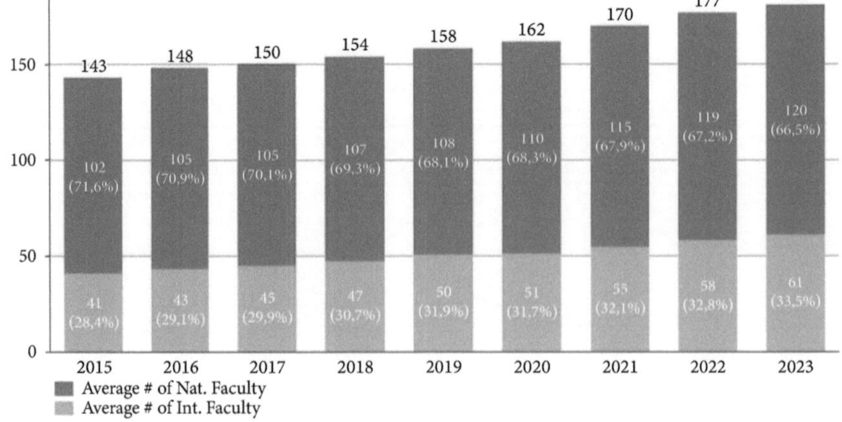

Figure 2.2: Average number of national and international faculty members among the 46 schools in the FT MiM ranking for which data is continuously available, 2015–2023

is in the five schools from Spain and Portugal). In contrast, faculty internationalization is woefully small in countries such as Germany, Hungary, and the Czech Republic. True, these countries are represented by a few schools only, making it difficult to draw definitive conclusions. However, given that those schools included in the analysis can be considered leading business schools in their respective environments, the inference that faculty internationalization in the B-schools from these countries in general is lagging behind does not seem far-fetched.

Second, as an overall observation, faculty internationalization at these leading European B-schools is primarily *from within the region*. Considering all 43 European schools taken together, most of their international faculty are from other European countries. Even in France with its high degree of B-school internationalization, well over half of all international faculty come from European countries. Schools in Portugal and Spain are noteworthy in that relatively few international faculty members come from direct neighbour countries with which they share a land border; instead, most international faculty come from non-neighbouring European countries. In smaller landlocked European countries such as Austria, Hungary, and the Czech Republic, the share of international faculty coming from Europe is over two-thirds; in Switzerland it even exceeds 90%.

What has driven the growth in faculty internationalization, primarily from within the region, in European B-schools? Before going into details, it is worth noting that this development has taken place in a favourable institutional context. In the European Union, the free movement of workers—a development that began in the 1960s and accelerated in the early 2000s—has made it progressively easier for employees to work in other EU countries. The creation of a common European Higher Education Area as a result of the so-called Bologna reforms since 1999 has fostered not only student mobility by providing comparable degree structures, but also staff mobility by providing greater transparency and recognition of qualifications. Staff mobility has also benefited from the fact that English has become the lingua franca of higher education in general. On the political level, given their skill shortages, many European countries have enacted policies to attract highly qualified employees from abroad, benefiting academics in business as well as other disciplines. These skill shortages are exacerbated by demographic factors, specifically the retirement in recent years of academics born during the baby boomer period from 1946 to 1964.

In addition to these wider background factors, there are specific demand-side and supply-side factors that have contributed to the increase in the international composition of B-school faculties. With respect to the former, management, business administration, and related disciplines (such as finance and accounting) have grown even faster than many other academic disciplines. Business schools have expanded rapidly, fuelling demand for new faculty members and pushing up prices (in the form of compensation and benefit packages). Differentials in compensation levels and career opportunities between countries make it attractive for new faculty members to cross borders and accept jobs where the prospects are brightest. Differentials in the geographic distribution of particular types of expertise, in turn, have made it attractive for B-schools to search for new faculty members from those countries with traditional strengths in the areas concerned. For example, many European B-schools (in particular from countries such as France, Belgium, and the Netherlands) have recruited young academics that have emerged from institutions with strong engineering and operations research traditions in the Middle East in order to fill positions in areas such as transportation research, logistics and supply chain management. Others have drawn academics with a mathematics, statistics, and data science background from schools in Asia to fill roles in business analytics, information systems, and related areas where demand has grown in recent years.

Furthermore, in their quest for reputational status from international and national accreditation agencies, B-schools have also been under pressure to recruit faculty in order to fulfil expected faculty sufficiency ratios. For example, accreditation guidelines from the Association to Advance Collegiate Schools of Business (AACSB) stipulate fairly exacting requirements with respect to faculty sufficiency in each degree programme. In its 2020 accreditation standards, AACSB has also reinforced its emphasis on internationalization, for example by requiring schools to show evidence of a 'global mindset' (a criterion that was not part of the 2013 standards). EFMD, in turn, considers the ratio of international faculty as one among several important indicators of a school's degree of internationalization, a central requirement for schools that aim for European Quality Improvement System (EQUIS) or EFMD programme accreditation. Faculty internationalization is also a criterion in some rankings that schools use in order to track and enhance their reputation. For example, the proportion of international faculty (in addition to international students) is one of the indicators that the *Financial Times* has been using in many of its rankings, starting with its introduction of the Global MBA ranking in 1999. Since then, B-schools have begun to use international indicators (including faculty internationalization) as strategic KPIs. These pressures have contributed to 'institutional isomorphism', the tendency of organizations to look alike as they conform to the same institutional norms (DiMaggio & Powell, 1983).

At the same time, supply-side factors have also played a role in the increasing internationalization of B-school faculty. Many young academics have sought employment in countries with a reputation for excellence in research and education, and for career progression opportunities (Mantai

& Marrone, 2023). Because continental European B-schools have regained some of the ground ceded to North American institutions in earlier decades (Richter, 2024) over the past 20–25 years, the prospect of securing a job in one of the former group of schools has gained in relative attractiveness for academics from around the world. In the advanced stages of their doctoral programmes many candidates willingly enter the global academic job market, in which those with the greatest ability to move in order to secure the 'best' jobs at the most prestigious institutions are at an advantage over those who are less mobile. International market mechanisms have developed considerably over the past 25 years, with a plethora of international academic career events organized by academic associations, accreditation organizations, international doctoral networks, and a range of widely accessible academic recruitment services and websites. At the more senior level, specialized search agencies have significantly grown their international recruitment practices for positions at the full professor and B-school leadership levels. In sum, the trend towards greater internationalization of faculty in many European B-schools has been supported by powerful socio-economic and institutional factors.

CLOUDS ON THE HORIZON: COUNTER-DEVELOPMENTS AGAINST FACULTY INTERNATIONALIZATION IN B-SCHOOLS

In contrast to the trends indicated above, in recent years signs have emerged suggesting that faculty internationalization may not be as pervasive as it may appear at first sight, and that the trend towards increasing faculty internationalization may slow down or even reverse. First of all, as our analysis has demonstrated, in most countries—with the possible exception of France and the UK—faculty internationalization tends to be primarily 'within-region'. While a pure count of nationalities among faculties in European B-schools suggests a high degree of internationalization, these faculties are far from offering a representative cross-section around the globe. Furthermore, there are marked differences between countries in terms of faculty internationalization. The evidence suggests that in many Central and Eastern European countries, faculty internationalization in B-schools tends to be considerably lower than is the case in Western Europe. Language, culture, and history, as well as political and socio-economic factors, provide at least partial explanations for the different speed of development. In sum, while faculty internationalization has been an important feature of business school development in many European countries, it is not a universal phenomenon.

Second, the schools included in Figure 2.2 are largely elite institutions located in a limited number of advanced Western European economies. Those schools that vie for a place in the international rankings and/or seek accreditation from international quality assurance organizations have developed faster in terms of their faculty internationalization; however, these schools represent a small sub-segment of all HEIs in the area of business and management. In sum, even within particular countries, different schools are developing at different speeds in terms of their internationalization efforts. Some observers even hold the elitist, competitive, and market-oriented approaches to internationalization responsible for the uneven progress in terms of internationalization of higher education at large, as the former tend to emphasize the economic benefits of internationalization at the expense of its educational and social ones (de Wit, 2015).

Third, within some of the Western European countries, forces have come into play in recent years that have made faculty internationalization more difficult or are likely to do so in future. An obvious case in this regard has been the exit of the UK from the European Union and its resulting effects, such as reduced access to EU research funding. Although UK-based business schools remain places with high levels of faculty internationalization, many foreign academics—in particular those from Continental Europe—have begun to consider their options or have already relocated elsewhere. From 2015 to 2023, the average annual growth rate in faculty internationalization among the five UK-based schools included in the analysis above was just 0.8% per annum. (albeit from a high starting point) as compared to 2.3% per annum among the 38 continental European schools and 4.8% per annum among the three B-schools from Asia-Pacific (starting from a low basis). Furthermore, new global geopolitical tensions have led many EU states to erect barriers against new faculty recruitment from countries outside the EU with which relationships—for various reasons—have tensed in recent years, such as China or Russia. Wars in the Ukraine and the Middle East and political and economic tensions in other regions (Southern Africa, Latin America) have driven academics out of these countries, but few of those have found employment in European B-schools. Ultimately, conflict and unrest hinder faculty internationalization as they create uncertainty and limit freedom of movement.

Finally, several EU member states have begun to develop higher education policies that may not be intended at restricting faculty internationalization per se, but that could well result in doing so. For example, in 2023 the Dutch government at the time presented proposals according to which a considerable proportion of courses included in undergraduate programmes would have to be taught in Dutch. While these new requirements have not come into law at the time of writing this chapter, they are hotly discussed in the academic community in the Netherlands. During the parliamentary debates in the summer of 2024, the proposed internationalization law for Dutch higher education has sparked significant concerns among Dutch parliamentarians. Key issues include fears of mass redundancies at universities, increased regulatory burdens, and potential accessibility challenges for students due to expanded use of enrolment restrictions. There are worries about the impact on regional economies, particularly in border areas, and the financial consequences for institutions facing potential decreases in student numbers. Their implementation would require universities to pay greater attention to Dutch language considerations in faculty recruitment and development in order to retain flexibility in their staffing and workload management decisions. As a result, faculty considering a move to the Netherlands would face additional hurdles, as they would have to invest in the development of language skills precisely at a time when many of them are still uncertain about their longer-term career and development prospects. Similar developments have been taking place in other European countries (e.g. Denmark) for a number of years already (Wright, 2022). There are also less tangible cultural factors that play a role in this context. With the rise of populism and of right-wing political parties in large parts of Europe and a public debate that centres around how best to curb migration, the atmosphere for international faculty has become less welcoming, even if politicians argue that high-skilled workers are exempt from these policies. The bureaucratic hurdles in getting visas, work permits, and the like for non-EU faculty and their family members in many European countries speak louder than words.

In sum, the political environment in many European countries has gradually become less favourable to faculty internationalization in recent years, in particular with respect to faculty members from outside Europe. The case of the Netherlands demonstrates how political decisions, such as the proposed internationalization law, can have far-reaching effects on the ability of universities to attract and retain international talent. This situation is not unique to the Netherlands but reflects broader tensions across Europe between the benefits of internationalization and concerns about preserving national identity, language, and educational access for domestic students.

These political factors create a complex environment for universities trying to balance international engagement with local needs and political realities. Universities must often adapt their strategies to navigate changing political landscapes while striving to maintain their global competitiveness and academic standards. Unfortunately, there is little evidence to suggest that this trend is likely to reverse in the near future. However, the mere pressure of faculty shortage, combined with continued encouragement and support from sector organizations, creates incentives for leading B-schools that are intentional about their development to overcome the hurdles against faculty internationalization, and in the process differentiate themselves from the competition.

MULTI-MARKET BUSINESS SCHOOL REALITY AND THE VALUE OF INTERNATIONAL FACULTY

In addition to the political, cultural, and socio-economic factors discussed above, gradual yet profound changes have been taking place with respect to the faculty models among many B-schools in Europe. Specifically, many schools have taken steps to shift their activity profiles away from a predominant focus on research and pre-experience education, in order to pay greater attention to external (often regional) engagement and non-traditional forms of education. These shifts have played out differently across different geographies and types of B-schools, yet they have had implications for the relative attractiveness of faculty from international versus domestic backgrounds, and their management.

Academic institutions in general, and B-schools in particular, operate in four markets at the same time. These four markets represent different stakeholders and activities that business schools engage with to fulfil their mission of education, research, and impact. Balancing these markets is crucial for a business school's overall success and relevance in the academic and business communities. Each of these markets have their own institutional logics that determine how best to compete and position within them. Consequently, they require different types of faculty composition depending on the institutional context of the schools concerned and their mission focus.

The image in Figure 2.3 illustrates four key markets that business schools typically operate in:

1. **Market for faculty:** This market focuses on attracting and retaining academic talent. It is associated with traditional academic research, including publishing scholarly articles, securing research grants, and providing doctoral degrees. This market is crucial for maintaining a school's academic reputation and research output.
2. **Market for students:** This market revolves around education degree programmes such as BSc, MSc, and MBA. It represents the core educational offering of business schools, attracting students seeking formal qualifications in business and management.
3. **Market for thought leadership:** This market involves applied research and outreach activities. It includes research centres, consulting

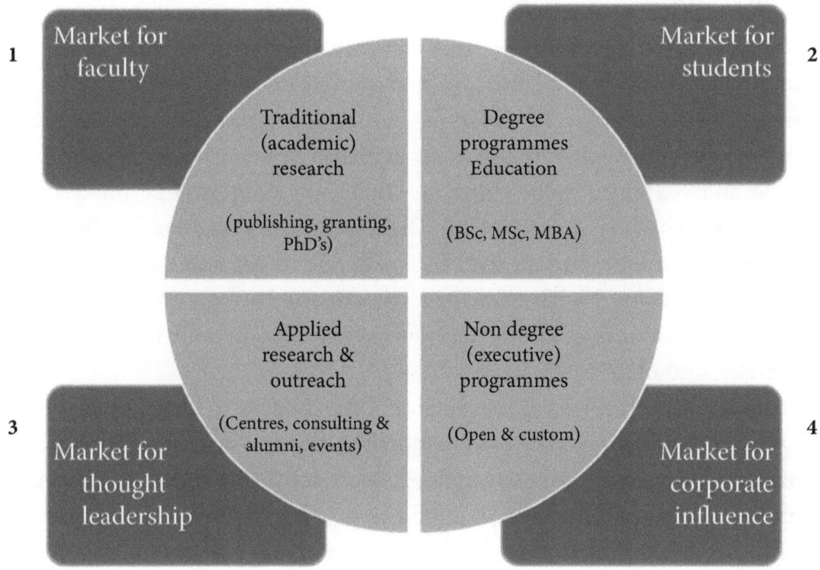

Figure 2.3: Markets in which B-schools operate. Adapted from a figure by Birkinshaw (2016). Reproduced with permission

services, alumni engagement, and various events. This market positions the school as a source of innovative ideas and practical insights for the business community.

4. **Market for corporate influence:** This market focuses on non-degree (executive) programmes, often customized or open-enrolment courses for working professionals and organizations. It is about providing targeted education and training to meet specific corporate needs, enhancing the school's influence in the business world.

Traditionally, faculty at many B-schools, and early to mid-career faculty in particular, essentially focused on the first two of these two markets, with roughly equal weight attached to them. For example, promotion criteria heavily emphasized productivity in research and education, in addition to a smaller 'citizenship' component (contribution to academic administration). The weight between these tasks, and the relative importance of quality-oriented versus quantity-oriented indicators, differed according to the type of institution concerned. Over the progression of their careers, faculty would assume additional responsibilities in the other two areas of external thought leadership (outreach and applied research) and (where applicable) executive education. They would also take on a broader set of managerial and administrative responsibilities.

In the traditional model, the basic criteria and approaches to managing faculty apply to domestic and international staff in the same way, although there may well be hidden (and sometimes even overt) differences between the two groups. For example, young foreign faculty members may often enjoy an initial advantage in recognition or status over domestic faculty members when they first join, as their very 'foreignness' makes them attractive for the hiring institution. There are costs associated with this attractiveness, though, and any advantage tends to get lost over time as the challenges associated with their presence in the foreign country increase such as with increasing family and caregiving responsibilities, dual career challenges, and other such factors.

However, the traditional career model has begun to shift, as B-schools put greater emphasis on thought leadership, impact, and engagement, and on post-experience or more specialized, less traditional forms of education. Elements of this shift have included a greater differentiation and unbundling of roles, the emergence of dedicated career tracks (e.g. in teaching and education, research, engagement), and a greater emphasis on engagement, outreach, and impact at earlier points in faculty members' careers. Institutions increasingly recognize that activities in the four spheres described above require different types of faculty and differentiated career tracks for faculty. In the Netherlands, for example, a new initiative for 'recognition and reward' of faculty was initiated a few years ago.[1] The essence of this initiative is to create a more inclusive, diverse, and balanced academic environment that values a range of contributions beyond research outputs. It represents a significant shift in how academic careers are structured and evaluated in the country, with potential implications for the broader international academic community. Dedicated career tracks for educators may rely more heavily on language skills and embeddedness in national education contexts, making it more difficult for international faculty members that may not be fully fluent in the language of the country in which they work. The same may hold for teaching in non-degree executive education programmes, in particular in open-enrolment programmes. Similarly, applied research and outreach activities may benefit from or even require an embeddedness in local networks and connections with stakeholders in the region that foreign faculty members need to build up over time in order to be as effective in these activities as their domestic colleagues. Clearly, there are opportunities for education and engagement in the international context where the nationality of the faculty members involved may be less critical, yet given the greater range of stakeholders that B-schools increasingly serve, they need to have a pool of faculty members that ensures their flexibility and responsiveness. Some schools may fear that the time and the opportunities for development that international faculty members often require sits at odds with these needs. In order to achieve their faculty internationalization objectives and their strategies of increased engagement and flexibility simultaneously, B-schools need to develop and implement new, targeted approaches for managing their early to mid-career faculty.

STRATEGIC IMPLICATIONS FOR B-SCHOOL LEADERS FOR ATTRACTING, MANAGING, AND RETAINING EARLY AND MID-CAREER FACULTY

Given the developments discussed in the previous sections, what are viable approaches to faculty internationalization for European B-schools that also face increasing expectations from their local, national and regional stakeholders? From our point of view, unguided or passive approaches to recruiting and retaining faculty—'we just hire whom we can get'—are not commensurate with the magnitude of the challenge that these institutions face. They need to put in place dedicated strategies for recruiting, managing and retaining international faculty. We outline six complementary approaches, organized along a typical faculty development lifecycle.

Enlarging the Pool of International Candidates

B-schools should use more targeted approaches in order to get access to a wider set of candidates for faculty positions from international markets. For example, they may develop reciprocal recruitment partnerships with schools of similar standing from abroad in order to give privileged access to candidates coming out of their PhD programmes. Such a strategy can be beneficial for both institutions as long as they are well-matched, as the ability to place PhD students at good international institutions is an objective for many research-oriented schools with strong programmes. This approach does not have to be limited to the initial recruitment level. The Wharton-INSEAD alliance,[2] which fosters faculty collaboration between the two schools, has also enabled faculty members whose early development did not progress as quickly as anticipated, to find employment and re-set their tenure clock at the respective partner institution. Many other schools make proactive use of international research and doctoral education networks such as EIASM (the European Institute for Advanced Studies in Management)[3] in order to create awareness among prospective international candidates for recruitment. Some B-schools can also tap in a more targeted way into the pool of potential international faculty who already live in their country region or have a particular affinity for it. For example, they may offer research workshops that are especially geared towards those who had initially arrived in the country as migrants.

Recruiting International Faculty and Supporting Their Integration

International faculty members, in particular those arriving from far-flung backgrounds, often require extra attention during the recruitment phase and support during the early years of their employment. Academic institutions can earn a strong employer brand if they recognize and meet these needs as best as possible. Young faculty members often respond best to offers of support if these come from, or at least involve, their natural peer group (i.e. other young faculty members). Buddy networks among international faculty can work well. Institutions can support international faculty by providing information and support for finding housing, schooling, or childcare options; tax and legal advice; or other such measures, and this kind of support should also extend to family members. A particularly salient point for many international faculty members is support for their partners with respect to matters of visa, work permit, and other bureaucratic hurdles. Employers that go out of their way in making these processes simpler have a real advantage over those that throw their hands up and let employees deal with these matters by themselves.

Relatedly, business schools should also offer support for language training at the appropriate level: proposing to faculty members that they can sit in on language classes for the same students whom they are supposed to teach may not be a compelling proposition, but dedicated courses that faculty members (and their family members) can take at their own time may be more attractive. Tandem teaching programmes in dual languages where a domestic and an international faculty member teach the same course in parallel in two different languages, and over time swap language sections, may also be an effective integration mechanism.

Introducing International Faculty Members to the Academic Ecosystem (Research, Education, and Outreach/Engagement) in the Local and Regional Context

Academic institutions are often not cognizant of the implicit knowledge required for young academics to operate effectively in the country where they work. Many universities offer helpful teacher qualification programmes which may introduce participating faculty members to the latest pedagogical ideas. However, what is often missing from these programmes is an introduction into how the quality assurance system in the country concerned works, or a basic overview of the local education system. Likewise, many B-schools may provide support for faculty members to attend international research conferences, but underappreciate the difficulty that foreign faculty members face in trying to operate in the national research environment. Attending an Academy of Management Conference that takes place thousands of miles away is likely to feel much more natural for a new colleague from Asia or Africa who has joined a B-school in Germany or in Spain than to attend a workshop of the German Academic Association for Business Research (VHB), or of the Spanish Academy of Management (ACEDE), that may take place in a neighbouring city. Research directors, department heads, and senior faculty members should make it their responsibility to introduce international colleagues to the relevant networks and help them get access. This is particularly important when it comes to applying for research funding from national sources, where an intimate understanding of the system, the application process, and the particular 'dos and don'ts' in the country concerned can be decisive for success. As outreach and engagement with external stakeholders becomes more important, creating access for new faculty members—wherever they may be from—to external stakeholders (e.g. corporate partners) is also crucial. All too often, senior faculty members (who are more likely to be from the home country, rather than from abroad) and corporate relations offices of B-schools guard contacts with businesses and other stakeholders as their property. They should utilize these contacts in order to make young, foreign faculty members a success.

Facilitating Greater Flexibility in Career Development

Given the development towards greater differentiation in academic roles in many European countries, there is a systemic need for greater flexibility in career paths and for 'managed permeability' between different roles. These needs may apply for faculty members regardless of background, yet they may be particularly acute when it comes to international faculty members. For example, foreign faculty members who develop a programme of engagement and outreach—a daring endeavour for the reasons described above—may require more time (in the form of an extended promotion and tenure clock) that allows them to do so, or otherwise they may not be willing to do so in the first place. Of course, this example may not apply to more traditional research-oriented institutions that encourage early-career faculty to focus single-mindedly on research and teaching. However, even within that traditional model, some flexibility may help institutions to attract and retain international faculty more easily. For example, earlier access to opportunities to be involved in executive education, which are often reserved for more senior faculty, can help to demonstrate to international junior faculty that they are being valued by the institution where they are employed and that the extra remuneration that such opportunities may carry can be an extra boon for them.

Use Development Tools for Faculty Internationalization

B-schools can do more to help their faculty members—in particular their domestic ones—to gain international experience. For example, the Erasmus+ programme supports mobility of teaching staff who want to gain teaching experience in another European country, and B-schools can tap into these opportunities more proactively. In the same way that B-schools develop agreements with international schools for student support, they may also do so for the purpose of staff exchange. When they grant sabbaticals, they may specifically tie these to a stay abroad. Senior faculty should open doors for junior faculty members to spend some time at reputable international research institutions. There are also great international development programmes in the area of teaching, such as the International Teachers Programme (ITP) run by the International Schools of Business Management (ISBM) consortium together with EFMD.[4] Participation in such international experiences may not change the internationalization statistics, but they enable faculty members to build important international networks which can be of great benefit further down the line. They also demonstrate employer commitment and contribute to faculty retention.

Enhancing International Faculty Retention and Managing Faculty Exits

With international faculty members, encouraging them to stay for long periods of time—and even permanently—is often particularly difficult, as individual priorities (e.g. family concerns such as caregiving responsibilities for elderly parents) may shift over time. In addition, the very international experience that foreign faculty members accumulate may increase their attractiveness in their respective home country. In order to be able to hold on to their international faculty members, institutions need to demonstrate (on a continuous basis) that they are serious in their desire and efforts to make these international faculty members a success. Access to promotion opportunities—not just from junior to mid-career positions, but also to senior professorial and to leadership roles—is as important as continuous re-affirmation and development support. When international faculty members do leave, B-schools (departments, research groups) should seek to maintain the relationship with them by offering permanent visiting faculty status, and take the opportunity to build new connections with the institutions that these faculty members join. In the same way as B-schools manage their international alumni networks, they can establish networks of 'faculty alumni' and use their former faculty members as ambassadors. International faculty members tend to have a higher degree of mobility than domestic ones, but B-schools can use that very mobility to good effect.

CONCLUSIONS

In this chapter, we asked ourselves two questions. First, what is the future of faculty internationalization in European B-schools? We believe that the internationalization of faculty will remain important for European B-schools. However, we need to acknowledge that a confluence of external as well as internal factors mean that the positive trend we have seen in previous years is unlikely to continue at the same pace. In addition to socio-economic, institutional, and market-related factors, the introduction of more diversified faculty models may make faculty internationalization more challenging. We believe that faculty internationalization for European B-schools is likely to become more nuanced overall, and more difficult for schools that are not at the top of the reputational hierarchy. B-schools need to develop and implement dedicated and differentiated approaches to faculty internationalization.

Second, we asked what strategies B-schools can adopt to meet these challenges and manage faculty internationalization successfully. In order to be effective, these approaches should be clearly aligned with the competitive strategies of the schools concerned (Guillotin et al., 2016) in the multiple markets they operate in. A school's impact agenda and its international faculty agenda may become more effective when they converge into the emerging global citizenship agenda (Van Rompay-Bartels & Tuninga, 2023). B-schools that manage to successfully recruit, retain, and integrate international faculty members will continue to do well. Despite challenges such as cultural adaptation, the integration of international faculty significantly enhances a business school's global competitiveness and relevance, ensuring that students are well-prepared for the realities of international business.

ACKNOWLEDGEMENTS

We thank the *Financial Times* business school ranking team for sharing the anonymized faculty nationalities data from their FT ranking database and Babette Lohuis (RSM) for her assistance with the data analysis.

NOTES

1. https://recognitionrewards.nl/.
2. https://insead.wharton.upenn.edu/.
3. https://www.eiasm.net/.
4. https://itp-schools.com/.

REFERENCES

Baruch, Y. (2013). 'Careers in Academe: The Academic Labour Market as an Eco-System'. *Career Development International*, 18/2, 196–210.

Birkinshaw, J. (2016). 'Innovation in Business Education: New Offerings, New Ways of Working'. Keynote at the AACSB Conference, Madrid, October.

Buckner, E., Denenberg, J., Gelashvili, M., Kontelli, M., Rodriguez, A. M., Wang, L., & Zhang, Y. (2022). 'The Internationalization of Higher Education in the Wake of COVID-19: A Rigorous Review of the Literature on Short-Term Impacts'. CIHE Perspectives No. 20. Center for International Higher Education (CIHE), Boston College.

Çalıkoğlu, A., Jones, G. A., & Kim, Y., eds. (2023). *Internationalization and the Academic Profession: Comparative Perspectives*. Springer.

de Wit, H. (2015). 'The Future of Internationalization of Higher Education in Europe'. *International Higher Education*, 83, 2–3. DOI: 10.6017/ihe.2015.83.9073.

DiMaggio, J. P., & Powell, W. W. (1983). 'The Iron Cage Revisited: Institutional Isomorphism and Collective Rationality in Organizational Fields'. *American Sociological Review*, 48/2, 147–160.

Ding, Y. (2022). 'Reinventing the Internationalization of Business Schools in the Post-COVID-19 Era'. In E. Cornuel, ed., *Business School Leadership and Crisis Exit Planning*. Cambridge University Press, 217–232.

Engwall, L., ed. (2023). *Internationalisation in Higher Education and Research: Perspectives, Obstacles, Alternatives*. Springer.

Finkelstein, M. J., & Jones, G. A., eds. (2019). *Professorial Pathways: Academic Careers in a Global Perspective*. Johns Hopkins University Press.

Fumasoli, T., Goastellec, G., & Kehm, B. M., eds. (2015). *Academic Work and Careers in Europe: Trends, Challenges, Perspectives*. Springer.

Guillotin, B., Mangematin, V., Minto, N., Burton, R. M., & Sharkey Scott, P. (2016). *Strategic Internationalization and Competitive Alignment*. Fox School of Business Research Paper No. 17-032. EFMD Research Conference, Barcelona, 10–11 October.

Lepori, B., Lambrechts, A. A., Wagner-Schuster, D., & Zahradnik, G. (2023). 'The European Tertiary Education Register, the Reference Dataset on European

Higher Education Institutions'. Nature Scientific Data. https://www.nature.com/articles/s41597-023-02353-2.
Mantai, L., & Marrone, M. (2023). 'Academic Career Progression from Early Career Researcher to Professor: What Can We Learn from Job Ads'. *Studies in Higher Education*, 48/6, 797–812.
Richter, A. (2024). 'The European Business School Sector: Phoenix Rising from the Ashes?' *EFMD Global Focus*, 18/1, 17–22.
Trapczyński, P. (2016). 'De-internationalisation: A Review of Empirical Studies and Implications for International Business Research'. *Baltic Journal of Management*, 11/4, 350–379.
Van Rompay-Bartels, I., & Tuninga, R. S. J. (2023). 'Toward a Model of Global Citizenship in Business Education'. *Journal of Transnational Management*, 28/1–2, 5–34.
Wright, S. (2022). 'Danish University Governance Reforms: Internationalisation and De-internationalisation'. *European Journal of Education*, 57, 96–108.
Zaheer, S. (1995). 'Overcoming the Liability of Foreignness'. *Academy of Management Journal*, 38/2, 341–363.

3

Shaping Perspectives

The Impact of the Pandemic on the Evolution of Internationalization at Home in Higher Education Institutions

CATHERINE PEREIRA-VILLA

INTRODUCTION

Stretching as far back as 1966, the scientific literature on higher education, business education, business schools, internationalization, and globalization spans diverse topics ranging from market orientation and internationalization (Jaworski & Kohli, 1996) and strategies on the acquisition of competitive advantages through internationalization (Johanson & Vahlne, 1977) to the application of contingency theory in business strategy (Hofer, 1975). The themes extend further to encompass discussions on profitability (MacMillan et al., 1982), organizational theory (Larsen & Olaisen, 2013), and accreditation impact (Lejeune & Vas, 2009). The publications found in Scopus since 1986 on the terms mentioned before yield 2,589 documents, of which 281 use the term 'internationalization at home' (IaH) and a further 26 also address the COVID-19 pandemic.

The scholarly discourse on business education and internationalization includes the development of distinctive skills (Prestwich & Ho-Kim, 2007), considerations of image, networks, plurality, structural change (Fugate & Jefferson, 2001), and the nuanced management of organizational change (Parker, 2002; Worley & Lawler III, 2006). Furthermore, the literature extends into explorations of leadership dynamics (House et al., 2002), the enhancement of performance metrics, and the examination of explicit and implicit perspectives on internationalization (Foster & Carver, 2018).

Catherine Pereira-Villa, *Shaping Perspectives.* In: *Management Education and the Rise of Uncertainty of Global Business.* Edited by: Eric Cornuel, Oxford University Press. © Oxford University Press (2025).
DOI: 10.1093/9780197794470.003.0004

An additional layer of complexity is found when the research explores the dynamics of management education.

Amid this scientific conversation, the world found itself thrust into the COVID-19 pandemic in March 2020—an unprecedented event that shaped profound changes across the human economic, social, educational, environmental, and cultural interactions, with repercussions that reverberate over a protracted period (Marinoni & van't Land, 2020).

Among the transformations that COVID-19 propelled, there was a surge in the adoption of digital modes of interaction and communication. Virtually overnight, academic activities pivoted to remote platforms, marking a paradigm shift in education.

Simultaneously, there emerged an upswing in omnichannel strategies to reach markets for goods and services, coupled with disruptions across all facets of private and public transportation as international borders closed in response to government-imposed virus containment measures. These measures, including the implementation of 'restrictions to human mobility' (Dueñas et al., 2021), limited the possibility for students—prepared and eager—to embark on international mobility. Consequently, educational systems underwent a metamorphosis, from elementary schools to institutions of higher learning, compelled to transition rapidly into online teaching-learning scenarios, as delineated by Mishra et al., (2020). Thus, the global higher education sector found itself navigating an accelerated digital transformation, a response to the demands presented by the initial challenges posed by the pandemic (Dwivedi et al., 2020).

According to UNESCO, the impact was staggering as higher education institutions (HEIs) in 185 countries were completely shuttered in April 2020, affecting upwards of one billion learners globally (Marinoni & v'ant Land, 2020). This monumental shift underscored the need for adaptability and resilience within higher education, as institutions grappled with the demands imposed by the pandemic.

While technology emerged as a potent and indispensable ally in the face of COVID-19, integration into academia implied several challenges. Specially, concerns arose regarding equitable access to the necessary technological resources for students (García-Morales et al., 2021). In turn, this required a re-evaluation of internationalization efforts, urging a more inclusive approach than ever before.

The challenges were twofold: emanating from the university to the student and reciprocally, requiring students and faculty to take on board the imminent changes. Despite the pre-existence of the concepts and practices of 'internationalization at home' (IaH) (Crowther et al., 2000), technology acted as a catalyst, augmenting this framework and affording countless students the opportunity to explore the world from their computers.

In this context, several questions arise: Are we gravitating more towards technology at the expense of physical mobility? Is internationalization as accessible as our aspirations dictate? Does an oversaturation of the 'online' space exist? Are we effectively stewarding the course of internationalization and the development of intercultural skills? What do the future trends in the intersection of education and technology hold? These inquiries constitute a fraction of the complex realities we explore in this chapter.

INTERNATIONALISATION AT HIGHER EDUCATION INSTITUTIONS (HEIS) BEFORE COVID-19

We cannot address the effective management of internationalization in HEIs and the challenges they confront without an examination of past events and reflecting on internationalization in the period following COVID-19.

Undoubtedly, the forces of internationalization and higher education are interwoven operating in a symbiotic relationship (Scott, 1998). Within the context of internationalization models in business activities, firms extend beyond their national boundaries to augment profits, collect insights from diverse markets, exchange technological expertise, mitigate risks, strengthen revenue networks, and seek foreign business partnerships. This phenomenon is described by the Uppsala Internationalization Model (Johanson & Vahlne, 1977). A parallel trend is discernible in HEIs, wherein internationalization becomes a strategic requirement to forge partnerships offering expanded choices for international exchanges and collaborations among students and professors (Khan et al., 2014).

However, Khan et al. (2014) also highlight that industry demands pivot towards graduates possessing heightened proficiency in cross-cultural communication, global leadership, and open-mindedness (soft skills). Consequently, HEIs must extend their internationalization strategies to encompass professors, students, academic programmes, and research projects to generate impact through teaching, research, and social outreach. This aligns with the recognition that one of the main challenges for business schools lies in addressing the industry's requisites for future professionals. While current internationalization strategies predominantly focus on structural aspects such as international research, diverse student and faculty composition, global partnerships, networks, and corporate connections (El Garah et al., 2023), there exists a gap in nurturing personal global perspectives and skills essential for future professionals. Internationalization, in its multidimensional character, emerges as both an issue and a challenge that requires acknowledgement and integration within business schools.

In the field of higher education, a frequently referenced definition of internationalization is provided by Knight (2004): 'The process of integrating an international, intercultural, or global dimension into the purpose, functions, or delivery of post-secondary education'. Knight further argues that 'internationalization is changing the world of higher education, and globalization is changing the world of internationalization' (Knight, 2008). This transformation is fuelled by various factors, including the evolution of advanced communication and technological services, heightened international labour mobility, increased emphasis on the market economy and trade liberalization, and a focus on the knowledge society and lifelong learning (Knight, 2004). This definition provides insights that before the pandemic, the world grappled with challenges that persist today.

In the 2000s, internationalization was predominantly veering towards the mobility of students. To actualize the goal of internationalization, certain countries needed a consensus on strategies aligned with universities' missions. Although IaH had already been associated with an international and intercultural competency without studying abroad in 1999 (Beelen, 2011), the US Congress introduced the CIBERs programme (Centers for International Business Education and Research) to strengthen business education. This initiative sought to propose strategies for business schools to adopt in internationalizing their curriculum, reflecting the urgency of developing intercultural competencies.

The Table 3.1 illustrates the work on CIBERs experiences at Memphis State University and Southern Illinois University. It delineates proposed internationalization strategies aligned with universities' missions, encompassing global awareness, global understanding, and global competence (Kedia & Cornwell, 1994).

Scrutinizing Table 3.1, it becomes evident that internationalization should not be conceived for a select few or confined to administrative spheres; rather, it can be seen as a comprehensive undertaking involving faculty and administration, academic programmes, students, business, and community. Notably, accessibility and technological considerations were absent from these strategies, underscoring their increasing importance post-pandemic.

In 2011, Jos Beelen provided a critical perspective of the outcomes of the 3rd International Association of Universities (IAU)[1] Global Survey on Internationalization in Higher Education. One important question in the study asked: 'In the internationalization policy/strategy, which of the actions has a higher priority?' Among 17 policies or strategies, international respondents affirmed that the four highest priorities included outbound mobility opportunities for students (studies, internships, among others), international student exchanges and attraction of international

Table 3.1. INSTITUTIONAL MISSION AND RELATED INTERNATIONALIZATION STRATEGIES

Institutional Mission	**Faculty and Administration**	**Academic Programmes**	**Students**	**Business and Community**
Global Awareness	• Internationalize existing functional area faculty • Support from dean and administrators	• International topics are integrated with existing courses	• Area studies • Language studies • Travel abroad • Internationalize domestic student body • Recruit international students	• Export-oriented programmes • Programmes on the international business environment
Global Understanding	• Add international business faculty • Reward international teaching and research	• Add a general international course • Courses in functional areas of international business • IB concentration	• Study abroad programmes • Foreign language programmes abroad	• Market development programmes for specific countries
Global Competence	• Develop an International Business Department	• Graduate international business degrees • Master's in international business studies • International MBA • Undergraduate international business degrees, e.g. Foreign Language and International Trade Programme	• Overseas internships • Extended stay programmes • Work abroad programmes	• Sophisticated international business training to enable executives to function abroad

Source: Kedia & Cornwell (1994). Reprinted by permission of the publisher (Taylor & Francis Ltd.).

students, international research collaboration, and strengthening content international/intercultural studies. At the time, IaH ranked at ninth place (Beelen, 2011).

The survey further explored the attention and resources allocated to various internationalization activities in institutions. In response to the question 'Among the following internationalization activities, which are the five that receive the most attention and resources in your institution?' and 'What are the three most important bases for internationalization in your institution?', IaH did not emerge as a high priority.

The survey yielded several insights: the prominence of internationalizing the curriculum as a cornerstone of internationalization; an apparent overlap between the terms 'IaH' and 'internationalization of the curriculum'; and the perception of an internationalized curriculum as a benchmark of quality rather than as a tool for teaching and learning (Beelen, 2011). More recently, the fifth survey echoed the importance of internationalization for HEIs; identified international cooperation and capacity building as the main benefit (the first time this is the case); found that the risks were unequal access and the difficulty to assess the quality of courses and programmes; the main drivers for internationalization were 'business and industry demand', 'demand from foreign HEIs', and 'government policies'; and the obstacles included, 'insufficient financial resources', 'bureaucratic difficulties', and the 'lack of knowledge of foreign languages'. Also, the top priority in international activities was mobility, followed by strategic partnerships and research collaborations (Marinoni, 2019). The survey also found substantial geographical differences in articulation agreements with low percentages in Latin America and the Caribbean, a growing offer of online programmes—particularly in North America—and stable funding for internationalization in high-income countries. The survey also found contrasts in internationalization of research based on HEIs focus, with responsibilities allotted mainly to academic staff—who make up less than 5% in Latin America and the Caribbean, but has the highest percentages in Asia, the Pacific, and North America. In addition, the overlap between IaH and internationalization of the curriculum continues. Also, while internationalization policies are common in HEIs, clear strategies associated with it are less frequent, and mobility continues to be both unequal and inaccessible for many (Marinoni, 2019).

The sixth survey released in April 2024 provides us with a view of internationalization after COVID-19 which reflects a stronger need for HEIs 'to strategically connect'; other institutional priorities and financial constraints as drivers of a decreased focus on internationalization; differences by region in terms of budgets; and student involvement in the internationalization process. Internationalization plans at the faculty and departmental levels are rare, while in general there is growth in the number of staff dedicated to internationalization in most HEIs. The survey also found that IaH increased in strategic importance and typically leveraged extracurricular activities, particularly through more interactions with international students using virtual means; intercultural/international experiences on campus; and intercultural skill building workshops for staff and students. The pandemic also seems to have promoted more international partnerships particularly in Latin America and the Caribbean and in private universities.

Going back to IaH, Beelen and Jones redefined the concept in 2015, emphasizing that it is not solely about providing mobility opportunities but is crucial in domestic learning environments, ensuring inclusivity for all students. Their definition posits that 'internationalization at home is the purposeful integration of international and intercultural' (Beelen & Jones, 2015), offering a nuanced perspective distinct from the earlier definition by Crowther et al. (2000): 'Any internationally related activity with the exception of outbound student and staff mobility'. These definitions imply that the infusion of random elements into a programme is insufficient to ensure success or meaningful impact, underlining the role of purposeful integration in IaH. Beelen and Jones further emphasize, supported by the Erasmus Impact Study (2013), that staff development would be a key factor in the success of IaH. The most recent Erasmus impact study supports Beelen and Jones' recommendation that all staff, even those with international experiences through mobility, would require support in aspects of internationalization practice within domestic, intercultural contexts of the home curriculum[2] (EU Commission & Directorate-General for Education Sport and Culture, 2018).

However, COVID-19 arrived and in 2022, the IAU issued its Second Global Survey Report: Higher Education one year into the COVID-19 pandemic. The study found that internationalization had been negatively affected mostly in terms of student exchanges (-39%) and staff mobility (-37%); 31% of universities had revised their internationalization strategies, while 43% meant to do so; 56% of universities developed new assessments measures; the most predominant international activities were found to be collaborative online learning (COIL) and virtual exchanges; and staff training in intercultural competences increased in 44% of the HEIs (Jensen et al., 2022).

Focusing on Latin America and the Caribbean, a region with low rates of internationalization, despite the relatively late onset of the pandemic, certain universities showcased agility in adapting to the COVID-19 outbreak (Gonzalez-Perez et al., 2021). A contributing factor to this swift adaptation was the prior development of technological capabilities and organizational flexibility, empowering universities to transition to remote learning.

Throughout the pandemic, mobility hinged on the use of digital tools to facilitate virtual experiences, thereby democratically expanding access to international education for vulnerable groups. Recognizing that an international education sector fixated on physical mobility lacks inclusivity (Castiello-Gutiérrez et al., 2022), the focus on online technologies, while rapid, did not equate the virtual experience of international students to an in-person encounter (Cordova et al., 2021). Challenges inherent in IaH persisted, including the difficulty of exchanging ideas with professors and classmates, forfeiting the access to campus facilities, and to cultural knowledge of the host country. Consequently, international students faced homesickness, limited language skills, and heightened awareness of cultural differences during the pandemic (Schueller & Şahin, 2023). The disruption of study, research, and campus activities, coupled with financial pressures, emerged as predominant concerns for students (UNESCO, 2021).

Regarding executive education, the conditions of MBA students was particularly challenging. Networking activities, integral to MBA programmes, play a crucial role in students not only acquiring new knowledge but also establishing diverse relationships that can shape their future careers. The detrimental impact on networking abilities, a consequence of the pandemic's restrictions, proved dramatic for MBA students. While hybrid education emerged as a potential solution to mitigate some of the drawbacks of virtual learning, the uncertainty persists regarding the point where there may be oversaturation of online interaction, and how the evolution of virtual teaching capabilities might influence internationalization of HEIs in the emerging markets (Cordova et al., 2021).

In 2022, UNESCO introduced the concept of 'virtual student mobility' (VSM) as a technology-driven form of mobility that facilitates cross-border and/or interinstitutional exchanges for academic, experiential, cultural, and/or emergency contexts (UNESCO, 2022). However, in all parts of the world the challenge lies in envisioning and implementing inclusive policies and programmes that extend beyond VSM. This entails leveraging innovative tools for internationalization through the widespread application of big data, cloud computing, and artificial intelligence (Jiang, 2021).

ACCESSIBILITY AND INCLUSIVE AND PURPOSEFUL INTERNATIONALISATION

Internationalization in higher education has faced scrutiny due to issues related to access, equity, diversity, and sustainability. A notable concern is the disconnect between global academic programmes and their local impact. This asymmetry is evident, especially in conditions where students are geographically distant, leading to a gap between mobile and non-mobile students. This disparity is particularly concerning as internationalization tends to reach a small elite of students, leaving the vast majority—99% of the world's student population—largely untouched (Castiello-Gutiérrez et al., 2022; Schueller & Şahin, 2023).

The reliance on mobility alone has proven insufficient in achieving the goals of internationalization for HEIs. To address these challenges, universities are urged to adopt more inclusive and innovative approaches in communication and cooperation, fostering collaborations in all aspects, to reshape international education with a focus on IaH (de Wit & Jones, 2018). This transformative approach emphasizes investing in digital technologies, developing online resources, providing digital and networking tools to both professors and students, and endorsing a hybrid combination of online and traditional teaching.

According to UNESCO (2021), high-income countries were better equipped to navigate the disruptions brought about by the pandemic. This resilience was attributed to increased government funding and a surge in domestic enrolment. Among the 57 countries surveyed, 14 primarily high-income countries in Europe and North America reported an increase in student enrolment. In contrast, 14 countries experienced a decrease of 20% or less, with six of them falling into the lower-middle-income category. While the growth in government support for higher education and the rise in domestic enrolment in some countries were important, reduced international mobility and the suspension of scholarships and funding for internationalization posed challenges to further enrolment growth (UNESCO, 2021).

Examining another part of the world, Ekaterina Minaeva and Larisa Taradina conducted a study in 2021 to investigate the impact of COVID-19 on the internationalization efforts of Russian universities, positioned as significant players on the global stage. The study revealed that the initial months of the pandemic posed challenges to internationalization for both metropolitan and regional universities in Russia. Many students opted to defer their studies for one to two years to experience international education in a traditional setting rather than engaging in online courses abroad (Minaeva & Taradina, 2022). Despite these difficulties, Russian universities implemented various strategies including digital initiatives for international research collaboration, an expansion of low-cost and accessible international online events, the development of digital infrastructure to enhance the domestic curriculum, the training of Russian educators on internationalization practices, and the cultivation of a resilient university culture. This adaptability led to new practices on virtual education, online student communities, and hybrid degree programmes. As a result, Russian universities were proactive in sustaining internationalization efforts (Minaeva & Taradina, 2022).

In the case of the United States, McKinsey & Company (2022) conducted research that involved surveying 600 faculty members and 800 students from public and private nonprofit colleges and universities in the United States. The research focused on the use and impact of eight different classroom learning technologies that were driving transformative changes in education including: group work with virtual collaboration; tools based on connectivity and community building; augmented and virtual reality; machine learning through Apps and chatbots; customised lessons based on students' progress; risk mechanisms for student monitoring; and classroom interactions and exercises, including gamification.

The study highlighted that during the pandemic, students expressed a preference for engaging and efficient tools. A significant majority (60%) reported that all the classroom learning technologies they had used since the onset of the pandemic had positively impacted their learning and grades. Classroom exercises were cited by 80% of students, and 71% noted machine learning–powered teaching assistants as the most effective learning technologies. The research emphasised several takeaways for the future of learning: the importance of stakeholders aligning on goals for using specific learning technologies, considering student access to technology before tool deployment, providing high-quality support to facilitate adoption by students and faculty, and agreeing on impact metrics and initiating measurements in advance of tool deployment (McKinsey & Company, 2022).

In the case of Latin America, a study by Cordova et al. (2021) identified the main strategies employed by universities to address the challenges posed by the pandemic in terms of internationalisation. These strategies included an increase in activities associated with IaH including COIL, the development of new virtual programmes, reinforcement of online exchange programmes with regional partners, partnerships with non-academic institutions (e.g. Coursera), and the creation of courses in different languages. The study also confirmed the significant negative impact of the pandemic on both inbound and outbound mobility (Cordova et al., 2021). Overcoming the hurdles posed by the pandemic demanded substantial efforts to sustain international cooperation (Castiello-Gutiérrez et al., 2022).

Despite the challenges, COVID-19 has also been a catalyst for reinvention and opportunities for HEIs. These include overhauling educational and pedagogical models along with learning strategies, transitioning from student mobility to virtual platforms, reaching larger audiences through inclusive mobility, providing connectivity and training programmes to students and staff, increased participation of students and faculty in online events, enhanced regional virtual mobility, the introduction of virtual student exchange and study abroad programmes, the expansion of COIL, the establishment of new partnerships and agreements that were difficult to reach before, the adoption of blended learning approaches, the organisation of international virtual seminars, and hosting local virtual events with international speakers (Charoensap-Kelly & Punyanunt-Carter, 2023). The recalibration of internationalisation strategies showed resilience and adaptability, highlighting the capacity of universities to face challenges and seize opportunities in a rapidly evolving context.

In recent years, the advance in information technologies has played an important role in expanding student coverage and inclusivity. This technological progress has not only increased the competitiveness of internationalisation efforts but has also leveraged the cost-effectiveness of virtual modes of education (Castiello-Gutiérrez et al., 2022). One such example is that of Universidad de La Sabana in Colombia, which has embraced technology and innovative approaches to harness collaborative efforts from academic department heads, adjunct faculty, administrative staff, the internationalisation office, and international allies to promote a more accessible, inclusive, and globally connected 'purposeful internationalisation' (Castiello-Gutiérrez, 2019). The commitment of the university to promote internationalization as part of its mission reflects a comprehensive and inclusive approach, reallocating resources to enhance internationalisation. Some key initiatives include COIL to foster cross-cultural collaboration and an enriched learning experience, exposure to diverse perspectives within courses to enhance the global dimension of the curriculum, and the frequent use of learning analytics platforms and real time surveys to analyse student engagement, obtain valuable insights for continuous improvement, and avoid oversaturation of the online space. Other university activities include the widespread use of tools for interaction to facilitate communication, course management, and enabling effective collaboration among students, faculty, and staff; promoting business and cultural visits in virtual formats; extending the opportunity for second language development; and exposure to diverse teaching styles through courses designed and lectured by the international faculty at partner institutions. Other activities include the broadening of the university's buddy programme to include virtual mobility, remote networking sessions, and the use of asynchronous teaching methods to accommodate different time zones, ensuring inclusivity for international participants. These strategies also align with current industry needs, providing students with valuable insights and skills demanded by the market.

FUTURE TRENDS IN INTERNATIONALISATION AT HOME

Promoting responsibility, university leaders are urged to champion IaH policies and programmes that prioritise students unable to travel but who seek access to quality international education. Key recommendations in this pursuit include embedding internationalisation into the core missions of universities; incorporating internationalisation in annual planning and budget at institutional and unit levels to guarantee resources; considering IaH activities as instances for embedding tools for teaching and learning; making an intentional use of pedagogies to implement different combinations of interaction and interactivity to promote learning; blending physical and virtual learning mobility—including internships—to create innovative and inclusive educational experiences; leveraging learning opportunities from research collaborations abroad to foster a global perspective and enhance academic quality; and implementing measures to reduce costs to institutions, students, and other stakeholders (Hudzik, 2022). These recommendations entail exploring efficient and cost-effective approaches to internationalization through sharing workload and resources with international partners; considering contracting out certain functions to external providers, including outsourcing specific administrative functions; developing campus cultural and language enrichment through international students, with a focus beyond their revenue value; fostering a sense of community and inclusivity; connecting to community diversity to promote on-campus learning; and integrating community-based, cross-cultural opportunities at home to create a more inclusive and globally aware learning environment. An additional perspective would be the use of artificial Intelligence resources as a personal coach to develop improved writing, conversation, and reading comprehension skills in English and other languages by students and faculty. All the recommendations underline the importance of flexibility, efficiency, and strategic thinking in adapting internationalisation practices to evolving contexts. By embracing innovative approaches and reevaluating established norms, institutions can enhance the accessibility and sustainability of international education initiatives and contribute to stewarding the course of internationalisation.

A good example of effectively stewarding internationalisation is that of the Quality Services of EFMD, which introduced in 2023 a model for internationalisation that transcends considerations of nationality mix. Instead, the model emphasizes the importance of recognising the local context, particularly in emerging markets, and is built on a foundation of profound respect for diversity. The model is organised into four overarching categories: policy (to address issues influencing strategy, reputation, and governance); content (encompassing aspects of the learning and development process); context (considering issues arising from the varied backgrounds of stakeholders); and elements of the broader network in which the school participates (El Garah et al., 2023).

In a world where globalisation has permeated almost every corner, it is fundamental to acknowledge the pressures to redefine standards and prepare for the potential impacts of a volatile business environment and the rapid development of schools in emerging economies. Technology emerges as an ally with business schools increasingly leveraging IT to overcome obstacles such as the cost of faculty and student mobility, as well as political and cultural challenges, among others.

A notable trend in internationalisation is the emergence of virtual visiting scholars, providing a contemporary solution to the barriers presented by physical mobility. Schools in some developed countries are now able to share their online faculty development workshops with online visiting faculty, fostering collaboration and knowledge exchange in a digital space. Another innovative initiative is the inclusion of virtual international guest speakers, allowing students and teachers to connect through screens without the need for overseas travel (El Garah et al., 2023). This paradigm shift not only enhances accessibility and inclusivity but also reflects the adaptability of educational institutions to the evolving conditions of global management education.

Certain studies assert that the ability to innovate and transform are pivotal factors for academic and international development. This underscores the necessity of fostering an innovative university culture and cultivating new skills among both academic and managerial staff. Additionally, there is a pressing need to capitalize on specific opportunities facilitated by digital tools, such as online and blended degree programmes, collaborative online initiatives with foreign institutions, the establishment of international student communities, the creation of digital services, and the implementation of robust platforms for virtual teaching. Moreover, comprehensive training programmes on internationalisation practice for teaching and administrative staff are important to assure readiness for the technological era in which we are currently immersed.

An additional way to enhance internationalisation lies in securing legislative and financial support from national governments. Simultaneously, collaboration programmes with technology companies within the private sector can foster development of new educational products that effectively address the challenges posed by globalisation, digital transformation and the need to design educational experiences using the metaverse, and techniques based on digital twins, among others. In this regard, it is essential to integrate strategic and operational initiatives to promote the competitiveness of universities on the international stage. This comprehensive approach could ensure that institutions are well-positioned to leverage opportunities and navigate the complexities of the global higher education.

CONCLUSION

There is indeed much to explore in the dynamic context of IaH. While there is no magic formula, certain patterns and trends have emerged emphasising the growing impact and role of technology. However, technology alone is not the focal point. In today's global society, the imperative for business schools is to prioritise the development of global citizens. To nurture global citizens, the emphasis has shifted towards soft skills, recognising the importance of face-to-face internationalisation for honing communication and leadership skills. The evolving context also demands inclusiveness, acknowledging the role of students as active participants in a transformed world marked by new learning tools that are in constant flux. It's worth noting that a lack of awareness stands out as a significant hurdle to the adoption of new learning tools in higher-education institutions, underscoring a challenge that needs attention (McKinsey & Company, 2022).

The educational landscape will require from HEIs the disposition to transform their teaching, research, and social outreach taking on board IaH as a tool for integrating purposefully international and intercultural skills in teaching and learning.

Considering students, faculty, HEIs, and the industry as key stakeholders in the challenges and opportunities of IaH, the following conclusions emerge from the reflections of this chapter:

1. Developing global citizens is a paramount goal for business schools, necessitating a focus beyond technical knowledge.
2. The recognition that soft skills, especially in face-to-face interactions, is crucial for preparing students for effective communication and leadership in a global context.
3. Students seek inclusiveness and desire to be active participants in a world that is constantly transforming, and this requires adapting new learning tools and methodologies to curricula.
4. Awareness and successful adoption by faculty and staff of internationalisation practice and new learning tools and heightened communication within institutions.
5. Fomenting virtual international communities and networking opportunities for students and faculty.

6. Leveraging opportunities for strategic collaboration among HEIs, industry partners, and government entities to address challenges and opportunities.
7. Embracing the commitment to continuous learning and adaptation that a global education requires to stay abreast of market needs, emerging trends, and technologies to promote academic quality.
8. Structuring the use of artificial intelligence coaches to personalise learning and further language skills.

As the landscape of IaH evolves, these conclusions provide a foundation to navigate the challenges and embrace the opportunities that lie ahead. The context suggests placing the institutional mission as the cornerstone of the strategic direction for global engagement and educational objectives.

The meaning of internationalisation is dynamic over time and intricately woven into the fabric of globalisation which demands adaptability, inclusiveness, and collaboration in the context of education. In turn, inclusiveness and collaboration point towards a cooperative approach to enhance the collective impact and resilience of higher education in a competitive world. There is also a need to acknowledge that technological expansion is reshaping education; therefore, many countries are adopting online and hybrid learning models in response to disruptions, marking a transformative shift in education (UNESCO, 2021). Universities will need to make strategic investments in digital technologies providing faculty and students with engaging interactive digital tools to promote comprehensive learning experiences. Fortunately, leveraging new technologies presents opportunities for cost savings, particularly in mobility-related expenses, and the integration of face-to-face and online initiatives offers a flexible and cost-effective approach to education.

To conclude, it is important to invite further reflection and research to pave the way for the advancement of the field of internationalisation in higher education and shaping perspectives of IaH. Future research could explore questions such as: How does the depth of learning differ between complete cultural immersion and partial immersion? What strategies can transcend barriers such as visa restrictions, currency volatility, geographical isolation, and social instability for a truly international learning experience? Can investments in virtual learning technologies, IaH, affordable exchange programmes, and research cooperation offer viable alternatives? What ethical issues arise in internationalisation, particularly concerning contextual fairness? How can the disparities in geographical, financial, social, and political conditions be addressed to ensure the quality of international education? How can we overcome mindsets associated with specific regional conditions and intellectual prowess?

ACKNOWLEDGEMENTS

I would like to express my appreciation and gratitude to María Carolina Alvarez Guzmán, Lina Rocío Ramos Pachón, and Sharon Alexandra Álvarez Pérez, members of the internationalization and research teams of the International School of Economic and Administrative Sciences. I am thankful for the engaging and productive discussions we had regarding their experiences, aiming to ensure a more inclusive and purposeful internationalisation of students, faculty, and staff during and after the pandemic.

The assistance provided by Sharon and Lina was particularly valuable when assembling ideas and discussing experiences with learning resources. They played a crucial role in making technological tools more accessible to a diverse student body, promoting inclusion, and fostering cross-cultural experiences through virtual mobility to shape managerial prowess.

NOTES

1. Created under the auspices of UNESCO in 1950.
2. Between 2014 and 2018, two million students and staff in higher education undertook a learning, training, or teaching period abroad with the new Erasmus+ programme.

REFERENCES

Beelen, J. (2011). 'La internacionalización en casa en una perspectiva global: un estudio crítico del Informe del 3.er Estudio Global de la AIU'. *RUSC: Universities and Knowledge Society Journal*, 8/2, 85–100.

Beelen, J., & Jones, E. (2015). 'Redefining Internationalization at Home'. In A. Curaj, L. Matei, R. Pricopie, J. Salmi, & P. Scott, eds., *The European Higher Education Area: Between Critical Reflections and Future Policies*. Springer International Publishing, 59–72.

Castiello-Gutiérrez, S. (2019). 'Purposeful Internationalization: A Common-Good Approach of Global Engagement'. *Journal of Comparative & International Higher Education*, 11, 93–95.

Castiello-Gutiérrez, S., Aguilar, M., & Jurado, C. (2022). *Internationalization of Higher Education after COVID-19: Reflections and New Practices for Different Times*. UPAEP University.

Charoensap-Kelly, P., & Punyanunt-Carter, N. M. (2023). 'Renewing Pedagogical Research and Practices: Helping International Students Succeed Post-COVID-19'. *International Journal of Communication*. https://www.researchgate.net/publication/366822114.

Cordova, M., Floriani, D. E., Gonzalez-Perez, M. A., Hermans, M., Mingo, S., Monje-Cueto, F., Nava-Aguirre, K. M., Rodriguez, C. A., & Salvaj, E. (2021). 'COVID-19 and Higher Education: Responding to Local Demands and the Consolidation of E-Internationalization in Latin American Universities'. *Academia Revista Latinoamericana de Administración*, 34/4, 493–509.

Crowther, P., Joris, M., Otten, M., Nilsson, B., Teekens, H., & Wächter, B. (2000). *Internationalisation at home: A Position Paper*. Citeseer.
De Wit, H., & Jones, E. (2018). 'Inclusive Internationalization: Improving Access and Equity'. *International Higher Education*, 94, 16–18.
Dueñas, M., Campi, M., & Olmos, L. E. (2021). 'Changes in Mobility and Socioeconomic Conditions During the COVID-19 Outbreak'. *Humanities and Social Sciences Communications*, 8/1. https://doi.org/10.1057/s41599-021-00775-0.
Dwivedi, Y. K., Hughes, D. L., Coombs, C., Constantiou, I., Duan, Y., Edwards, J. S., Gupta, B., Lal, B., Misra, S., Prashant, P., Raman, R., Rana, N. P., Sharma, S. K., & Upadhyay, N. (2020). 'Impact of COVID-19 Pandemic on Information Management Research and Practice: Transforming Education, Work and Life'. *International Journal of Information Management*, 55, 102211. https://doi.org/https://doi.org/10.1016/j.ijinfomgt.2020.102211
EU Commission & Directorate-General for Education Sport and Culture. (2018). *The Erasmus Impact Study*. EU Publications.
Foster, M., & Carver, M. (2018). 'Explicit and Implicit Internationalisation: Exploring Perspectives on Internationalisation in a Business School with a Revised Internationalisation of the Curriculum Toolkit'. *The International Journal of Management Education*, 16/2, 143–153.
Fugate, D. L., & Jefferson, R. W. (2001). 'International Perspective: Preparing for Globalization—Do We Need Structural Change for Our Academic Programs+'. *Journal of Education for Business*, 76/3, 160–166.
El Garah, W., Naude, P., & Osbaldeston, M. (2023). 'An Emerging Market Perspective on the Internationalisation of Business Schools'. *Global Focus*, 17/1, 29–34.
García-Morales, V. J., Garrido-Moreno, A., & Martín-Rojas, R. (2021). 'The Transformation of Higher Education After the COVID Disruption: Emerging Challenges in an Online Learning Scenario'. *Frontiers in Psychology*, 12. https://www.frontiersin.org/articles/10.3389/fpsyg.2021.616059.
Gonzalez-Perez, M. A., Mohieldin, M., Hult, G. T. M., & Velez-Ocampo, J. (2021). 'COVID-19, Sustainable Development Challenges of Latin America and the Caribbean, and the Potential Engines for an SDGs-Based Recovery'. *Management Research: Journal of the Iberoamerican Academy of Management*, 19/1, 22–37.
Hofer, C. W. (1975). 'Toward a Contingency Theory of Business Strategy'. *The Academy of Management Journal*, 18/4, 784–810.
House, R., Javidan, M., Hanges, P., & Dorfman, P. (2002). 'Understanding Cultures and Implicit Leadership Theories Across the Globe: An Introduction to Project GLOBE'. *Journal of World Business*, 37/1, 3–10.
Hudzik, J. K. (2022). *Post-COVID Higher Education Internationalization: Prospects and Priorities*. STINT Internationalization Seminar. February 2022. Michigan State University.
Jaworski, B. J., & Kohli, A. K. (1996). 'Market Orientation: Review, Refinement, and Roadmap'. *Journal of Market-Focused Management*, 1/2, 119–135.
Jensen, T, Marinoni, G, & van't Land, H. (2022). *Higher Education One Year Into the COVID-19 Pandemic: Second IAU Global Survey Report*. International Association of Universities.
Jiang, H. (2021). 'Opportunities and Challenges: Internationalized Higher Education in the Pandemic and Post-Pandemic Age'. *Journal of Foreign Languages and Cultures*, 5/2, 152–154.
Johanson, J., & Vahlne, J.-E. (1977). 'The Internationalization Process of the Firm: A Model of Knowledge Development and Increasing Foreign Market Commitments'. *Journal of International Business Studies*, 8/1, 23–32.

Kedia, B. L., & Cornwell, T. B. (1994). 'Mission Based Strategies for Internationalizing U.S. Business Schools'. *Journal of Teaching in International Business*, 5/3, 11–29.
Khan, M., Bank, D., Okon, E., Al-Qaimari, G., Olivares, S., & Treviño-Martínez, S. (2014). *Diverse Contemporary Issues Facing Business Management Education*. IGI Global. https://doi.org/10.4018/978-1-4666-6449-4.
Knight, J. (2004). Internationalization Remodeled: Definition, Approaches, and Rationales. *Journal of Studies in International Education*, 8, 5–31.
Knight, J. (2008). *Higher Education in Turmoil: The Changing World of Internationalization* (Vol. 13). Brill.
Larsen, T. J., & Olaisen, J. (2013). 'Innovating Strategically in Information and Knowledge Management: Applications of Organizational Behavior Theory'. *International Journal of Information Management*, 33/5, 764–774.
Lejeune, C., & Vas, A. (2009). 'Organizational Culture and Effectiveness in Business Schools: A Test of the Accreditation Impact'. *Journal of Management Development*, 28, 728–741.
MacMillan, I. C., Hambrick, D. C., & Day, D. L. (1982). 'The Product Portfolio and Profitability—A PIMS-Based Analysis of Industrial-Product Businesses'. *Academy of Management Journal*, 25, 733–755.
Marinoni, G. (2019). *Internationalization of Higher Education: An Evolving Landscape, Locally and Globally: IAU 5th Global Survey*. DUZ Academic Publishers.
Marinoni, G., van't Land, H., & Jensen, T. (2020). 'The Impact of COVID-19 on Global Higher Education'. *International Higher Education, Special Issue* 102.
McKinsey & Company. (2022). 'How Technology Is Shaping Learning in Higher Education'. https://www.mckinsey.com/industries/education/our-insights/how-technology-is-shaping-learning-in-higher-education.
Minaeva, E., & Taradina, L. (2022). 'Internationalization in Russian Universities During the Pandemic of COVID-19: Lessons for Succeeding in the New Reality'. *Higher Education Quarterly*, 76/2, 293–310.
Mishra, L., Gupta, T., & Shree, A. (2020). 'Online Teaching-Learning in Higher Education During Lockdown Period of COVID-19 Pandemic'. *International Journal of Educational Research Open*, 1, 100012. https://doi.org/https://doi.org/10.1016/j.ijedro.2020.100012.
Parker, L. D. (2002). 'It's Been a Pleasure Doing Business with You: A Strategic Analysis and Critique of University Change Management'. *Critical Perspectives on Accounting*, 13/5, 603–619.
Prestwich, R., & Ho-Kim, T.-M. (2007). 'Knowledge, Skills and Abilities of International Business Majors'. *Journal of Teaching in International Business*, 19/1, 29–55.
Schueller, J., & Şahin, B. B. (2023). 'Considering the Complexities of Virtual Student Mobility as an Approach to Inclusive Internationalisation in the Post-Pandemic Period'. *Perspectives: Policy and Practice in Higher Education*, 27/3, 96–104.
Scott, P. (1998). 'Massification, Internationalization and Globalization'. In Scott, P. (Ed.) *The Globalization of Higher Education*, 51–62.
UNESCO. (2021). *COVID-19: Reopening and Reimagining Universities: Survey on Higher Education Through UNESCO National Commissions*. https://unesdoc.unesco.org/ark:/48223/pf0000378174.
UNESCO. (2022). *Virtual Student Mobility*. https://Www.Iesalc.Unesco.Org/En/Mve4/.
Worley, C., & Lawler III, E. E. (2006). 'Designing Organizations That Are Built to Change'. *MIT Sloan Management Review*, 48, 19–23.

4

Locally Relevant, Globally Inspired

What 'Glocal' Means for a Business School

MARION DEBRUYNE

The movement towards internationalization has been powerful and provided direction to the evolution of a vast amount of business schools in the last decades. It's a movement that very few within the global business community would question. Yet it begs the question of whether it is a move towards something or also away from something. When a business school becomes more international, does it at the same time become less local?

Does the support for internationalization imply the demise of local relevance? Is it an either/or or an and/and question? Or is there a way for a business school to be combine both? In this chapter, I discuss how the movement towards internationalization created tensions with the local mission of business schools. I argue that those tensions are not fictions, yet that local and global are not at opposite ends of the spectrum.

Asking the question whether there is a real dilemma between being local and being international is increasingly relevant. As much as there has been a strong movement towards internationalization in higher education, increasingly there is a countermovement arising. The question whether the internationalization of higher education has negative repercussions for society is part of a societal debate in quite a few countries. Has internationalization gone too far and led to unintended and negative consequences? In the Netherlands, some political parties have openly questioned whether universities should continue to be as open to international students as they are today, pointing towards the cost for society in terms of local housing, public funding for higher education, and so on. In Belgium, limits to English language education and the proportion of international students are part of government negotiations. In other countries, immigration and visa policies have put restrictions on the access and prospects

Marion Debruyne, *Locally Relevant, Globally Inspired.* In: *Management Education and the Rise of Uncertainty of Global Business.* Edited by: Eric Cornuel, Oxford University Press. © Oxford University Press (2025).
DOI: 10.1093/9780197794470.003.0005

for non-domestic students. The underlying premise in each of these debates is that the internationalization of higher education has negative repercussions for local stakeholders. Even for schools in regions where these pressures do not exist, it is useful to pro-actively ask what the stance of a school is towards local stakeholders and how the local community affects its legitimacy.

Rather than unequivocally talking the talk of internationalization, business school leaders should be building another narrative as well. That narrative should firmly establish that contrasting local and global constitutes a false dichotomy. At the same time, that narrative also defines a new way forward. It demonstrates the way that business schools can have local relevance while being international.

LOCAL RELEVANCE

Before asking ourselves what it means to be locally relevant, it is a useful exercise to look back a few decades to the era when many business schools were created. What one will conclude is that local relevance is part of the origin and founding purpose of many business schools.

Very few business schools are 'born global'. Most in fact are quite clearly 'born local' and the ambition to be international emerged only later on. Merely the fact that participants needed to physically get to campus provided relevance to local proximity. Business schools have a natural 'catchment area' around their campus that is not unlike the one that characterizes any retail business. It is this 'retail' model that has led to a very fragmented global landscape of thousands of business schools, even though the core product (an undergraduate or master's degree in business) is by and large the same in all these schools. Amongst this large number of schools, a select group can distinguish themselves as local leaders: the premier business school in their city, region, or country that can claim the strongest reputation (yet often not the highest market share). Yet this select group of local leaders is still large and quite fragmented. An even selecter subgroup of schools has regional or global appeal and can be considered first-tier internationally.

The idea of local relevance transcends mere convenience and proximity, though, and permeates the historical mission of many business schools. For many that mission contains the core belief that the business school has a role to play in its local environment and its legitimacy revolves around impact on the local community. (I'm using the word 'local' loosely here as it may apply to a city, region, country, depending on the context.) For example, quite a few business schools in France find their roots within the local chamber of commerce. The business school was intended to be a source of employable and well-educated talent to the existing business community. Alternatively, business schools are often seen as engines of entrepreneurship that can drive growth and innovation in a region and contribute to prosperity. That ecosystem perspective is also core in the argument that business, government, civil society, and higher education interact to drive innovation, the so-called quadruple helix model.

The origin story of Vlerick Business School also clearly illustrates the societal relevance and impact that drove its inception, growth and reputation. The Belgian school was created in the 1950s and received its name through its founder Andre Vlerick. In the years after World War II, it was critical to rise from the ashes of the devastation caused by war and build the foundations of a strong European economy, which later on would become a unified economy as shaped by the European Union. Belgium, and its capital Brussels, today are home to the European Parliament and many EU institutions that emerged from this union. The Marshall Plan was part of the effort to rebuild the economy. Officially the European Recovery Program was an American initiative established in 1948 to provide foreign aid to Western-Europe to re-build the infrastructure and economy. Young up-and-coming economist and politician André Vlerick was assigned the mandate for the implementation of this Marshall Plan in Belgium. The same motivation of economic relaunch that existed behind the Marshall Plan also led him to create what is now known as Vlerick Business School. The reasoning was that a strong economy needed a strong entrepreneurial foundation, with a lively entrepreneurial spirit and well-educated entrepreneurs. The owners and next generations of the many family businesses in the region could benefit from learning the theories and knowledge emerging from overseas. as being taught across the pond in US-based MBA programmes. Moreover, those entrepreneurs running growing businesses needed qualified and well-trained young talent to join their ranks and support their growth. Completely in line with this thinking, the first Vlerick programmes were targeted at entrepreneurs on the one hand and young university graduates on the other hand. Local impact therefore was central to the school's purpose and original founding beliefs.

Vlerick's story in that sense is surely not unique. For many schools, there's been historical value in closeness to the local business community and local talent and the goal of local relevance is rooted in the history of the school. Schools were founded to serve and strengthen their community and the legitimacy of business schools is built on the value generated for the local ecosystem as well as the leading role a business school can play in that ecosystem. Many business school deans will recognize this narrative in the discourse from alumni that were part of the history of their school and represent the cohorts from an earlier era. In fact, it can be hard to convince those alumni who are proud of their school's position as local leader that this local impact is not sufficient in today's world. Resource dependency on these historical stakeholders sometimes even hampers schools in their internationalization efforts.

OPEN TO THE WORLD

Over time, local relevance was no longer seen as sufficient to legitimize a business school. The forces of globalization permeated the campus walls and convinced business school leaders that they needed to open up beyond their local stakeholders and take a broader point of view. As business became more global, so did business schools. And as the concept of globalization and global business became firmly rooted into the curricula of MBA programmes, it also became firmly rooted into the belief system of business education itself. Internationalization became a strong driving force in the development of business schools over time. Accreditation bodies such as EFMD reinforced this movement by making internationalization an explicit cornerstone and prerequisite of accreditation as described in the EQUIS standards. The emphasis on internationalization as criteria in business school rankings such as the *Financial Times*' various rankings contribute to the same movement.

'Internationalization' is a term that carries multiple meanings. The many areas of impact can be seen in the EQUIS internationalization dimensions. International business schools produce research that adheres to international standards and has relevance that goes beyond the local ecosystem. They are an active participant and contributor to the international research community. Their faculty base is diverse in terms of the nationality and international experience of its members. They attract students with diverse international backgrounds and provide them with international learning experiences and career opportunities. They work together with schools in other countries to enrich the learning journey of their students through exchanges, trips, and joint degrees. In their executive education activities, they attract client from different countries for whom they develop programmes that demonstrate an understanding of international business and integrate the international reality in which their customers operate.

Considering these multiple dimensions of what it means to be an international business school, it can feel like a gargantuan task for incumbents with a strong local heritage to make progress on all fronts. Internationalization is a transformational journey for those schools with local roots and a history that is entrenched into a local ecosystem and community. It's also a journey that never ends and does not lead towards the same destination with the same intermediary checkpoints for all schools. More likely, each school individually needs to determine its own relevant model of internationalization, depending on its context, portfolio of activities, history, and so on. In that respect, it should be acknowledged that some schools have intrinsic advantages that make the internationalization journey easier while others face stronger headwinds. Location is important. For example, it's clear that for schools located in a cosmopolitan metropole the possibilities are greater than for those located in a remote corner of the world.

Nevertheless, the direction of travel is clear for all. As internationalization is an integral part of accreditations and rankings, it has also become an integral part of a school's reputation and status. Any business school leader who is not preaching internationalization most definitely goes against the tide. Yet with the push towards internationalization being as strong as it is, it is also easy to get caught up in it the effort while losing sight of the reason and reasoning behind it. After all, business school leaders are prone to the lemming effect just like any business leader. The risk is for internationalization to become a normative effort that checks the boxes yet does not touch the heart and soul. When instrumentalized and utilitarian, internationalization loses its purpose.

I would argue that an internationalization narrative and strategy that prioritizes purpose over expansion can incorporate internationalization in a historically locally-oriented purpose. Just as an innovation narrative that is anchored within the roots of an organization has more chance to succeed, an internationalization narrative that embraces instead of denies the roots of a school can be better embedded for success. It comes with the consideration that being international is at the heart of creating local value.

We quite easily fall into the trap of stereotyping schools as 'local' or 'international', yet there is no necessary contradiction between being local and international. The conclusion that local and global are opposite ends of a spectrum is quickly made yet does not have to be true. Should we deny local relevance to be seen as truly credibly international? I will argue the opposite and present three ways for schools to be 'glocal': globally inspired, locally relevant.

LOCAL RELEVANCE REVISITED, THROUGH AN INTERNATIONAL LENS

Even at a time when digital learning possibilities remove geographical barriers for learning, the on-campus model remains resilient. The shock of the COVID-19 pandemic forced providers and consumers of business education to adopt digital learning on a massive scale. While schools had to make the transition very quickly, they succeeded in doing so and learned a lot along the way about how to create effective digital learning. Yet the appetite for in-person persists. Of course, in-person learning does not limit schools to local students. More than ever, applicants are willing to move abroad for their MBA or specialized master's degree and consider schools around the world. But what about the short courses and learning moments that are part of lifelong learning? Accessible options in the proximity of learners cater to the appetite for in-person learning and offer a sustainable solution that does not require travel. Moreover, they offer schools the opportunity to add value by translating universal insights to the local context and enable participants to bridge the gap between theory and practice. Learning impact can be enhanced with recognizable examples, familiar cases and integration of the local ecosystem. At the same time, schools that have an international outlook can combine this with providing broader international inspiration and embedding learning and insights that live up to international standards and incorporate state-of-the art global research. Business schools can find a point of differentiation in bringing universal ideas and knowledge into the local context and translate theory to practice in a way that speaks to what is going on in the immediate environment of participants. In fact, doing so can provide a gateway away from the sameness that characterizes the curricula of business schools. Every school operates within its unique context, and the same is true for its participants. Taking knowledge that is universal in concept and developing an understanding of its contextualization enables participants to put that knowledge into action while developing a deeper understanding of its implications. When schools succeed in delivering that contextualization, their internationalization agenda serves a local purpose at the same time.

Opening Minds and Hearts

Our role and obligation is to educate future leaders who can operate and thrive in a globalized world. That mission is though not exclusively 'global for global' and can include 'global for local'. In other words, it serves both international students as well as domestic students and represents another way in which internationalization serves a local purpose.

At Vlerick Business School this narrative of internationalization is behind the credo 'Open to the World'. We are based in Belgium, a small and open economy that sits centrally within Europe both geographically as well as symbolically as major European institutions are based in Brussels. Doing business from Belgium requires an openness that goes beyond borders, as the domestic market is most often too small to provide the necessary scale for companies to be competitive. Business education that has the ambition to be relevant should match the international outlook of the business surrounding it. Bringing the world inside the classroom prepares students for the international environment in which they will be expected to operate as they advance their careers. Not being international would do them a disservice in reflecting the reality of the business world they are entering. International content, international faculty, and a broad diversity of students create the environment that reflects this reality. Having more than 50 different nationalities on campus brings with it a richness of experiences that is not without challenges yet at the same time incredibly valuable.

Raising the Bar

Local leadership can be a very comfortable hammock for schools to stay and linger. As schools internationalize, they open themselves up to a broader and more diverse group of peers. That wider scope pushes schools forward and out of the status quo. Having this international outlook is a way for schools to measure themselves against a different yardstick. That means that internationalization prevents falling into the complacency trap. It brings inspiration, opportunities to collaborate and new and diverse perspectives.

An illustrative example of this is the FOME alliance, an alliance of ten major business schools from Asia, Europe, and North America. Standing for 'Future of Management Education', the schools that are part of the alliance are all driven to be at the forefront of developments in terms of digital learning innovation. By joining forces, they created a platform that enables all members to advance. The platform allows for knowledge sharing and benchmarking, the exchange of thoughts and experiences, and cocreating and co-experimenting.

CONCLUSION

This chapter offers a plea to revisit the model of internationalization for business schools—one that does not deny, yet incorporates and embraces, local relevance and dismisses the false dichotomy that has been created between what we call local schools and international schools. Schools that aim to have local relevance are more effective in delivering on that promise from an international vantage point. On the other hand, schools that embrace internationalization by denying local relevance do so at the peril of losing legitimacy in the eyes of local stakeholders. Moreover, let's ask ourselves how we can be more than isolated islands that are completely removed from the place we are located in. On the contrary, from this place of privilege that we occupy, connecting with what's going on outside of the campus walls can be part of our societal mission.

It would be a mistake and a missed opportunity if we all deny the fact that we operate from a certain context, and all become location-agnostic global schools. This chapter offers some ideas for schools to become 'glocal' by being international and local at the same time. The goal is certainly not to present an exhaustive set of ideas on how to be a glocal school, as it is for each school to build their own vision of what that would entail for them. Yet the mere objective is to illustrate that presenting local and international as conflicting with one another is at best an incomplete view. Instead, I suggest a revisited Internationalization narrative that is rooted in the collective purpose of a school and incorporates its local context and stakeholders as much as it reflects a global point of view.

5

US MBA Programmes

Clearing the Runway for Global Business Leaders

ISABELLE BAJEUX-BESNAINOU AND OLIVER HAHL

INTRODUCTION

Few graduate-level business students are more impassioned and venturous than international students coming to the United States. They come, invigorating the economy and the talent pool, with many choosing the popular Master of Business Administration (MBA) programme. Their sights are set on gainful positions at multinational corporations, consulting firms, and entrepreneurial endeavours in a golden land of opportunity. They make fastidious preparations, coordinating new living arrangements and financial commitments in an entirely new country. Some may prepare by learning about certain cultural differences and American norms in advance, but few arrive with a thorough understanding of everything that will be expected of them academically, socially, and professionally. Uncertainties and risks exist for them, but these spirited future leaders look beyond the hurdles and race forward.

Many arrive inspired by ambitions to launch their professional careers in the US. Immigrants who come seeking economic and social mobility are described as 'integral to the American success story', with nearly half of all Fortune 500 companies founded by legal immigrants or children of immigrants, according to 2023 data (Doolittle, 2024).

International students receive crucial support for achieving their goals through the efforts taking place at their MBA programmes. In aviation terms, the MBA programmes are comparable to airports that the students first select, before taking flights heading to different 'destinations', their careers. The faculty are pilots in the cockpit, and the staff are flight attendants, both helping our students take off. It is essential that the US

Isabelle Bajeux-Besnainou and Oliver Hahl, *US MBA Programmes.* In: *Management Education and the Rise of Uncertainty of Global Business.* Edited by: Eric Cornuel, Oxford University Press. © Oxford University Press (2025).
DOI: 10.1093/9780197794470.003.0006

MBA programmes clear the runway by addressing communication issues, raising awareness of potential obstacles, and broadening their outlook on the future.

Internationalization strategies play an important role in helping students, both domestic and international, along their journeys from MBA students to global business leaders. American programmes need internationalization if they are to prepare their students to assume the top roles in business management and leadership. In turn, there is a mutual benefit to the US, as it remains competitive through the great contributions of MBA graduates.

Because of the depth of the job opportunities in the US, it is perfectly acceptable for some US business schools to allow graduates to focus on domestic career paths. This chapter describes why internationalization is valued by MBA programmes in the US and how some programmes are implementing internationalization strategies to achieve global competitiveness, for which the international student plays a critical role. University leaders have prioritized two strategies: first, attract and nurture international students; and second, equip all students with international experiences through the MBA programmes.

US programmes benefit from pursuing these efforts, despite not needing to do so at the same level as their European counterparts, for example. Because there is high demand for MBA programmes in the US and ample job supply for the MBA graduates within the US market, MBA programmes from top business schools could fill their classes with domestic students alone. However, there is a high value of having international and domestic students in the same classrooms as their experiences complement each other.

The chapter is divided into three sections: first, discussing the current US MBA market and its attractiveness to international students; second, explaining why internationalization is important to these programmes; and third, outlining what tactics support internationalization. Overall, we seek to highlight the underlying value of the US MBA as a beacon to students around the world, which in turn allows the US economy to flourish. The programmes open a door to internships, a thriving job market, and significantly higher earning potential. Even if graduates do not stay in the US to work, the programmes enable students to meet people and grow their professional networks with influential organizations and alumni around the world. Along the way, we will share a few stories of our alumni from Carnegie Mellon University's Tepper School of Business, who were drawn to the freedoms and wealth of American life and achieved their goals with great success.

WHY A US MBA FOR INTERNATIONAL STUDENTS?

Higher education is among the major sources of revenue in the US economy. International students coming to the US for higher education contributed US$44 billion in revenue to the country's economy in 2019, which was comparable to the nation's exports in corn, soybeans, and textiles combined (Bound et al., 2021).

US business schools are competitive in attracting research and teaching talent. As a result of PhD programmes being able to attract top international students who in turn provide a strong recruiting pool for faculty members, the elite US business schools attract strong researchers. These researchers are often among the most prominent academic leaders in their fields, contributing to cutting-edge research and thought leadership. The Sveriges Riksbank Prize in Economic Sciences in Memory of Alfred Nobel 2015–2023 has gone consistently to individuals who were affiliated with US institutions at the time of the award (The Nobel Foundation, August 2024). Nine Nobel Prize recipients have been on the Tepper School's faculty (Tepper School of Business, 2024). Students in the US classrooms benefit from learning cutting edge knowledge and are constantly challenged to question the status quo. Moreover, by comparison to some global competitors, classroom sizes tend to be smaller, allowing students to receive direct and personalized guidance. It becomes a virtuous cycle that perpetuates the quality of many US business schools.

Studying in the US evokes the enduring appeal of influential corporations that are creating the next big innovation and startups that thrive on entrepreneurial spirit. The MBA programme in the US remains a highly sought-after educational path, drawing more than 155,000 students annually, according to the Association to Advance Collegiate Schools of Business (AACSB) (Byrne, 2022). The MBA, with its focus on business skills and leadership development, stands out as an important credential.

Several compelling reasons underlie the MBA's popularity. The rapid pace of change in today's knowledge economy is one incentive, attracting certain professionals who need new skills and the strategic thinking required to seek career advancement to senior roles. As the job market becomes increasingly competitive, there is persistent demand for the broad business knowledge that MBA programmes offer. These programmes equip students with expertise in areas such as finance, marketing, operations, and strategic leadership, which are crucial in navigating complex business environments.

Along with the benefits of this education, the type of students attracted to the US MBA are seeking a rewarding business career. They tend to earn higher salaries compared to those with only a bachelor's degree and are positioned for promotions, ascent to senior management roles, and other forms of career advancement. The majority of graduates succeed in leveraging the degree to make a career change, and 85% rate the value of their programme as 'good to outstanding', according to a 2022 report from the Graduate Management Admission Council (GMAC). This report also shows that North American full-time MBA students received a 50% median compensation increase from pre-MBA to post-graduation: from US$80,000 to US$120,000 (Cote, 2022).

At the Tepper School of Business, the MBA Class of 2023 achieved a new record average base salary of US$156,500 (Tepper School of Business, 2023). In 2022, MBA graduates received an average starting salary of US$120,000, more than 57% higher than the US$69,320 average for workers with only a bachelor's degree; graduates from top-ranked MBA programmes, of which Carnegie Mellon is one, could earn starting pay packages (including bonuses) of US$200,000 and higher, according to Graduate Management Admission Council data (Fore & Thomas-Oxtoby, 2024). This difference is even more striking when you consider that MBA salaries are calculated at graduation while the average salary of a bachelor's graduate is calculated over a lifetime.

A team from the networking platform LinkedIn, along with Economic Graph, came across data that revealed 'the career-boosting power of an MBA', including one finding that MBA grads from the class of 2012 were 139% more likely to secure a VP-level role within 10 years of graduation than those with a bachelor's alone (Borden & Faraut, 2023). The findings prompted LinkedIn to design a new US MBA ranking in 2023 that primarily focuses on how programmes translate into long-term career success, examining the five criteria of job opportunities, the ability to progress in one's career, network strength, leadership potential, and a diverse learning environment (Bisoux, 2023). Carnegie Mellon ranked 17. In publishing its inaugural 'Top MBA Programs 2023', LinkedIn posits that despite the upfront cost of US$200,000 or more for the best US business schools, 'it is an investment worth making' (LinkedIn News, 2023).

The traditional MBA programme in the US is an intensive full-time programme, usually over two years, that delivers a strong foundation in business principles and leadership and requires a full-time commitment. The ideal candidate has a bachelor's degree followed by about five years of work experience. Part-time options are prevalent and targeted to working professionals who can readily apply what they learn to their current positions. Dual MBA programmes are an alternative to the traditional coursework and provide a combination of MBA studies with another graduate degree, such as an MD, a JD, or an engineering master's degree. Students are seeking to integrate their expertise in a field with business knowledge to enhance their career prospects and earning power. Employers highly value MBA degrees when hiring. A Statista survey showed that 91% of employers hired MBA graduates across all industries (Dyvik, 2024).

Globally, universities offer MBAs in various formats. Most European schools offer one-year MBA programmes, contrary to the two-year US model. This model allows for an internship in the summer between the first and second years. This internship can be pivotal for international students to gain more exposure to US companies and become more adapted to the US culture.

However, there are some risks, both for the US business schools, and the international students that should not be ignored. There is a growing perception in the higher education community that political risks, such as US government policies on visas and immigration, have impacted enrolment of international students and could spiral to limit even more international student enrolment in the future. Because of complications with the sponsorship of work visas and permanent residencies, it can be difficult for firms to hire international students graduating from US institutions. As a result, the US is beginning to see more and more competition from other countries (Sutherland & Chakrabarti, 2023). Some prospective students are straying to universities in nations that are easing this burden. Countries such as Canada have already established initiatives that seek to attract international students and seem to have an easier process (Zwetsloot et al., 2019). Uncertainties in these policies have the potential to shape the composition of MBA cohorts, potentially dampening international demand, influencing the demographic and cultural diversity.

Prospective MBA students must weigh the potential return on investment of a graduate degree against its costs and risks. The high costs of tuition and living expenses in the US relative to opportunities in students' home countries pose a discernible deterrent. Factors such as expected earning potential post-graduation, career advancement opportunities, and the reputation of the programme all contribute to these calculations.

Kalpesh Kapadia, a Tepper School alumnus, provides a nice illustrative example of the benefits of a US MBA for international students. He came to the US in 1995, after working as an engineer at one of India's leading firms. He earned a master's degree in industrial engineering and operations research at New Jersey Institute of Technology in 1996 and then worked as a production engineer for a year before coming to the Tepper School.

Kapadia's education, along with his personal experiences as an international student, was pivotal in what would become a phenomenal career in global technology and finance. His MBA led to Wall Street, where he became recognized as the top analyst in 2004 across all sectors by the *Wall Street Journal* and went on to found Equanum Capital in 2005. He became CEO and cofounder of the startup Deserve, a mobile-first credit card platform launched in 2013, which he based on the challenges of building a credit profile as a young man arriving in the US.

'One of the most important takeaways from the Tepper School was the network of relationships I built with classmates, faculty, and alumni', Kapadia said. 'These connections have been instrumental in advancing my career. I secured my first job on Wall Street through alumni, and I received my first investment in my company from a Tepper alumnus at Accel'.[1]

We have established the rich economic opportunities along with the quality-of-life benefits that the US presents for business leaders. Although the path presents students with certain risks, particularly in that securing a job after graduation is not guaranteed, aspiring leaders feel compelled to proceed. Not all US MBA programmes internationalize, but those programmes at leading universities that do tend to put great care and attention into the design and implementation of their internationalization efforts. Next, we will take a look at why internationalization is important to those schools.

WHY INTERNATIONALIZE THE US MBA PROGRAMMES

Carnegie Mellon University has built a strong international reputation among US institutions. It often places highly in the 'most international' rankings, such as *Quacquarelli Symonds* (QS) and *US News and World Report*, with QS giving the university a near-perfect score of 99.8 among US institutions for proportion of international students ('Most International Students', 2022; Collier, 2023). The MBA at Carnegie Mellon is distinctly global, with around 56% of enrolment coming from 30 different countries for the graduating class of 2024, and graduates of our programme are hired by top-tier firms in technology, finance, and consulting, primarily in the US (Tepper School of Business, 2024).

Lyenda Delp is representative of how former international students are applying their education to drive success in the US. She came from Kingston, Jamaica to Carnegie Mellon's MBA programme in the 1990s, and she currently leads BlackRock's financial institutions group in the Americas to deliver asset management and advisory and risk management capabilities to sophisticated clients in the insurance industry. When asked what she gained from her MBA programme, her response was, 'So much!'

'The most impactful skills were to problem-solve critically, analyse rigorously, engage diverse and robust perspectives, recognize individuality, and know when to generalize, as well as when not to.' Both Iin and out of the classroom, I learned to persevere in seeking solutions even during crises or just when things are tough', said Delp[2]

Prior to her MBA, Delp had earned a bachelor's degree in chemistry and biochemistry and worked for two years as a credit analyst at a bank reviewing loan applications. Upon earning an MBA, she joined Deloitte Consulting, then Goldman Sachs, eventually joining BlackRock in 2009. Under her leadership, her BlackRock team more than doubled the amount of assets managed in the Americas for insurance clients and firmly established a position as an industry leader.

We have discussed the beneficial symbiotic relationship between US MBA programmes and their international students, which in turn translates to benefits within the US economy and its international workforce of highly skilled talents.

University rankings wield significant influence over institutional priorities and student choices, and rankings publications take different approaches to evaluating internationalization as a factor. The *Financial Times*' Global MBA ranking rewards programmes with higher percentages of international students, faculty, and board members, and those that leverage global partnerships to provide robust opportunities for their students to study and work abroad. In contrast, *US News and World Report*'s Best Business Schools ranking methodology (2024) does not recognize or reward internationalization efforts and traditionally emphasizes factors such as placement, salary, reputation, grade point average, and test scores.

These differences help to explain why US institutions take different approaches to integrating international perspectives into their curricula. Programmes that seek to be competitive globally actively enrich their educational environments with different cultural perspectives, both to generate international experiences and attract a globally diverse student body. While some MBA programmes prioritize extensive internationalization efforts, including study abroad programmes, global partnerships, and culturally diverse curricula, others may be limited. US schools vary widely in how they offer and present global opportunities.

The international students bring to campuses a wide array of cultural experiences that help broaden and deepen discussions inside and outside of the classrooms. International students also increase the quality of the student body since many top students from non-US countries apply to US MBA programmes. Attracting this international talent is a benefit to the US companies as recruiters target these high-quality graduates. To summarize, the international students coming to US MBA programmes benefit from the overall student experience, are of high quality, and usually secure amazing job opportunities. This virtuous cycle increases the school's rankings and prestige.

This prestige is what attracted Marc Onetto to Carnegie Mellon. He is principal at Leadership from the Heart and Mind consulting firm and a retired senior vice president of worldwide operations and customer service at Amazon, under CEO Jeff Bezos. Working for GE early in his career, he led the globalization and quality transformation effort as vice president and general manager of the global supply chain for medical systems, making an impact 1992–2002 when the company's value rose 3,000% and earning recognition for his efforts in the autobiography of then-GE chairman and CEO Jack Welch (Deep, 2014).

A Paris native who earned a master's degree in engineering from Ecole Centrale in the city of Lyon, Onetto came to the US in 1973 to pursue an MBA at Carnegie Mellon. He described his desire to attain the MBA degree as follows:

> My father always admired the USA and often told me I should go and experience life there. He had served in the French Free Air Force in World War II, was trained as a pilot in the USA in 1943, and kept strong, positive memories of his life there. In the mid-1970s, the USA was really the centre of the world for business success, and so it was evident for me to consider a US university to complement my education with a business degree. Secondly, I was attracted by the quantitative approach to business proposed by Carnegie Mellon University. I knew it would fit very well with my strong French academic scientific education. At the time, Carnegie Mellon's business school was very much a world leader in proposing this new scientific approach to business education. Finally, one of the alumni of my French university had just graduated from Carnegie Mellon's business school. He convinced me this was the best choice for me.[3]

Recruited first by Exxon upon earning the MBA, Onetto said he benefited greatly from the highly data-driven approach to business management he learned and the international diversity of his classmates. The global perspective he gained was particularly valuable, according to Onetto:

> Beyond my academic education, the business school also gave me a very important life experience. For the first time in my life, I was exposed to working in teams with people from all over the world. I still remember how surprised I was to see people proposing creative solutions with a different approach. I still remember my colleague [for one team project] from Japan. Interacting with him really taught me to deal with diverse cultural and education backgrounds. This turned out to be extremely useful for me when later in life I became in charge of worldwide operations at GE and Amazon with hundreds of thousand people all over the world.[4]

Even US MBA students who do not stay in the US after graduation increase their job prospects and career opportunities. Government-sponsored scholarship programmes from non-US countries serve to attract and support talented students in studying abroad, including in the US. Through sponsored students, universities gain not only the rich cultural and diplomatic benefits that come from international relationships but also the attractive financial benefit of enrolling fully funded students. The Department of State developed the EducationUSA network of hundreds of advising centres in more than 175 countries and territories (EducationUSA, 2024). These coordinators are a point of contact when universities seek advice regarding recruitment of students in a specific region or country. Similarly, prospective students can be encouraged to contact these advising coordinators to ensure they receive reliable information on their MBA search and application process to study abroad (EducationUSA, 2024).

At Carnegie Mellon, alumni have helped us connect to both government-sponsored and corporate-sponsored students. Tad Brinkerhoff, the Tepper School's assistant dean of master's programmes, has worked on these sponsorships in recent years and developed support for incoming sponsored students.

The Indonesia Endowment Fund for Education, known as 'LPDP', led to an important sponsored-student programme between Indonesia and Carnegie Mellon following a conversation between one Indonesian CMU alumnus and Brinkerhoff.[5] LPDP is an agency of Indonesia's federal government tasked with overseeing the education endowment fund. The Indonesian constitution outlines that at least 20% of the state budget go to education (Lembaga Pengelola Dana Pendidikan, 2024). Government-sponsored students from Indonesia receive support not only for the programme tuition but also for their housing expenses.

It is common for Carnegie Mellon to draw sponsorships from corporations in Japan and Korea based on our reputation and strengths in quantitative areas. Corporate sponsorships from Japan and Korea have come from the electronics, energy, finance, semiconductor, and utilities sectors. Both countries also have provided government-sponsorships for students in finance.

These sponsored students are highly desirable. While a clear advantage is receiving full tuition from the sponsor, there are a list of other benefits sponsored students bring to the institution.[6] They have already been vetted by their sponsors as quality students who also have strong leadership potential. As they earn the degree, these students exhibit strong motivation and commitment to the programme, knowing they are backed with support from their employer. The sponsor usually tends to the students' financial needs, alleviating any of these potential issues from the institution. The students receive jobs with their sponsors upon graduation, helping the institution to efficiently and successfully meet post-graduation placement goals. Finally, graduates become alumni that help to develop the institution's important corporate and government connections globally.

Regardless of where they find work, the contributions of MBA graduates flow back into the global economy in the form of progress and innovation. We have discussed why students seek out an MBA and why the US programmes want to attract them. We will now describe the internationalization tactics these programmes use in the US to 'clear the runway' and prepare MBA graduates for 'liftoff' in their careers.

THE TEPPER SCHOOL AS A CASE STUDY FOR INTERNATIONALIZATION OF US MBA PROGRAMMES

Developing global understanding among students in the MBA programme requires robust initiatives, along with the faculty and staff who will implement and support them. Successful internationalization must aim to reach all students. The goal is to imbue them with a keen understanding of business, economic, political, and ethical issues of the world and develop a sophisticated understanding of a variety of cultural norms and customs.

MBA programmes in the US that value internationalization place a high value on the students themselves. As shown through our previous examples of Tepper School alumni, the learning environment is enriched by the individuals' backgrounds, cultural knowledge, and insights that the students bring with them to the business school and share with other members of the university community. We will now show that internationalization encompasses at least two strategies: first, attract and nurture international students, and second, equip all students with international experiences.

Attracting and Nurturing International Students

International students go to great lengths to apply to, vet, and attend US MBA programmes and carry with them cultural perspectives that enriches the classroom once they arrive and acclimate to their programmes. For these reasons, a strategy of internationalization is focused on attracting and nurturing these student populations.

At the Tepper School, incoming MBA students who are new to the US are extended the opportunity to participate in our Business English and Cultural Immersion (BECI) Summer Program. The BECI programme is designed to the specific needs of MBA students acclimating to US academic culture and life.

The BECI programme takes place over nine weeks prior to the start of the fall semester, first delivering online sessions on business-oriented language, writing, and communications skills for several weeks, and then meeting in person for the last two weeks of the programme to instruct them in cultural immersion activities together after their arrival in the US. Brinkerhoff and an English-as-a-second-language practitioner are among the BECI organizers providing guidance in business presentation competence, negotiation and persuasion techniques, and cross-cultural communication (Davis, 2024b). The students are introduced to individuals including fellow students, faculty members, and community members who can help advance their career network, which is a crucial aspect of their future job search.

Presenting the Case of the International-Student Entrepreneur

US business schools distinguish themselves through their ability to nurture entrepreneurial thinking and foster innovation. Many have established centres and programmes dedicated to entrepreneurship, offering vital resources, mentorship, and funding for nascent ventures. The opportunity to consider entrepreneurship as a post-MBA career is not limited to US students, who grow up in a culture that celebrates the entrepreneurial spirit and successes, but also can be open to international students. Access to capital and other resources are readily available in the US. However, cultural limitations often cloud their willingness to see entrepreneurship as an avenue for their career and the relational skills needed to pursue such a career.

As one example of someone who overcame these challenges, we present Ozioma Aniagu, a Tepper School graduate of the class of 2024. Aniagu started a career in her home country of Nigeria as a state department field agent before moving to Toronto to be a software engineer. After five years developing software solutions, she entered the Tepper School's MBA programme intending to advance in the technology sector, but her plans changed. Through two entrepreneurship courses, she created an idea for a new product inspired by traditional African cooking. 'I have all of these classmates and professors to talk to, and all of these resources here, so I am going to commit to designing this product', said Aniagu, who earned an MBA in 2024 and is planning a product launch in 2025 (Davis, 2024a).

A shift to entrepreneurialism is not unusual for US MBA students who often find support and encouragement to develop new businesses. Unlike domestic students, however, Aniagu said she struggled 'with small talk and the social nuances of business school' as an international student (Davis,

2024a). She credited her MBA programme for helping her further advance her communication skills and giving her practice to develop interpersonal skills on her path to leadership.

Developing Inclusiveness and Belonging

Cultural differences, while valued by the institution, can be a barrier for some students that allow differences to affect peer relationships. They may feel challenged to develop working relationships with students whose identities or practices do not align with their home countries' beliefs and policies. These differences could relate to culture, religion, gender, sexual identity, societal status, and other numerous backgrounds and situations. Indeed, the very definition of leadership—seen as an inclusive, collaborative, team-based position in America—can be at odds with other cultures that perceive leadership as directive and controlling (Hofstede, 1992; Hoppe & Bhagat, 2007).

Many scholars over the years have examined closely the challenges faced by international students and found that student wellness is influenced by their peer networks, funding and finances, ability to communicate, feelings of loneliness, sense of belonging, knowledge sharing, strength of purpose, and ability to maintain the motivation to cope with the daily challenges of undertaking a graduate programme (e.g. Bound et al., 2021; Lorenzetti et al., 2023; Martirosyan et al., 2019). Students look to the institution for support through, not simply resources, but also direct and explicit guidance on making the most of opportunities.

Campus life presents excellent opportunities to offer co-curricular programmes that can help support the wellness of international students. At the Tepper School, such co-curricular programmes also expand upon the inclusive leadership concepts and career planning presented in our MBA programme. One co-curricular offering we established is the Accelerate Leadership Center (ALC) at Carnegie Mellon, where students can access coaching, educational events, and a leadership development certification. Key components of the ALC are one-to-one leadership coaching, one-to-one peer communication coaching, immersive leadership programmes, and interactive workshops.

Through their experiences at the ALC students build their professional identities; develop their skills to be innovative, collaborative, and inclusive leaders; and increase their personal confidence by focusing on the foundational capacities of emotional intelligence, cultural humility, and constructive dialogue.

Overarching challenges faced by international students are related to adjusting to an unfamiliar environment, forming personal and business networks, and succeeding in a new US-based business culture. Speaking up, as well as small talk, is a challenge for some, as one example provided by Rebecca Lamperski, executive director of the ALC. Some international students who sought coaching from the ALC first needed to start with strategies to speak up during class and team projects, and then to work on how to build relationships at networking and recruiting events.[7]

A second co-curricular set of activities are related to diversity, equity, and inclusion initiatives, which are proactive movements that seek to prioritize the sanctity of every student and faculty member to pursue their work without bullying or harassment based on their background. McKinsey & Company (2022) defines these three terms as 'closely linked values held by many organizations that are working to be supportive of different groups of individuals, including people of different races, ethnicities, religions, abilities, genders, and sexual orientations'. Some institutions refer to these efforts by the acronym DEI, but at others, including the Tepper School, we also encompass the concept of 'belonging' to the discourse. These initiatives are led by the Tepper Together task force and follow a strategic plan outlining our diversity, equity, inclusion, and belonging (DEIB) goals and actions (Tepper School of Business, 2022). The Tepper School's David L. Major, associate dean of DEIB, helps students differentiate belonging from inclusion by explaining it as 'a way of feeling at home' and being a part of the decision-making in what we do.[8] 'When I introduce myself and DEIB to MBA students at the start of their program, I really focus on this feeling of belonging because these students need to feel "at home" in our space', he said. International students are a part of the diversity and understand the DEIB concepts as pertinent to global views of identities and differences, Major explained. Every student, including international students, plays an important role in the plan. Our graduates leave the university having experienced a DEIB plan in action and gained related leadership knowledge that will one day enhance their future work environments.

By aspiring to instil the inclusive leadership mindset in all our MBA students, we nurture a campus culture that welcomes and supports differences. It brings learning benefits to individual students and helps to develop great organizational leaders. A support system needs to be comprehensive in its reach to students, beginning with the recruitment phase, then guiding students through the enrolment and academic achievement phases, then ensuring post-graduation placement, and lastly connecting graduates to prosperous alumni networks. Those alumni worldwide would maintain their university connection over a long period of time and, with success, will contribute to a thriving alumni network over generations.

Equipping All Students with International Experiences

Some of the competitive MBA programmes worldwide integrate capstone projects and study abroad programmes to instil students with management competencies and provide international exposure. Before students can navigate these intense and complex opportunities to positive outcomes, they need preparation, no matter whether the students are domestic or international, and the curriculum alone will not address this educational need.

Learning centres are one way that MBA programmes can deliver multicultural resources. The teachings of these centres must be closely aligned with the MBA programme curriculum.

As an example of the types of experiences that a learning centre can offer in helping students develop cultural skills, the ALC partnered with the Graduate Business Association to host a cultural meal practice event. At this event, students participated in a dinner party featuring an array of tables based on the cuisine and culture of different countries. At each table, the students learned about and were able to practice the dining customs and etiquette, such as how to eat certain foods with your hands at an Indian table or how to use the many utensils in a full place setting on an American table.

Student activities that embrace international cultures and spotlight the unique backgrounds of members of the community, such as cultural meals and workshops, serve dual purposes: to prepare all students with a foundation for global understanding and to nurture, respect, and celebrate the individuals who travelled far and crossed international borders to be a part of the cohort.

Beyond these types of experiences in which students engage locally, students may also gain hands-on experiences through short-term study abroad courses. In a course like this, students are put into groups and connected with a company in a different country. They spend the first half of the semester scoping out a project with the 'client'. These virtual connections are then complemented by a 12-day, in-country experience where the students work directly with the company, often in their offices, to increase cultural immersion. This in-country time is crucial. The students navigate cultural differences in a professional environment and gain a glimpse of business culture in a country they have not visited previously. They fulfil the role of engagement managers to develop and execute a project, all the while managing client expectations and team goals. These courses serve as capstone courses, allowing students to use all of the skills they have learned in the first 18 months of their programme to tackle a real-world problem.

Examples of these programmes include projects in Brazil, Chile, Germany, South Africa, and South Korea, with others planned for the future.

While much of the MBA programme for international students helps them develop knowledge about US culture and to prepare them for the US job market, the experiences discussed above serve two additional purposes: first, allowing non-US students to experience other cultures to which they have had less exposure; and second, positioning non-US and US students alike to develop and apply the cultural skills they need to better lead global teams and firms. This global perspective, which starts with international students studying in the US, is critical to all business leaders now and in the future.

CONCLUSION

This chapter has described the benefits of US MBA programmes for international students, along with reasons why these programmes are seeking out students from across borders to enrich the learning experiences at institutions. In support of these benefits, we have shared some tactics to support international students in MBA programmes and encourage all students in these programmes to gain international experiences.

There are challenges to building internationalization into MBA programmes, but if students succeed in achieving a degree and job placement, their careers will take off and facilitate business growth. This growth helps to invigorate the US economy as well as the institutions. In the US, we have been fortunate, so far, signalling to international students with the bright promise of industry, innovation, and unique career opportunities for which the nation is known.

All future business leaders are going to need to understand diverse perspectives and navigate cultural differences. We have presented some reasons and methods in support of internationalization, knowing that American innovation comes from clearing the runway to bring different ideas and individuals together.

NOTES

1. Personal communication, 16 August 2024.
2. Personal communication, XXX.
3. Personal communication, 19 August 2024.
4. Personal communication, 19 August 2024.
5. Personal communication, 21 August 2024.
6. T. Brinkerhoff, personal communication, 21 August 2024.

7. Personal communication, 22 July 2024.
8. Personal communication, 19 August 2024.

REFERENCES

'Best Business Schools'. (2024). *US News and World Report*. https://www.usnews.com/best-graduate-schools/top-business-schools/mba-rankings.

Bisoux, T. (2023). 'A New Way to Assess the ROI of an MBA'. Association to Advance Collegiate Schools of Business, 18 December. https://www.aacsb.edu/insights/articles/2023/12/a-new-way-to-assess-the-roi-of-an-mba.

Borden, T., & Faraut, J. (2023). 'How (and Why) We Launched the All-New LinkedIn Top MBA Programs Ranking'. LinkedIn News, 14 November. https://www.linkedin.com/pulse/how-why-we-launched-all-new-linkedin-top-mba-programs-ranking-w0qme/.

Bound, J., Braga, B., Khanna, G., & Turner, S. (2021). 'The Globalization of Post-secondary Education: The Role of International Students in the US Higher Education System'. *Journal of Economic Perspectives*, 35/1: 163–184.

Byrne, J. (2022). 'By the Numbers: How Rare Is Your MBA Degree?' *Poets and Quants*, 22 April. https://poetsandquants.com/2022/04/27/size-of-top-u-s-mba-programs-by-enrollment/.

Collier, S. (2023). '10 US Universities with the Most International Students'. *Quacquarelli Symonds*, 1 June. https://www.topuniversities.com/blog/10-us-universities-most-international-students.

Cote, C. (2022). 'The ROI of an MBA: Is the Degree Worth It?' Harvard Business School Online, 22 November. https://online.hbs.edu/blog/post/roi-of-an-mba#:~:text=In%202022%2C%2085%20percent%20of,provide%20a%20return%20on%20investment.

Davis, S. (2024a). 'From Intelligence Field Agent To Entrepreneur, Tepper School MBA Student Pursues Her Dream'. Carnegie Mellon University, 3 May. https://www.cmu.edu/tepper/news/stories/2024/may/commencement-profile-ozioma-aniagu.html.

Davis, S. (2024b). 'Tepper School Hosts First Annual Business English and Cultural Immersion Program for International MBA Students'. Carnegie Mellon University, August. https://www.cmu.edu/tepper/news/stories/2024/august/immersion-program.html.

Deep, S. (2014). 'Vintage Education'. *Carnegie Mellon Today Archives*, 14 December. https://www.cmu.edu/cmtoday/issues/january-2015-issue/giving-back/vintage-education/index.html.

Doolittle, S. (2024). 'The Land of Opportunity'. *Boston College Law School Magazine Online*, Winter. https://lawmagazine.bc.edu/2024/02/the-land-of-opportunity/.

Dyvik, E. (2024). 'Percentage of Companies That Hired MBA Graduates from 2008 to 2022'. Statista, 4 July. https://www.statista.com/statistics/233189/hiring-rate-of-mba-graduates/.

EducationUSA. (2024). *Global Guide*. US Department of State. https://educationusa.state.gov/us-higher-education-professionals/recruitment-resources/global-guide.

Fore, P., & Thomas-Oxtoby, S. (2024). 'MBA Grads Reliably Earn a Six-Figure Salary in These Six Industries'. *Fortune*, 7 August. https://fortune.com/education/articles/mba-grads-reliably-earn-a-six-figure-salary-in-these-6-industries/.

Hofstede, G. (1992). 'Cultural Dimensions in People Management'. In V. Pucik, N. Tichy, & C. Barnett, eds., *Globalizing Management: Creating and Leading the Competitive Organization*. Wiley, 66–76.

Hoppe, M. H., & Bhagat, R. S. (2007). 'Leadership in the United States of America: The Leaders as Cultural Hero'. In J. S. Chhokar, F. C. Brodbeck, & R. J. House, eds., In *Culture and Leadership Across the World: The GLOBE Book of In-Depth Studies of 25 Societies*. Routledge, 475–535.

Lembaga Pengelola Dana Pendidikan (LPDP). (2024). Ministry of Finance of Indonesia. Updated 21 August. https://lpdp.kemenkeu.go.id/en/tentang/selayang-pandang/.

'LinkedIn Top MBA Programs 2023: The 50 Best US Business Schools To Grow Your Career'. (2023). LinkedIn, 14 November. https://www.linkedin.com/pulse/linkedin-top-mba-programs-2023-50-best-business-schools-e2ece/.

Lorenzetti, D., Lorenzetti, L., Nowell, L., Jacobsen, M., Clancy, T., Freeman, G., & Oddone Paolucci, E. (2023). 'Exploring International Graduate Students' Experiences, Challenges, and Peer Relationships: Impacts on Academic and Emotional Well-Being'. *Journal of International Students*, 13/4, 22–41.

Martirosyan, N. M., Bustamante, R., & Saxon, D. P. (2019). 'Academic and Social Support Services for International Students: Current Practices'. *Journal of International Students*, 9/1, 172–191.

'Most International Students'. (2022). *US News and World Report*, Fall. https://www.usnews.com/best-colleges/rankings/national-universities/most-international.

Nobel Foundation. (2024). 'All Prizes in Economic Sciences'. The Nobel Prize, 27 August. https://www.nobelprize.org/prizes/lists/all-prizes-in-economic-sciences/.

Sutherland, P., & Chakrabarti, M. (2023). 'Why So Many US Educated Foreign Students Don't Stay for Work'. WBUR, 26 June. https://www.wbur.org/onpoint/2023/06/26/why-so-many-u-s-educated-foreign-students-dont-stay-for-work.

Tepper School of Business. (2022). *2022–2027 Tepper Together DEI&B Strategic Plan*. Carnegie Mellon University. https://www.cmu.edu/tepper/the-intelligent-future/assets/docs/tepper-together-dei-strategic-plan.pdf.

Tepper School of Business. (2023). *2023 Full-Time MBA Employment Report*. Carnegie Mellon University. https://www.cmu.edu/tepper/recruiting-and-partnerships/recruit-at-tepper-school/mba/full-time-employment-statistics/index.html.

Tepper School of Business. (2024). *2024 Full-Time MBA Employment Report*. Carnegie Mellon University. https://www.cmu.edu/tepper/recruiting-and-partnerships/recruit-at-tepper-school/mba/full-time-employment-statistics/index.html.

'What Is Diversity, Equity, and Inclusion?' (2022). McKinsey & Company, 17 August. https://www.mckinsey.com/featured-insights/mckinsey-explainers/what-is-diversity-equity-and-inclusion.

Zwetsloot, R., Dunham, J. Arnold, Z., & Huang, T. (2019). 'Keeping Top AI Talent in the United States: Findings and Policy Options for International Graduate Student Retention'. Center for Security and Emerging Technology, December. cset.georgetown.edu/research/keeping-top-ai-talent-in-the-united-states/.https://doi.org/10.51593/20190007.

6

Navigating Change

The Impact of the COVID-19 Pandemic on the Internationalization Strategies of Business Schools

ADRIANA KUDRNOVA LOVERA, RITA RIBEIRO, AND SOFIA SALGADO PINTO

EMBRACING GLOBAL CONNECTEDNESS IN THE ERA OF COVID-19

In recent decades, business schools worldwide have sought to provide a truly global education, preparing students to lead in an increasingly interconnected world. For many schools, this international focus potentially opens doors to prestigious rankings and accreditations, attracts diverse faculty and students, enhances cross-cultural understanding, and fosters innovative research collaborations. However, the onset of the COVID-19 pandemic in early 2020 brought international activities to a sudden standstill. Borders closed rapidly as governments sought to contain the virus, leaving countless international students and staff scrambling to return home or be stranded abroad for months (Matthews, 2020). For business schools, this period was marked by uncertainty and tough choices; for instance, how to safeguard students while keeping operations running. This unprecedented challenge forced business schools to find new ways to maintain global partnerships, engage students through distance learning, and adapt to the realities of remote work. Were these challenges and changes a turning point for the internationalization strategies of business schools?

Despite the significance of these challenges, there remains a gap in research regarding how schools have navigated these complex changes. One international study investigated the pandemic's impact on the internationalization of higher education institutions, and provided broad insights drawn from large-scale survey responses (Marinoni et al., 2024). Other

Adriana Kudrnova Lovera, Rita Ribeiro, and Sofia Salgado Pinto, *Navigating Change*. In: *Management Education and the Rise of Uncertainty of Global Business*. Edited by: Eric Cornuel, Oxford University Press. © Oxford University Press (2025). DOI: 10.1093/9780197794470.003.0007 works have focused on specific aspects of this impact, such as work by Osbaldeston and Kudrnova Lovera (2023), which examines the challenges faced by schools during the pandemic and discusses potential shifts in the practice and assessment of internationalization. Our study delves into the specific strategies and innovations employed by international business schools. Understanding these responses is crucial, as it can provide insights for business schools worldwide to build more resilient and adaptable internationalization strategies. By examining what was done and why, we can better grasp the extent to which schools can rethink and reshape their global education offerings in response to unprecedented disruptions.

This chapter presents a study that employs qualitative research methods to examine changes in internationalization strategies of business schools resulting from the COVID-19 pandemic. We selected a sample of diverse schools in different countries with mature levels of internationalization to examine the topic. First, we contextualize the concept of internationalization through a review of the literature, and then present the methodological framework and research approach are presented. Empirical findings are showcased next, followed by our comprehensive analysis and interpretative insights. We then present our thinking about the future of internationalization. Ultimately, we aimed to uncover how strategies continue to evolve, offering deeper insight into the way schools are adapting to the current global landscape. By doing so we fill part of the existing research gap, providing new insights into the unique approaches and innovations adopted by international business schools during this period of rapid change.

UNDERSTANDING THE BIG PICTURE—INTERNATIONALIZATION: WHAT DOES IT REALLY MEAN?

A review of the literature reveals that while internationalization is considered an important dimension of many schools, there are differences in how it is defined and analysed. Confusion about the meaning of the term led Knight from the University of Toronto to examine the evolution of the concept and develop one of the most widely cited definitions, 'the process of integrating an international, intercultural or global dimension into the purpose, functions or delivery of post-secondary education' (Knight, 2003, 2). Knight's definition underscores that internationalization is a process and has a multifaceted nature.

In parallel, the term 'comprehensive internationalization' emerged in the mid-2000s and was popularized by the American Council on Education (ACE) through its various publications (ACE, 2002; 2005; 2006). ACE defines comprehensive internationalization as 'a strategic, coordinated process that seeks to align and integrate policies, programmes, and initiatives to position colleges and universities as more globally oriented and internationally connected institutions'.[1]

Building upon Knight's foundational work (Knight, 2004), a study commissioned by the European Parliament in 2015 on the state of internationalization in higher education led to the reconsideration of the concept and expansion of Knight's definition, adding 'in order to enhance the quality of education and research for all students and staff and to make a meaningful contribution to society' (de Wit et al., 2015, 29). De Wit et al. add a purpose of internationalization in a definition still often cited today.

These widely used definitions acknowledge that internationalization is an ongoing process rather than a static goal. They include a normative element about the impact of the process on society. The European Parliament's definition focuses on the enhancement of education and research quality together with providing a meaningful contribution to society. Meanwhile, the ACE definition focuses on developing institutions that are resilient, inclusive, and just.

However, some scholars argue that these definitions are limited. Hawawini (2016) considers the standard definitions frequently cited in higher education, such as those by Knight, the European Parliament, and ACE, and argues that these are too focused on inward-looking criteria, which does not allow for a comprehensive consideration of the connections between an institution and partners in the global knowledge economy, lacking the dynamic process of reciprocal enrichment. In the case of business schools, Hawawini (2016) considers the criteria used by the *Financial Times* ranking of the top 100 global MBA programmes and observes that geographic location and market characteristics explain the prevalence of inward internationalization (and higher internationalization scores) in Europe.

Further extending the discourse, Mittelmeier et al. (2021) argue that past definitions of internationalization have led to a categorization of activities in binary terms, internationalization at home versus internationalization abroad, and that a third category of internationalization at a distance should be considered, given the rise in technology-supported opportunities. More recently, Marginson (2023) critiques Knight's definition of internationalization by arguing that it is too broad and lacks specificity, failing to account for the complexities and power dynamics inherent in the global landscape of higher education.

Different definitions provide complementary perspectives on the internationalization of higher education institutions. No single definition is sufficient to fully explain and support a comprehensive analysis of the process. Some authors explore the internationalization of schools through specific models and formats adopted by institutions, while others consider multidimensional frameworks to support its analysis.

Evolving Strategies and Models of Internationalization in Business Schools

While business schools have faced challenges in defining effective internationalization strategies, numerous authors have explored the various formats and business models of internationalization in higher education. Ricart captured this uncertainty in 2011, noting then that 'we are still struggling to define the right business model in this important dimension. Twenty-five years of internationalization and the process is more open than ever' (Ricart, 2011, 552). This reflects a broader sentiment about the complexity of navigating internationalization.

Soliman et al. (2019) found that in the case of English business schools, internationalization strategies develop in various phases: an initial period in which initiatives are controlled by operational managers and are not featured in a university's strategy, a second period in which practices are managed by middle managers and mentioned in the strategy but not foregrounded, and a third stage in which it becomes a core strategic priority managed by senior managers. They also found that 'international strategy was deliberate in each strategic period, whereas it was emergent over a longer time frame of several strategic periods' (Soliman et al., 2019, 1421).

Hawawini (2016) describes five forms of international reach:

1. The import model: schools that bring the world to their campus
2. The export model: schools that send students and faculty abroad; online courses
3. Academic joint ventures: institutions located in different countries design and deliver programmes jointly
4. Academic partnerships, alliances and consortia: institutions that collaborate on various initiatives such as exchanges, joint programmes, research
5. Campuses abroad: establishing a physical presence abroad, temporarily or permanently

Osbaldeston and Kudrnova Lovera (2023) discussed the various models of internationalization among EQUIS-accredited schools and the structure behind the model:

- Full internationalization at home: single school
- 'Sister' schools: dual schools

- ‘Founding’ or ‘fledgling’ schools: new school in a developing country/region
- Joint venture: new school formed by two or more partners
- Multi-campus/global network: multiple/interlinked schools
- Selected partnerships/global alliance: multiple/network of schools

Frameworks for Evaluating Internationalization in Higher Education

Various frameworks for internationalization analysis and support exist. The ACE Model for Comprehensive Internationalization (ACE, n.d.) is structured around six target areas to advance the Teaching-Research-Service missions of institutions:

1. Institutional commitment and policy
2. Leadership and structure
3. Curriculum and co-curriculum
4. Faculty and staff support
5. Mobility
6. Partnerships

Another framework is provided by EFMD’s Quality Improvement System for international business schools, EQUIS. To help assess the degrees of internationalization, EQUIS developed a multidimensional model with 12 areas grouped into four broad categories: policy, content, context, and network (EFMD Global website, accessed July 2024).[2]

Policy

1. Strategy
2. Recognition/reputation
3. Governance/advisory board

Content

4. Curriculum/learning resources
5. Research and development
6. Competencies

Context

7. Faculty/visiting professors
8. Students/exchanges/alumni
9. Professional staff

Network

10. Executive education/clients/recruiters
11. Alliances/partners
12. Activities abroad

The EQUIS model offers a structured and comprehensive approach to analyse internationalization in business schools. Each of the 12 areas can be assessed on a low-medium-high scale and mapped in a spider diagram in order to provide schools with a concrete tool to assess their current state or progress over time. These models and frameworks demonstrate the complexity and diversity of internationalization efforts in business schools, providing a rich foundation for analysis.

This section has presented definitions of internationalization, various formats, and frameworks for analysis. It acknowledges the multidimensionality of internationalization and the diverse perspectives through which it can be analysed. By capturing these essential elements, we proceed with the study of the changes observed during the COVID-19 pandemic.

BEHIND THE SCENES OF OUR STUDY

As we saw in the last section, there is no universally accepted definition of internationalization among business schools. However, based on existing definitions and contributions, we distilled the essential elements to guide our analysis. Our aim was to identify and understand the changes in policies, processes, and initiatives within the functional areas of business schools: teaching and development, research and innovation, and various services and activities.

The COVID-19 pandemic presented a unique opportunity to observe how business schools responded to a crisis, particularly in areas directly impacted by lockdowns and travel restrictions. To explore the shifts in internationalization strategies of business schools in this period, we adopted a qualitative approach, which allowed us to understand how the schools' decisions were shaped by the specificities of their context. Our research unfolded in three phases, each designed to gather detailed insights into these changes.

Phase 1: Identifying Initial Changes

In the first phase, we aimed to capture a broad view of the landscape by conducting a literature review alongside qualitative interviews with deans and associate deans from a diverse range of business schools. The review of existing literature allowed us to understand the existing body of research on internationalization in higher education. It helped identify commonly used definitions and approaches by universities and business schools, as well as the main topics addressed.

Building on this foundation, our interviews focused on identifying shifts in internationalization processes and initiatives in response to the COVID-19 lockdowns. This phase helped us understand the initial challenges and responses, focusing on government regulations and school policies, as well as changes concerning students, staff, programmes, alliances, and other activities during the pandemic. We gathered insights into the challenges schools face, such as navigating government regulations and adapting to new operational realities and explored how schools initially adjusted their policies and priorities. This provided a foundational understanding of the immediate impacts of the pandemic on internationalization efforts and set the stage for further exploration in subsequent phases.

Phase 2: Tracking Strategy Evolution Over Time

In the second phase, we conducted follow-up interviews three years later with some of the participants. These interviews allowed us to track the evolution of their internationalization strategies over time and identify any shifts in priorities or new challenges that emerged. By engaging with the schools throughout this extended period, we captured a wide range of responses and adaptations, providing a rich understanding of how diverse factors such as geographic location, institutional size and structure, and governance influenced their actions and initiatives. This inclusive and longitudinal approach ensured that we gathered a complete picture of the ways business schools responded to the pandemic. It also allowed some reflection from school leaders on the decisions made during the peak of the crisis, as well as an assessment of the long-term effects of some changes.

Phase 3: Analysis and Synthesis of Internationalization Strategies

The third phase involved a comprehensive analysis and synthesis of the data collected in the previous phases. We aimed to identify new or different initiatives that sustained internationalization at each school. This phase allowed us to identify common themes and patterns, as well as unique approaches that could serve as inspiration for other institutions. This analysis provides valuable insights into the evolving nature of internationalization strategies in business schools and highlights the factors contributing to their resilience and adaptability during the pandemic.

Given the annual and multi-annual nature of higher education cycles, this project spanned several years, starting in 2021 and concluding in 2024. The study employed a qualitative research method, collecting data from semi-structured interviews with top business schools around the globe during the post-COVID period (starting in 2021 with a follow-up in 2024). Each business school agreed to participate in the longitudinal study, allowing us to track changes over time and understand how business schools adapted their strategies and structures throughout different stages of the pandemic.

The Schools in the Spotlight

Several characteristics were considered when selecting the schools for the study. We sought to look at institutions where internationalization is a central element of their activities and strategic vision. Thus, we considered the purpose of internationalization at each institution (e.g. fostering global connections among institutions, elevating colleges and universities to a global level, enhancing the quality of higher education, and impacting society). Furthermore, all selected schools are five-year EQUIS accredited institutions, the highest possible accreditation in a system that uniquely requires schools to meet a standard on internationalization. Although this focus on accredited institutions might introduce some bias, it ensures that the schools under analysis are actively and intentionally engaged in international activities at a high level. Indeed, all the schools studied have a clear international strategy.

Furthermore, we sought to capture the experiences of a wide range of schools across various contexts. Diversity within the sample was intended to explore the unique challenges faced by schools and how various school characteristics may influence decisions during the pandemic and its aftermath. Therefore, to understand the context of the changes and initiatives observed, we outlined several key characteristics of the schools and their potential implications:

- **Geographic location**: The campus location can affect access to international networks and partnerships.
- **Institutional structure**: Whether a school is stand-alone or part of a larger university can influence its governance, autonomy, resources, and strategic priorities.

- **Campus configuration**: The existence of single or multiple campuses, along with their locations, can impact a school's global reach and operational complexity.
- **Ownership type**: Public versus private ownership can affect funding, autonomy, and international collaborations.
- **Size**: The number of core faculty and students offers insight into the scale of operations and capacity for undertaking international initiatives.

Keeping these characteristics in mind allowed us to better understand how internationalization manifests across different business schools and the factors that may influence its implementation.

A brief description of each school will follow to provide context and support the understanding of our findings.

Skema Business School (France)

A private higher education and research institution under the status of a non-profit association, SKEMA was born in 2009 from the merger between Ecole Supérieure de Commerce de Lille (ESC Lille) and CERAM Business School, Sophia Antipolis. The importance of internationalization is clear in its mission of being a 'global school that prepares the business talents of the 21st century—responsible, mobile, multicultural, entrepreneurs with abilities to manage information, data and knowledge'. It has nine campuses spread along five continents (one in Brazil, one in the United States, one in South Africa, two in China, one in Dubai, and three in France), and an innovation centre in Canada. As of December 2022, SKEMA had nearly 11,000 students and 200 faculty. The school offers programmes at all education levels. SKEMA campuses pursue the same objective: to offer students a multicultural experience combining academic and international professional experiences. The school has a long-lasting international approach, evidenced by its initial accreditation by EQUIS in 2006 as ESC Lille.

School of Business, American University Cairo (Egypt)

This is a private business school and is one of five schools housed by the American University in Cairo, an independent not-for-profit higher education institution accredited in both the United States and Egypt. The university was established in 1919, and the roots of the School of Business date

Table 6.1. CHARACTERISTICS OF SCHOOLS IN THE STUDY

School	Geographic Location	Institutional Structure	Campus Configuration	Ownership Type	Size (faculty and student numbers as of 2022)
SKEMA	France	Stand-alone	Multi-campus (9) - several countries	Private	F-200 S-11,000
School of Business, American University Cairo_AUC	Egypt	Stand-alone	One campus	Private	F-100 S-1200
Peter B. Gustavson SoB, University of Victoria	Canada	University-based	One campus	Public	F-60 S-1500
Imperial College	UK	University-based	Multi-campus (2) - same city	Public	F-95 S-2500
QUT Faculty of Business and Law, Queensland University of Technology	Australia	University-based	One campus	Public	F-1000 S-11,500
Escola de Administração de Empresas de São Paulo da Fundação Getúlio Vargas-EAESP	Brazil	Stand-alone	One campus	Private	F-240 S-3600

back to 1947. AUC School of Business was accredited by the Association to Advance Collegiate Schools of Business in 2006, becoming triple-accredited in 2014 following its accreditations from EQUIS and AMBA (Association of MBAs). The school offers undergraduate and graduate degrees as well as executive education programmes. In December 2022, the school had 1,236 students, including 1,052 undergraduate students and 184 graduate students, in addition to 114 faculty members, including 61 full-time and 53 part-time. AUC School of Business was recently renamed AUC Onsi Sawiris School of Business.

AUC is committed to internationalization. The school states on its website, 'The internationalization strategy of the school is built on the principles of a Connect, Diversify, Glocalize (CDG) strategy whereby we connect the Middle East Africa region and the world, foster an intercultural learning experience, as well as produce and disseminate international knowledge for the benefit of the region'.

Peter B. Gustavson School of Business, University of Victoria (Canada)

A public, not-for-profit business school belonging to the University of Victoria, the school was first awarded EQUIS accreditation in February 2007 and has since maintained the quality label. The school offers programmes at all education levels and views internationalization as one of its strategic pillars. The Gustavson School of Business is intentionally small in numbers, and in 2022 had nearly 1,500 students and 60 regular faculty members.

Imperial College Business School (UK)

Part of Imperial College London, a public research university dedicated to science and technology, the school has two campuses in London and offers undergraduate and postgraduate education including an MBA, master's degrees in specific subjects, a PhD, and executive education. In 2022, Imperial College Business School had approximately 2,510 students and 95 full time faculty members.

The school has long held an international approach, having been internationally triple-accredited since 2012. In its strategic 2018–2028 document, the school reveals its strategic vision to 'be a world-leading business school with a diverse, engaged and supportive research and learning environment that leverages technology and entrepreneurship to benefit businesses and improve society'.

QUT Faculty of Business and Law, Queensland University of Technology (Australia) is

One of five faculties of the Queensland University of Technology, QUT is a public research university located in the coastal city of Brisbane. The QUT business schools include the QUT Graduate School of Business, as well as four discipline-focused schools: the School of Accountancy, the School of Advertising, Marketing and Public Relations, the School of Economics and Finance, and the School of Management. As of December 2022, QUT Faculty of Business and Law enrolled a total of 11,500 students and employed more than 1,000 faculty. It was the first Australian business school to earn triple-crown accreditation.

Escola de Administração de Empresas de São Paulo da Fundação Getulio Vargas (EAESP FGV) (Brazil)

EAESP FGV is a private higher education institution. It offers programmes from undergraduate, and master's to doctorate, offering courses in business administration and public administration. The school belongs to the Getulio Vargas Foundation (FGV), with its main office in Rio de Janeiro and a presence in São Paulo and Brasília. EAESP FGV offers educational programmes in over 100 cities in Brazil through a network of affiliate partner institutions, with executive education and MBA programmes in several areas of knowledge. FGV has 11 schools and 2 institutes dedicated to education. The EAESP is one of these schools and in 2022, registered approximately 3,600 students and 240 faculty members. Internationalization has long been part of EAESP's strategy. The school was triple-crown accredited in 2004.

STRATEGIES IN A SHIFTING LANDSCAPE

This section presents schools' key initiatives to navigate the evolving educational landscape. These include embracing digital transformation, forging new partnerships, and expanding the internationalization of their curricula. Additionally, schools placed a strong emphasis on student and faculty satisfaction and well-being, supporting these groups through a variety of programmes and policies. Management approaches were also adjusted to enhance decision-making processes and leverage lessons learned from past experiences. These findings illustrate the diverse ways in which schools responded to the pandemic, highlighting their efforts to sustain internationalization goals.

Digital Transformation

All schools reported a significant boost in digital adoption and transformation. This included substantial investments in technology and accompanying support for faculty and students. Beyond facilitating remote teaching and learning, several insights can be gleaned from the digital transformation that occurred during and after the pandemic. The digital shift enabled schools to pursue key internationalization objectives in novel ways.

Accessing New Markets

The adoption of technology for distance learning and the digitization of processes that were traditionally conducted in person and on paper have opened up opportunities to recruit students from regions that were previously inaccessible. For instance, AUC transitioned its executive education to a hybrid model, enabling entry into new markets across Africa, and reported planning to create more hybrid courses to support entry into those markets. Similarly, EAESP introduced hybrid formats at the start of programmes to support the transition of students from new regions and countries. Integrating a hybrid portion into its programmes was accompanied by additional support from the school to help students find housing and ease the transition to an eventual in-person format. The school also changed its mode of delivery for the school entrance exam, which unexpectedly increased participation and broadened the geographic diversity of applicants. The online exam format will be retained to maintain the benefits of a wider, more diverse applicant pool, provided it aligns with government regulations.

Accessing New Partnerships

The increased regularity of online activities reduced the resources needed to engage with partners in other parts of the world, enabling schools to establish connections with a wider range of institutions. AUC, for example, strengthened ties with universities across Africa, which in the past could not engage due to the resources required from those institutions for travel. While travel remains an option, the initial establishment of partnerships online has allowed for a broader focus, considering new partners within the same continent for schools in Africa and Latin America.

Distant and Hybrid Modes

Initially, all schools moved to online programme delivery. Some, like Imperial College, invested heavily in technology and were convinced that they would never go back fully to face-to-face. Meanwhile, QUT, with a decade of experience in postgraduate online education, saw no major disruptions to existing online programmes but had to expand its operations to cover all undergraduate and postgraduate programme offerings, which required a significant investment. SKEMA, for instance, eventually abandoned the hybrid format for most degree programmes but retained some online options, such as for executive training. Gustavson, traditionally a face-to-face provider, successfully launched an online programme in partnership with a Polish university (COIL) during the pandemic, and subsequent offerings followed.

Student and Faculty Satisfaction and Well-Being

Schools implemented various strategies to enhance student and faculty satisfaction and well-being, particularly during challenging periods of government-imposed campus closures. Initiatives included open campuses, enhanced support systems, and new learning opportunities to attract and retain international students and faculty, ensuring their needs were met both during and beyond the pandemic.

Attracting and Retaining International Students

Government policies on campus closures posed challenges for schools in attracting international students. SKEMA successfully retained international students due to a government policy that allowed them to keep the campus open. Imperial College introduced a student enhancement package, allowing students whose international experiences were disrupted to join a later cohort on an international experience within the next three years. The school has also created new online experiences that students can join even after graduation. EAESP faced student anxiety about returning to class and even saw demonstrations from students. Competitor decisions about opening up their campuses earlier affected these expectations of their students. In Australia, QUT faced a closed border policy and recognized the lack of government support for international students and filled the gap by providing additional support, including emergency bursaries and meals. Gustavson managed to retain some international students through its Co-op internship programme, with a dedicated staff that placed more students in internships during COVID than before, thanks to increased market demand.

Student Well-Being

SKEMA launched the SKEMA Care initiative, which considers the learner's satisfaction and experience. This has allowed them to better understand the learning needs, as well as the physical and social needs of students. International students were provided with hot meals and protected from isolation. SKEMA Care was developed with specific KPIs to assess performance on the learning experience of their students at all campuses. QUT moved all student support systems online, allowing for better monitoring and expansion of in-demand services. Creating welcoming environments for international students remained a priority for the school. Imperial College engaged closely with the Student Advisory Council to ensure student perspectives were considered during the implementation of changes.

At SKEMA, the focus on student well-being remained beyond the pandemic. Student support played a critical role that has led to the redesign of the Students Affairs Office into a new Student Experience Office, ensuring the same student experience across borders.

Attracting International Faculty

Attracting international faculty was already challenging for EAESP due to Brazil's economic and political situation. The crisis exacerbated this challenge, with some faculty leaving. However, the shift to online teaching created new opportunities for the school to recruit international faculty, as remote lecturing became an attractive option.

Supporting Faculty

Schools provided various forms of support to help faculty adapt to new teaching platforms and methodologies. Imperial College offered training to help faculty become comfortable with new online platforms and garnered their support for the shift to digital during the lockdowns. EAESP addressed the impact of the pedagogical changes by reducing teaching loads to allow time for adaptation and providing counsel and support. Gustavson introduced moderators to support online teaching and student experience.

Moderators ensured that the technology was working properly and interacted with students if any tech problems emerged. In addition, after the first lockdown, there was different anxiety from faculty and students about returning to the classroom. This prompted the introduction of additional mental health support for all. QUT had a design studio that created individual modules that anyone could use to learn, and design teams were available to provide direct support. In the first month, they had significant demand for their services, but this lessened as people acquired the necessary skills to use the new technologies on their own. AUC introduced the Happy School Initiative, focused on three elements: 'the Soul' to inspire and motivate for collaboration, innovation, and productivity; 'the Body', emphasizing people's health; and 'the Mind', promoting mental well-being.

Changes in Management Approach

In response to the pandemic, schools adapted their management approaches by prioritizing short-term decision-making and establishing crisis committees to handle rapidly changing situations. Institutions leveraged lessons from past crises to enhance their ability to quickly implement effective strategies, ensuring smooth operations during the COVID-19 pandemic.

Evolving Decision-Making Processes

Initially, schools reported the need for short-term decision-making. Schools were uncertain about the length of the crisis and were apprehensive about making long-term decisions, thus they opted for adaptation decisions on a daily basis. Schools were cautious about setting expectations and emphasized the importance of clarity and communication. Crisis committees, like those at Imperial College and SKEMA, met frequently to make daily decisions. Schools within larger universities also found that central leadership took more control, with committees set at the university level. Gustavson faced challenges when the University of Victoria suspended all international activities, leading to dissatisfaction among business school students who lost their international experiences. In addition, as the students changed their preferences over destinations, the school maintained its criteria for selecting international partners but expanded its network, including more partners from Europe and Latin America. QUT also saw some of its decision-making move to the university level, as the university sought to protect resources and ensure compliance with regulations.

Leveraging Lessons from Past Crises

The speed at which schools were able to adapt differed. Prior experience in managing crises helped some schools adapt more quickly to the challenges posed by the pandemic. AUC, for instance, leveraged lessons from nine years before, when Egypt went through a period of social, economic and political turmoil. The university was shut down and had to rapidly move classes online. Following that experience, the school prepared the necessary infrastructure for a future crisis, which eased its transition to online during the COVID crisis. Faculty and support services were prepared. QUT also relied on its experience managing a previous flooding crisis to guide its response to the pandemic; however, the COVID crisis added a layer of uncertainty in terms of its duration and a new health dimension. The school used its experience to guide its response particularly in terms of technology, people, teams and process management.

UNPACKING THE INSIGHTS

This section presents the insights derived from the analysis of the schools' strategies. One key finding was the significant influence of the national and institutional contexts, which often constrained or shaped what the schools could or could not do. These contexts forced schools to navigate the repercussions of their decisions while continuing to deliver their programmes. The shift to online learning across all the daily activities required extra investments in technology and support systems. In addition to this increased investment, the well-being of students, faculty, and staff emerged as a critical dimension to consider. The experiences during lockdowns and the subsequent return to campus provided valuable lessons about building resilient and supportive communities.

The Context: Navigating Constraints During the Pandemic

During the pandemic, schools operated within the constraints imposed by their respective universities and national contexts. The strategic decisions regarding campus access for international students—such as allowing them a place to stay during the day or providing a warm meal—were primarily determined by governments, followed by universities, with schools being the last to implement these regulations. This top-down decision-making process left many schools with little autonomy, severely restricting their ability to make independent decisions.

Notably, even though business schools are among the most internationally diverse, they were excluded from the decision-making process concerning restrictions on access for faculty and students. Consequently, schools were left to manage the repercussions of these strict access controls without having been part of the initial decision-making process.

The pandemic also highlighted the broader economic and social impact of internationalization within higher education. The national context exposed how deeply intertwined international students are with local economies. For instance, at QUT, the departure of international students significantly reduced the local workforce, demonstrating the critical role these students play not only in the education system but also in the community's economic well-being. This example highlights the significant ways in which internationalization impacts communities, beyond the academic realm.

The constraints imposed by national and university contexts were far more limiting than what the individual schools would have chosen if they had been given the freedom to decide or if they had been involved in making the decision. National policies had a greater impact on schools' operations than whether a school was independent or privately owned. It is particularly noteworthy how schools were constrained by school infrastructure limitations and daily operational decisions in responding to the new challenges posed by the pandemic. This underscores the importance of context in shaping the strategic responses of educational institutions.

These findings illustrate that institutional responses vary significantly based on their unique national and local contexts. Schools in less restricted countries may exhibit different initiatives compared to those in more constrained environments. Similarly, institutions in easily accessible regions versus those in distant or isolated locations, or those in large countries with extensive internal markers versus smaller nations, will face and respond to challenges in varied ways. Understanding these contextual differences is necessary to understand the diverse strategies adopted by schools and for anticipating how future crises might be managed. This perspective helps us appreciate the importance of context in shaping the strategic responses of business schools.

Accelerated Investment and Sense of Need

An unsurprising yet noteworthy outcome of this study was the rapid pace of investment and digital transformation across all schools. While some schools scaled their existing offerings, others undertook significant transformations of their infrastructure. We observed a substantial investment of resources—both financial and human—towards digital transformation, and these efforts proved highly effective. Schools moved quickly because of the urgent demands of the situation; however, without this pressing need, such changes might not have been initiated or even anticipated.

Schools adapted to online teaching with remarkable speed. Faculty members quickly adjusted to delivering courses online, and students swiftly adapted to distance learning. The transition, though fast, was generally smooth. Many schools implemented support mechanisms to facilitate this shift, assisting faculty in adopting new technologies, designing and producing teaching materials, and effectively conducting online sessions. These efforts helped ensure a mostly seamless experience for both faculty and students.

International faculty found new ways to engage, with increased opportunities for participation in mixed forums and invitations to various events. However, these changes did not significantly change the fundamental modes of course delivery.

Prioritizing Well-Being During Uncertain Times

During the pandemic, schools universally emphasized the well-being of students, faculty, and staff as a central concern. Signs of fear, isolation, panic, depression, and loneliness were monitored, with many schools implementing initiatives specifically designed to support the mental health of their students. These initiatives went beyond traditional counselling, as schools became aware of the vulnerability and mental strain on students and created new supports. Schools adopted a more attentive approach to student interactions, both during online classes and on campus, to ensure that any signs of distress were promptly addressed. In some cases, this was also made available to faculty and staff.

The pandemic underscored the vital role of universities as centres of social interaction, holding significant responsibility for the well-being of not only their students, faculty, and staff, but also their broader community—including partners, the local community, and families. This responsibility became even more pronounced in the face of international uncertainties and challenging environments.

Reflecting on their actions during this period, school leaders acknowledged that in hindsight, they should have prioritized the human aspect of their community more. Many expressed the belief that they could have done more to support the well-being of students, faculty, and staff, rather than focusing primarily on infrastructure and pedagogical concerns.

The social role of schools, particularly in the context of international experiences, became even more significant during this time, highlighting the importance of fostering a supportive and connected community.

Strengthening Community Connections

The pandemic offered lessons in three dimensions of community. First, it underscored the critical importance of placing students at the centre of international strategy. This involves prioritizing students' experiences, well-being, and exposure to different cultures, and recognizing how being far from their home can amplify these experiences. The focus on students became even more essential as they navigated the challenges of distance and isolation.

Second, the crisis highlighted the importance of communicating clearly with the internal community, comprising students, faculty and staff. Schools often took certain needs for granted, such as assuming that it was sufficient that everyone had a computer, when in reality, a good internet connection was the essential requirement for participating in a class or meeting. Or, when resuming after the lockdown, many schools did not adequately address the fear and anxiety of returning to campus. This reluctance to re-engage with normalcy became a crisis in itself, catching some schools off guard. This lack of communication left parts of the community feeling unsupported and unprepared for the transition back to in-person activities.

Third, the shift to distant interactions with both existing and new school partners revealed the potential for nurturing remote communities. Schools discovered that effective research, teaching and collaboration could extend beyond geographic boundaries, opening up new opportunities that had not been previously considered. The ability to form and sustain these distant connections demonstrated how technology could facilitate global collaboration, despite a physical separation. And although the technology for remote collaboration existed before, it was only during the pandemic that people became truly comfortable using it. This shift has had a lasting impact on how schools and their local communities interact, further emphasizing the evolving nature of community in a post-pandemic world.

WHERE DO WE GO FROM HERE?

Our study provided insights into the various decisions and initiatives taken by business schools at different moments of the COVID-19 pandemic. It highlighted the short-term limitations faced by institutions and how they navigated these challenges through adaptation and change. Additionally, we were able to gather post-crisis reflections from some of the interviewees, offering a deeper understanding of how past actions are shaping current decisions and the potential shifts in the internationalization landscape.

While internationalization may not have changed dramatically, the recent crisis has offered valuable lessons. This section explores key themes of geopolitics, ecology and the future of teaching and learning. We conclude the section with a diagram (Figure 6.1) that summarizes the dimensions already discussed.

The Significance of Internationalization

Despite the global shock of COVID-19 on schools worldwide, one thing remains clear: the fundamental purpose of internationalization in business education has not changed. Strong institutions continue to view internationalization as a core element of their strategy, and this perspective was not altered by the pandemic. The commitment to fostering global connections and enhancing the quality of education and research remains as strong as ever.

With international networks expanding to include new and diverse partners, internationalization now carries even greater significance. This expansion promotes more inclusive international communities, enriching the overall impact of internationalization efforts. Engaging with diverse cultures and perspectives allows people to develop global competencies and intercultural skills, enlarging their potential contribution to society. The pandemic has brought to light the importance of placing people at the centre of internationalization efforts to help ensure that academic and cultural experiences remain meaningful but also supportive of individuals' well-being. This focus may also foster more resilient strategies that are better equipped to withstand and adapt to future crises.

Geopolitics: Strategic Choices for Global Partnerships

The lockdowns demonstrated the potential for forming partnerships in different regions, as the need for constant travel and face-to-face meetings diminished. As an example, business schools in Africa and Latin America considered new partners in their same regions rather than seeking them in other continents. The pandemic fostered a more inclusive approach to collaboration, emphasizing openness to diverse partners, regardless of their geographic location or financial standing.

After the pandemic, geopolitical events continue to influence internationalization choices. Geopolitics will remain a crucial factor in decisions regarding faculty and student mobility, as well as in the choice of campus locations. These decisions may originate from the schools themselves or be shaped by government policies and international relations constraints.

Just as lockdowns did not stop internationalization efforts, neither will geopolitical events. Schools, faculty, students and entire communities will continue to adapt to these evolving conditions.

Ecological Considerations in International Strategy

Geographic destinations for internationalization are increasingly influenced by international relations, but also by ecological concerns related to long-distance travel. While ecological considerations are beginning to shape internationalization patterns, their influence is still in its early stages. Students and faculty look for the positive value of mobility. Ultimately, international mobility needs a balance of resources used and the value created by bringing together people with different cultures and perspectives. Although recognized as important, ecological factors have not yet significantly impacted the actual decisions of students or schools regarding internationalization. Currently only a few are weighing the environmental versus the social impact. We expect to see more schools do so in the future.

The Pandemic and the Future of Teaching and Learning in Higher Education

As we have seen in other industries, the digital transformation was boosted by the pandemic. The same is true in higher education. Just as business practices have evolved, so too has the landscape of teaching and learning. There is now a natural acceptance of online meetings among researchers, faculty, staff and students. However, the pandemic also underscored the importance of physical presence on campus, which remains essential for the academic community. Social interaction is crucial for both learning and well-being. This dual approach—embracing both digital and physical environments—will likely continue to shape the future of education and of internationalization.

The pandemic prompted significant changes in programme delivery methods, increasing accessibility through online platforms while highlighting the differentiation and value creation of face-to-face formats.

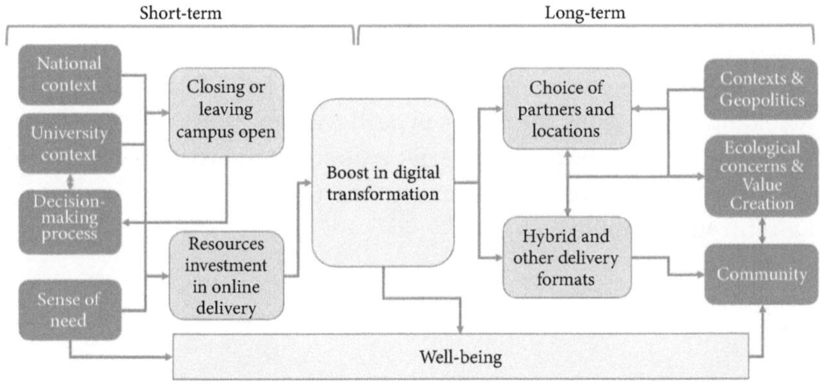

Figure 6.1: The short- and long-term impact of the pandemic on the internationalization of business schools

The outreach of executive education also expanded, with a shift to hybrid formats, increased collaboration with partners and companies, and greater accessibility for students from diverse geographies. This broader reach enabled distance learning to flourish at an unprecedented pace.

But what have institutions learned on top of enlarging the executive and post-grad market through good and well-designed online programmes? What changes are booming in the more demanding face-to-face courses? New generations of students are expecting more dynamic and innovative approaches. Artificial Intelligence will certainly have a role in the new developments of both digital and in-person learning formats.

Internationalization decisions are increasingly shaped by the context in which they are made, with geopolitics and national contexts playing a significant role. However, in the realm of higher education—and business schools in particular—preparing professionals for an increasingly uncertain and volatile environment requires the development of different skill sets. Internationalization provides a fertile ground for such a development and holds the potential to create impact in the communities involved. In this study, we have observed schools at mature levels of internationalization, and we anticipate the same to be true even in the early stages of a business school's internationalization journey.

The pandemic revealed that even the most traditional and change-resistant institutions, such as universities, can adapt when driven by a compelling need for change and a commitment of resources. Despite the widespread adoption of digital tools, there were no significant breakthroughs in innovative instructional technologies. But the current world situation requires more change in higher education. Internationalization can play a role in driving this change.

At the heart of internationalization should be a focus on people—understanding the skills societies will need and how those needs are evolving. Designing international strategies around these insights will not only impact the school's community and its partners but also contribute to long-term sustainability.

NOTES

1. ACE website, https://www.acenet.edu/Pages/default.aspx, accessed April 2022.
2. https://www.efmdglobal.org/wpcontent/uploads/EQUIS_Standards_and_Criteria.pdf

REFERENCES

American Council on Education (ACE). (n.d.). 'Comprehensive Internationalization Framework'. Accessed 24 July 2024. https://www.acenet.edu/Research-Insights/Pages/Internationalization/CIGE-Model-for-Comprehensive-Internationalization.aspx.

American Council on Education (ACE). (2002). *Promising Practices: Spotlighting Excellence in Comprehensive Internationalization.*

American Council on Education (ACE). (2005). *Building a Strategic Framework for Comprehensive Internationalization.*

American Council on Education (ACE). (2006). *A Handbook for Advancing Comprehensive Internationalization.*

de Wit, H., Hunter, F., Howard, L., & Egron-Polak, E. (2015). *Internationalization of Higher Education*. European Union. https://doi.org/10.2861/6854

EFMD Global. 'EQUIS Standards & Criteria'. (2024). https://www.efmdglobal.org/wp-content/uploads/2024_EQUIS_Standards_and_Criteria.pdf.

Hawawini, G. (2016). *The Internationalization of Higher Education and Business Schools.* Springer Singapore.

Knight, J. (2003). *Internationalisation: Meanings and Models* (15–35). www.sauvca.org.za

Knight, J. (2004). 'Internationalization Remodeled: Definition, Approaches, and Rationales'. *Journal of Studies in International Education*, 8/1, 5–31.

Marginson, S. (2023). 'Limitations of the Leading Definition of 'Internationalization' of Higher Education: Is the Idea Wrong or Is the Fault in Reality?' *Globalization, Societies and Education*. https://doi.org/10.1080/14767724.2023.2264223.

Marinoni, G., Bartolome, S., & Cardona, P. (2024). 'Internationalization of Higher Education: Current Trends and Future Scenarios'. https://www.iau-aiu.net/IMG/pdf/2024_internationalization_survey_-_executive_summary.pdf

Matthews, D. (2020, March 24). 'International Students Across Europe Face "Chaos"'. *Times Higher Education News.*

Mittelmeier, J., Rienties, B., Gunter, A., & Raghuram, P. (2021). 'Conceptualizing Internationalization at a Distance: A "Third Category" of University Internationalization'. *Journal of Studies in International Education*, 25/3, 266–282.
Osbaldeston, M., & Kudrnova Lovera, A. (2023). 'Management Education: Internationalization, Accreditation, and the Pandemic'. In M. Apaydin, J. D. Branch, M. M. Dent, & O. Regalado-Pezúa, eds., *The Internationalization of Higher Education: Concepts, Cases, and Challenges*. Information Age Publishing, 175–191.
Ricart, J. E. (2011). 'A Push for Research and Internationalization in European Business Schools'. *British Journal of Management*, 22/3, 550–554.
Soliman, S., Anchor, J., & Taylor, D. (2019). 'The International Strategies of Universities: Deliberate or Emergent?' *Studies in Higher Education*, 44/8, 1413–1424.

7

Finding Strategic Balance

Protecting Global and Local Legitimacy within an Internationalization Agenda

ROBINA XAVIER

DETERMINING STRATEGY IN UNCERTAIN TIMES

The world's universities and their associated business schools have proven highly resilient to global change. They have weathered many storms from global and local financial crises, government policy changes, geopolitical tensions and war, and, in recent times, a devastating global pandemic. Throughout this time, there have been many criticisms of their educational product (Pfeffer & Fong, 2002) and calls for reform. More recently, these criticisms are challenging the previously 'taken for granted' legitimacy (Carroll & Hannan, 1989) of educational institutions and their roles in future society.

So how should business schools continue to best respond and stay ahead in an internationally competitive environment while meeting the complex needs of both their local and international communities? What will they look like? What will they offer? Who will they serve?

This chapter will consider the importance of strategic balance in decision-making by individual schools and the wider business school network to ensure the legitimacy of the sector amidst highly uncertain global conditions. Iterative isomorphic innovation (Deephouse, 1999) will be explored as a way to progress change while protecting individual market players. The importance of maintaining strong stakeholder endorsement during change will be illustrated by recent challenges to the internationalization agendas of universities in the regions of Australia, Canada, and the United Kingdom and how powerful actors can use legitimacy challenges as a basis for radical

Robina Xavier, *Finding Strategic Balance.* In: *Management Education and the Rise of Uncertainty of Global Business.* Edited by: Eric Cornuel, Oxford University Press. © Oxford University Press (2025).
DOI: 10.1093/9780197794470.003.0008

reform. The protective powers of collaboration and network associations are also explored.

Management education emphasizes the importance of strategy to achieve organizational goals. All major international business accreditation systems such as the European Management Development Fund (EFMD) EQUIS framework also emphasize strategy in relation to business school operations and success. Strategy is featured in the very first chapter of the 2024 EQUIS Standards and Criteria, Chapter 1, Context, Governance and Strategy (EFMD, 2024). For EQUIS, a commitment to internationalization through strategy and operations is also critical with internationalization being one of the core transversal standards for all accredited schools.

Strategy can be seen as 'a set of guiding principles that, when communicated and adopted in the organization, generates a desired pattern of decision making' (Watkins, 2007). Competitive strategy is about being different, 'deliberately choosing a different set of activities that deliver a unique mix of value' (Porter, 1996, 64). Central to strategy is the role of decision-making. For contemporary business school leaders, decisions are being made in an environment of ever-increasing demands from an ever-increasing set of stakeholders including powerful funding agencies and regulators. Determining strategy is not done in isolation. Watkins (2007) suggests that decisions on strategy must always consider the network of partners with whom the organization works.

Within their strategy setting, organizations need to balance the benefits and costs of differentiation and conformity (Deephouse, 1999). Being different reduces competition as the organization is offering something in short supply in its sector. By being the same, the organization benefits from the halo of acceptance of the sector. This creates a strategic tension for decision-makers in mapping the organization's future: be different or be the same. To take advantage of both these elements, organizations that want to gain an advantage 'should be as different as legitimately possible' (148). It is both an art and science to know where that boundary lies.

As business schools consider their overall strategies and the role of internationalization in their futures, their desire and ability to innovate will be front of mind. Whether actually coined by Drucker or not, 'Innovate or die' remains a common catch cry. Innovation in business school strategy may not be as diverse or as distinctive as one might imagine given the discipline expertise available within business schools. While there are distinctive players such as IMD and INSEAD for executive education and Open Universities UK and Arizona State University for universal access, there is much similarity in practice and change is difficult (Hoffman, 2021). In times of great uncertainty, judgement on innovation will need to achieve organizational goals as well as accommodate changing sentiment on the role of a business school and its social licence to operate to ensure legitimacy is maintained. Again, the point of strategic balance is critical. Sentiment can and does change quickly and schools need sufficient flexibility in their strategy to respond accordingly.

FORCES FOR AND AGAINST SECTOR CHANGE: SECTOR OR STAKEHOLDER LED

While through an economic lens business schools could be considered the 'success story of the late twentieth-century education' (Pfeffer & Fong, 2002), further change remains necessary and is happening. It is unclear how much change is driven by a proactive drive to do things differently or a reactive response to demands of others. Miotto et al. (2020) suggest that business schools are focusing on developing strategies centred on educating responsible managers, somewhat in response to their own legitimacy challenges from over emphasizing pure economic benefit in the past.

Business schools have recognized the need to change their curricula, embedding an increasingly growing list of important issues such as climate change, social and income inequality, sustainability, energy transition, ethics, robot human interaction, and artificial intelligence. Many schools are using the UN Sustainable Development Goals as a framework to map their work (Miotto et al., 2020). Filling up the curricula either through embedding new content or adding electives is a common worldwide approach which tries to demonstrate ongoing relevance. While meeting the short-term needs, it is not substantially challenging the status quo in terms of a future focussed overall approach to business education.

In a recent article from Harvard Business School's Institute for Business in Global Society (Chang, 2024), Andy Hoffman argues the need for a fundamental shift in business education to ensure students become 'stewards of the market' and 'help us live our lives'. This builds on his earlier work (Hoffman, 2021) outlining 'nine broad categories of proposed changes for business schools:

1. Instil an ethos of management as a calling;
2. Rebuild the business school on a system of aspirational principles;
3. De-emphasize the core;
4. Move beyond simply monetary measures;
5. Train stewards of the market;
6. Reexamine the purpose of the corporation;
7. Discard misguided metrics and models;

8. Bring the government back in; and
9. Pay proper attention to citizenship.

Parker (2018) takes the reform agenda much further, calling for the development of an 'entirely new way of thinking about management, business and markets' with a key concept of 'organizing' (170) to underpin all operations.

Sector led change allows business schools to consider the needs of stakeholders both internal and external and change accordingly, with some degree of control over the change timeline. Resources can be allocated accordingly and capacity and capability for change assessed and addressed. Any and all change is difficult so the incentives for and against change will need to be clear for business school leaders as they map their future strategies. Hoffman (in Chang, 2024) highlights the enormous inertia present in the business education ecosystem, particularly in relation to the constraints of rankings and reward systems. He highlights the danger of one school trying to lead significant change all the way through to a full institutional overhaul, thereby changing the current isomorphic nature of global business education.

Being fundamentally out of step with key stakeholders is a critical threat to legitimacy and may limit the sector's options for self-determined change. The change timeline may also be forced upon the sector. While change is difficult, the sector should pay heed to the liability of obsolescence where such entrenched inertia can lead to a fundamental misalignment with the wider environment and key stakeholders and a subsequent higher failure rate (Ranger-Moore, 1997).

While each international system is different there remains more similarity in many of the global education systems than substantial differences. Calls for innovation through structural change, governance and oversight and strategy such as Hoffman's (Chang, 2024) are important for the future development of educational institutions but more difficult to achieve in practice.

SIMILARITY AS A STRENGTH: THRIVING AND SURVIVING THROUGH PROTECTING LEGITIMACY

Organizational legitimacy is linked to an organization's ability to thrive and survive (Ruef & Scott, 1998). It is defined as 'a generalised perception or assumption that the actions of an entity are desirable, proper, or appropriate within some socially constructed system of norms, values, beliefs and definitions' (Suchman, 1995, 574). Legitimacy can be considered in terms of acceptance (Brown, 1994), taken-for-grantedness (Carroll & Hannan, 1989), and reasonableness, appropriateness, and congruence (Meyer & Rowan, 1977). Legitimate organizations survive because stakeholders are more likely to supply resources to those that are perceived to be desirable, proper or appropriate.

Legitimacy is closely linked to the expectations of stakeholders on organizational action, in particular whether the actions represent 'the right thing to do' (Suchman, 1995, 579) and whether the organization has a right to continue operations (Bedeian, 1989). Legitimacy can be judged by evoking the value systems of stakeholders around 'collectively valued purposes, means and goals' (Meyer & Rowan, 1977, 349). If achieved, this legitimacy represents affective congruence where there is consistency between the organization's goals and values and those of its stakeholders (Choi & Shepherd, 2005).

Completely legitimate organizations have no threat of negative stakeholder evaluation as they are seen as organizations 'about which no question could be raised' (Meyer & Scott, 1983, 201). Their legitimation provides 'insulation from scrutiny' (Bansal & Clelland, 2004, 95), helping to reassure stakeholders that any untoward event such as a crisis is unusual. In the likelihood of such an event, Bansal and Clelland (2004) suggest stakeholders will rally around the organization, thereby significantly lessening the effect of the environmental incident. On the other hand, completely illegitimate organizations are likely to continually face threats both internally and externally. As outlined by Pfeffer and Salancik (1978, 194), 'when activities of an organization are illegitimate, comments and attacks will occur'.

Organizational and environmental actions and changes can lead to the questioning or loss of legitimacy. This can create a legitimacy gap where key public support for the organization's actions is lost and resources are withdrawn.

The process of external legitimation takes time and not all legitimation attempts meet with equal success. Hannan and Freeman (1989) suggest that longevity may be the key component in organizations achieving legitimacy, particularly for those who reach the taken-for-granted stage where the organization is legitimate by assumption (Henisz & Zelner, 2005). Older organizations develop dense webs of exchange relationships with relevant sectors of the environment and this provides protection to organizations by reducing selection pressures. Newer organizations, however, operate in an environment of uncertainty (Lounsbury & Glynn, 2001) without the social networks that can stabilize the new firm in its targeted markets.

In most industries, there is limited regulation with organizations free to set their own path within certain parameters. In this environment, ambiguity and uncertainty make the choice of appropriate strategies less clear. To address this, organizations create norms of strategic behaviour that key stakeholders come to accept (DiMaggio & Powell, 1983). This acceptance is noted and organizations start to imitate other successful organizations (Deephouse, 1996). Organizations also learn about successful behaviour of others through relevant networks (DiMaggio & Powell, 1983), including those relevant to business schools such as accreditation networks. On the other hand, organizations that demonstrate significantly different behaviour from others either through innovation or unique strategies run the risk of being deemed unacceptable by key stakeholders including regulators and the public. Deephouse (1996) demonstrated a positive relationship between strategic isomorphism and legitimacy. Organizations that conform to strategies used by other organizations are recognized by regulators and the general public as being more legitimate than those that deviate from normal behaviour.

While a newer type of organizational structure than a university, business schools can achieve and maintain legitimacy through an iterative isomorphic process. Business schools in different regions or different regulatory systems can select strategies to achieve their goals and the support of key stakeholders, and if those strategies are successful, they will be imitated over time. These strategies could incorporate all or some of Hoffman's proposed changes and reflect to different extents their local environment as well as globally significant and relevant areas under their internationalization approach. Knowledge of successful strategies is enhanced through national and international professional associations.

For schools implementing change, legitimacy can be protected by staying within a range of acceptability (Deephouse, 1999) with the selection of radically different strategies that move outside this range potentially putting the business school in peril. Conversely, no change may lead to the business school becoming irrelevant to its environment as external conditions change. Business school accreditation systems privilege continuous improvement sending an important signal through the network that all participants should expect and drive change.

While recognizing that once an organizational field becomes well established there is an inexorable push towards homogenization, Hambrick et al. (2004) argue that we should recognize that an industry is always subject to opposing pressures for heterogenization (as firms strive to achieve competitive differentiation) and homogenization (as firms strive to achieve legitimacy). However, in periods of great change and uncertainty, isomorphism is seen to drive further alignment to common standards as a protective shield. For business schools, a key question is whether the common standards will be the existing ones or a new set, and what resources are available to drive the development of any desired change.

WHEN INTERNATIONALIZATION STRATEGY AND GEOPOLITICS COLLIDE: AN UNFOLDING LEGITIMACY CHALLENGE

The iterative isomorphic process outlined above can be considered in terms of the internationalization agenda being implemented by the global business school network. There are many aspects to the internationalization of universities and business schools including student profiles, curricula, faculty, research, mobility, partnerships, connections with practice, and outreach. The EFMD has a well recognized model to help business schools enhance their internationalization through a multidimensional approach. Studies consistently show that internationalization is a top priority for universities and a strategic imperative for their leaders, but as demonstrated in a recent study of nearly 200 universities in Australia, the United Kingdom and Canada (Navitas-Nous Group 2023), confidence in the ability to successfully deliver an internationalization agenda remains less certain.

While there are exceptions in different regions, the internationalization strategies of business schools have received two key types of endorsement to support their legitimacy: regulatory (acceptance by the state agencies that formally regulate an organization) and public (acceptance by the general public) (Deephouse, 1996). However, in some regions, the strategic balance previously accepted may now be out of balance, signalling a potential legitimacy challenge (DiMaggio & Powell, 1983) that brings into question the continued endorsement of both these key players.

In many regions, there has been a growing presence of international students in business schools, often praised for enhancing soft diplomacy and the diversity of views in a globally relevant discipline. Economic benefits have also been recognized not only to the business school or parent university but to the surrounding communities through consumerism and a flexible workforce.

While only one dimension of internationalization, the prevalence of international students in universities and business schools has recently gained significant national interest in countries such as Australia, Canada, and the United Kingdom.

Only recently celebrated as Australia's largest services export and fourth largest export industry, Australian universities are currently facing a major challenge to their organizational legitimacy in relation to the proportion of international students enrolled in degrees. While aimed at universities as a whole, the prevalence of students in business and business-related studies are a key part of the challenge. The proportion of international students in the sector has been caught up in national discussions on overseas migration and the availability of affordable housing.

Louw (2024) suggests that chasing international student revenue has led Australian universities to neglect their core mission of delivering a high quality education to Australian domestic students. This view is widely portrayed through the media and has led to the Australian government recommending caps on the proportion of international students going forward. A nationwide cap is proposed as well as caps for individual providers and for individual campuses with effect as of 1 January 2025, less than three months from the planned passage of relevant legislation. The nationwide cap is expected to be approximately 50,000 less than the previous year with the potential impact for the country's largest universities of up to $85 million per year in lost revenue.

Australia has the highest proportion of international students of any large, developed country and the highest of all OECD countries with the exception of Luxembourg. Business students make up the overwhelmingly largest proportion of these students. Based on 2019 figures from the OECD, approximately 28.4% of tertiary students in Australia were international students, over a third higher than the next highest country (New Zealand, 20.8%) and almost three times the OECD average of 10.1% (Louw, 2024). In the group of highest ranked universities in Australia, on average more than one third of students (36.6%) were international students in 2023.

In the face of significant cost-of-living increases in Australia, public sentiment has changed quickly with open and frequent questioning of the impact of migration on housing shortages. While immigration covers all types of people who wish to move to a country either for short-term stays or permanently, international students have become an easily identifiable and highly vulnerable target not only for cost-of-living pressures, but for limiting opportunities for domestic students. While there is considerable evidence that disputes the fundamentals of much of the arguments being put forward, the narrative is now firmly entrenched and the national government is acting accordingly. Without announcing specific alternative policies, the major opposition party has doubled down on the proposed position suggesting that the Australian dream (of home ownership) is worth more than any export industry (Bragg, 2024).

The Canadian government's move in early 2024 to limit international students by restricting visas to 2023 levels has had an immediate and significant effect. Canadian enrolments are predicted to be below the government set caps by around 20% as students travel instead to other countries (Hare, 2024). The peak university body, Universities Canada has been reported as suggesting application numbers among its members were down an average of 40% (Hare, 2024) with questions now in the sector as to whether the governmental actions have irreversibly damaged the Canadian brand.

Similar challenges have been faced in the United Kingdom through policy change. With domestic tuition fees in the UK still frozen, the loss of international student income through changes to UK visa laws is likely to have a significant impact on the sector. The visa restrictions applied by the United Kingdom's Sunak government to limit the ability to bring family members or dependents on a student visa appear to be continuing to hamper recruitment with mid year application numbers close to 30% down in 2024 compared with 2023 (Adams, 2024). Based on trends, there are estimates of 150,000 fewer international students commencing their study in the 2024 autumn. The legitimacy of the sector was central to framing support for the policy change with suggestions that international students may be undermining the integrity and quality of the UK higher education system by using university courses as a cheap way of getting work visas.

Given the evidence of what has happened in both the UK and Canada, the impact within the Australian system is being described as 'economic self-sabotage' (Hare, 2024) and the sector is lobbying hard on the negative impacts such a change can bring.

Damaging signals have been sent to a market that is highly influenced by single country policy interventions. Within the global education ecosystem, changes in the market are picked up quickly with prospective students taking up opportunities in countries that are more welcoming than others. Reports by sector players suggest that a growing number of prospective international students are considering alternatives to Australia, Canada, and the UK with the shifts being attributed to immigration policies which have made studying less possible and/or attractive (The Economic Times, 2024). Between January and July 2024, student interest in these three markets has dropped approximately 20%–25%. While a challenge to Canada, Australia, and the UK, this provides growth opportunities for other countries.

As part of a wider narrative on the proportion of international and domestic students within any system, the assumed social licence of a university has been questioned. At least in Australia, the university sector has been conscience of changing community attitudes towards it for some years (Greenwood, 2022). Australians still have significant confidence in their universities, with approximately 70% of adult Australians in a recent survey believing that universities do a good job (Biddle, 2023). While this has been relatively stable during the COVID period, there has been considerable decline in confidence over the past 15 years. Once somewhat ignored in public debate, there is now an almost daily questioning of the actions of the university sector and its priorities by multiple stakeholders. In announcing the proposed caps on international education, the Australian Minister for Education, the Hon Jason Clare, MP said he was not only protecting the integrity of the system but the social licence for the system to continue to operate (Karp, 2024), with the strong implication that the sector has brought this need for change upon itself (The AFR View, 2024) through a significant misalignment with stakeholder sentiment. The taken-for-grantedness legitimacy of the university sector has now been challenged and the support of two major actors, the government and the public, is not assured. Self-determination is limited within the significant level of regulatory oversight being applied.

Greenwood (2022) suggests the university sector needs to talk more directly to the community about its role in society. In Australia, the peak university body, Universities Australia, has launched a major awareness raising campaign entitled Universities Matter, hoping to gain more community support for its future and the future of its government funding.

INNOVATING TOGETHER TO REDUCE RISK

Modern university governance would suggest that university risk registers in the regions outlined earlier would have contained risks on change to government policy. These would have been reviewed by governing bodies and mitigation strategies put in place. However, the severity of the change and the limited time from announcement to implementation was unlikely to have been foreseen and is likely to challenge all university growth strategies. This should serve as a warning to business school leaders.

Business educators will continue to debate the future of business curriculum and the best way to prepare the leaders of tomorrow but time may not be on their side if the prevailing forces of inertia prove too strong and self-directed change does not occur in a reasonable timeframe. The recent system shocks are a good reminder to our business schools that regulator and public sentiment can change quickly so the timeline for addressing needed change may be taken out of the hands of business schools if they don't continue to evolve and align with key stakeholder perspectives. Change to date has been slow and may need to move more quickly if the global business school network is to, at the very least, stay abreast of changing community expectations.

Business schools, whether stand alone or within university structures, need to consider all stakeholders when mapping their internationalization strategies and innovation agendas. The global social licence of the business school network is critically important, as is maintaining individual school legitimacy in local markets. Business school leaders need to assess the changing expectations of both domains in thinking about their purpose and deliverables and recognize that these will continue to change and, at times, conflict. Managing that conflict will require careful attention.

In times of significant uncertainty, isomorphism is common as stepping too far out of the norm for any one player can be dangerous. There is a role for key business schools in different markets to collaborate on initiatives to push more effectively against the prevailing inertia to drive the changes needed. This can assure not only the current legitimacy of operations and offerings but shore up legitimacy capital for the future. If successful, these practices are likely to be copied within the wider sector, giving protection to smaller or more vulnerable schools, including those who are yet to build their network strength.

National and international associations of business schools can do much to support these activities through providing key platforms for the exchange of ideas, lobbying for support and change as needed, and taking every opportunity to remind key stakeholders of the value placed in the social licence given to each school to operate. Business schools need to tell their own story of achievement and change, collectively and individually, or it will be told—and perhaps mistold—by others. The question posed by Deephouse (1999) as to whether it is better to be different or the same remains critical for each business school leader and the wider business school network leadership to consider. As a still relatively young sector, strategic balance is vitally important if legitimacy is to be protected and resources made available by key stakeholders for sustained growth.

REFERENCES

Adams, R. (2024). 'UK Universities Face Growing Struggle to Recruit International Students'. *The Guardian*, 12 July.

Bansal, P, & Clelland, I. (2004). 'Talking Trash: Legitimacy, Impression Management, and Unsystematic Risk in the Context of the Natural Environment'. *Academy of Management Journal*, 47/1, 93–103.

Bedeian, A. G. (1989). *Management* (2nd ed.). Dryden.

Biddle, N. (2023) 'Attitudes Towards Education in Australia'. ANU Centre for Social Research and Methods. https://csrm.cass.anu.edu.au/research/publications/attitudes-towards-education-australia.

Bragg, A. (2024). *Insiders*. Australian Broadcasting Corporation, 1 September.

Brown, A. D. (1994). 'Politics, Symbolic Action and Myth Making in Pursuit of Legitimacy'. *Organization Studies*, 15/6, 861–878.

Carroll, G. R., & Hannan, M. T. (1989). 'On Using Institutional Theory in Studying Organizational Populations'. *Administrative Science Quarterly*, 54, 545–548.

Chang, E. (2024). 'Is Business Education Serving Society? The Case for Transformation in a Changing World'. https://www.hbs.edu/bigs/is-business-education-serving-society.

Choi, Y., & Shepherd, D. (2005). 'Stakeholder Perceptions of Age and Other Dimensions of Newness'. *Journal of Management*, 31, 573–596.

Deephouse, D. L. (1996). 'Does Isomorphism Legitimate?' *Academy of Management Journal*, 39/4, 1024–1039.

Deephouse, D. L. (1999). 'To Be Different, or to Be the Same? It's a Question (and Theory) of Strategic Balance'. *Strategic Management Journal*, 20/2, 147–166.

DiMaggio, P. J. & Powell, W. W. (1983). 'The Iron Cage Revisited: Institutional Isomorphism and Collective Rationality in Organizational Fields'. *American Sociological Review*, 48, 147–160.

European Foundation for Management Development. (2024). 'EQUIS Standards and Criteria'. https://www.efmdglobal.org/wp-content/uploads/2024_EQUIS_Standards_and_Criteria.pdf.

Greenwood, M. (2022). 'Universities Need a Singular Focus on Rebuilding Their Social Licence'. *Australian Financial Review*, 29 May. https://www.afr.com/policy/health-and-education/universities-need-a-singular-focus-on-rebuilding-their-social-licence-20220526-p5aoq5.

Hannan, M. T., & Freeman, J. (1989). *Organizational Ecology*. Harvard University Press.

Hambrick, D. C., Finkelstein, S., Cho, T. S., & Jackson, E. M. (2004). 'Isomorphism in Reverse: Institutional Theory as an Explanation for Recent Increases in Intraindustry Heterogeneity and Managerial Discretion'. *Research in Organizational Behavior*, 26, 307–350.

Hare, J. (2024), '"Careful What You Wish For": The Hidden Hit in Foreign Student Caps'. *Australian Financial Review*, 7 August.

Henisz, W. & Zelner, B. (2005). 'Legitimacy, Interest Group Pressures, and Change in Emergent Institutions: The Case of Foreign Investors and Host Country Government'. *Academy of Management Review*, 30/2, 361–382.

Hoffman, A. J. (2021). 'Business Education as if People and the Planet Really Matter'. *Strategic Organization*, 19/3, 513–525.

Karp, P. (2024). 'Labor Rejects Report That International Students Will Be Capped at 40% of University Enrolments'. *The Guardian*, 8 August. https://www.theguardian.com/australia-news/article/2024/aug/08/labor-international-student-cap-jason-clare.

Lounsbury, M. & Glynn, M. (2001). 'Cultural Entrepreneurship: Stories, Legitimacy and the Acquisition of Resources'. *Strategic Management Journal*, 22, 545–564.

Louw, M. (2024). *Breaking Universities' Addiction to International Students*. The Menzies Research Centre.

Meyer, J. W., & Rowan, B. (1977). 'Institutionalized Organizations: Formal Structure as Myth and Ceremony'. *American Journal of Sociology*, 83, 340–363.

Meyer, J. W., & Scott, W. R. (1983). 'Centralization and the Legitimacy Problems of Local Government'. In J. W. Meyer & W. R. Scott, eds., *Organizational Environments: Ritual and Rationality*. Sage Publications, 199–215.

Miotto, G., Blanco-Gonzalez, A., & Diez-Martin, F. (2020). 'Top Business Schools Legitimacy Quest Through the Sustainable Development Goals'. *Heliyon*, 6/11. https://doi.org/10.1016/j.heliyon.2020.e05395.

Navitas-Nous Group. (2023). 'Thriving in a Hyper Competitive World'. https://nousgroup.com/assets/docs/Nous-Navitas-GSEIL-Report-2023.pdf.

Parker, M. (2018). *Shut Down the Business School: What's Wrong with Management Education*. Pluto Press.

Pfeffer, J. & Fong, C. (2002). 'The End of Business Schools? Less Success than Meets the Eye'. *Academy of Management Learning and Education*, 1/1, 78–95.

Pfeffer, J., & Salancik, G. (1978). *The External Control of Organizations: A Resource Dependence Perspective*. Harper and Row.

Porter, M. I. (1996). 'What Is Strategy?' *Harvard Business Review*, 74/6, 61–78.

Ranger-Moore, J. (1997). 'Bigger May Be Better, But Is Older Wiser? Organizational Age and Size in the New York Life Insurance Industry'. *American Sociological Review*, 62, 903–921.

Ruef, M., & Scott, W. R. (1998). 'A Multidimensional Model of Organizational Legitimacy: Hospital Survival in Changing Institutional Environments'. *Administrative Science Quarterly*, 43/4, 877–904.

Suchman, M. C. (1995). 'Managing Legitimacy: Strategic and Institutional Approaches'. *Academy of Management Review*, 20/3, 571–610.

The AFR View. (2024). 'Have Universities Brought Clare's Hard Cap on Themselves?' *Australian Financial Review*, 28 August. https://www.afr.com/policy/economy/have-universities-brought-clare-s-hard-cap-on-themselves-20240826-p5k5id

The Economic Times (2024). 'UK, Canada and Australia Losing Popularity Among International Students'. *Economic Times*. https://economictimes.indiatimes.com/nri/study/uk-canada-australia-losing-popularity-among-international-students/articleshow/112704503.cms?from=mdr.

Watkins, M. D. (2007). 'Demystifying Strategy: The What, Who, How, and Why'. *Harvard Business Review*, 10 September, https://hbr.org/2007/09/demystifying-strategy-the-what.

8

Creating Strong Innovation Ecosystems

How TUM Campus Heilbronn Is Driving Applied AI in Europe

GUNTHER FRIEDL

INTRODUCTION

Innovation ecosystems are dynamic networks where universities, businesses, startups, and governments collaborate to fuel technological advancements, entrepreneurship, and economic growth. In today's fast-moving fields such as artificial intelligence (AI), the importance of these ecosystems cannot be overstated. A well-connected and thriving innovation ecosystem can accelerate research, foster entrepreneurship, and create competitive advantages for entire regions.

One institution that exemplifies how universities can serve as catalysts for such ecosystems is TUM Campus Heilbronn, a part of the Technical University of Munich (TUM). TUM is Germany's largest and most prestigious Technical University. TUM Campus Heilbronn has been established in 2018 based on a donation by the Dieter Schwarz Foundation and specializes in digital transformation, management, technology, and entrepreneurship. Since its inception, TUM Campus Heilbronn has leveraged global partnerships, cutting-edge facilities, and an ambitious vision to become a key player in developing an AI-centred innovation ecosystem in one of Germany's most innovative regions.

The Heilbronn-Franken region in the German federal state of Baden-Württemberg, where the campus is located, is known for its 'hidden champions'—innovative, family-run small and medium-sized enterprises (SMEs) that lead in global markets. The synergy between these local industries, academic research, and global knowledge transfer makes the region

Gunther Friedl, *Creating Strong Innovation Ecosystems.* In: *Management Education and the Rise of Uncertainty of Global Business.* Edited by: Eric Cornuel, Oxford University Press. © Oxford University Press (2025).
DOI: 10.1093/9780197794470.003.0009

a hotbed for AI innovation, and TUM Campus Heilbronn is at the heart of this development.

THE ROLE OF TUM CAMPUS HEILBRONN FOR THE DEVELOPMENT OF AN INNOVATION ECOSYSTEM

Since its inception in 2018, TUM Campus Heilbronn has been at the forefront of addressing critical challenges in digital transformation and family business management, with a strong emphasis on AI and related digital technologies. The campus has grown rapidly, and as of December 2024 now hosts more than 1,000 students from the TUM School of Management and the TUM School of Computation, Information, and Technology. With over 70% of the student body coming from international backgrounds, TUM Campus Heilbronn has become a hub for global talent, offering an unparalleled platform for cross-cultural exchange and collaboration.

This international outlook has been instrumental in positioning the campus as a driver of innovation and knowledge exchange. Starting with the TUM School of Management in 2018, the strategic expansion to include the TUM School of Computation, Information, and Technology has further solidified its interdisciplinary capabilities. The establishment of the TUM's Heilbronn Data Science Institute bridges the gap between data science and management, providing a foundational pillar for the application of AI technologies in real-world business and industrial contexts.

Attracting Global Talent and Expertise

One of the key strategies behind the success of TUM Campus Heilbronn has been its ability to attract top-tier talent from around the globe. The diverse backgrounds and perspectives of students and faculty create a vibrant intellectual environment where creativity, innovation, and problem-solving thrive. This international diversity enables the campus to act as a melting pot of ideas, fostering a culture of interdisciplinary collaboration that is essential for tackling complex challenges in today's rapidly evolving technological landscape.

Faculty members at TUM Campus Heilbronn are often renowned experts in areas such as AI, digital business, and supply chain management. Many are active researchers, leading projects that address cutting-edge topics such as generative AI, predictive analytics, and digital platform ecosystems. Their work not only enriches the academic offerings but also integrates global best practices into the curriculum, equipping students with the skills needed to excel in competitive industries.

Faculty members bring with them robust international networks of collaborators, connecting the campus to leading research institutions, industry leaders, and innovation hubs worldwide. These connections create opportunities for students to participate in global research initiatives, industry internships, and entrepreneurial ventures. Since its inception, faculty members have already received two of the prestigious grants from the European Research Council (ERC).

TUM Campus Heilbronn's programmes integrate research-driven insights with hands-on experiences, ensuring that students are not only familiar with state-of-the-art technologies but also equipped to apply them effectively. Through workshops, hackathons, and collaborative projects, students are encouraged to develop innovative solutions to real-world problems, preparing them to take leadership roles in shaping the future of AI and digital business.

By aligning its focus with the needs of a globalized economy, TUM Campus Heilbronn is cultivating a new generation of leaders who are ready to drive technological and organizational innovation.

Building Global Research Partnerships

Beyond its educational mission, TUM Campus Heilbronn has become a key player in global research collaborations, establishing partnerships with top universities, research institutions, and industrial organizations worldwide. These partnerships not only enhance the quality of research conducted on campus but also position Heilbronn as a node of global innovation in AI and digital transformation.

TUM has forged research alliances with leading institutions in the United States, Asia, and Europe, ensuring that its faculty and students remain at the cutting edge of technological advancement. With respect to the Heilbronn Campus, these collaborations include for example the University of Oxford, Stanford University, ETH Zürich, HEC Paris, the Hebrew University of Jerusalem, Nanyang Technological University, and the National University of Singapore, and they focus on topics such as the regulation of AI, AI and data visualization, quantum sovereignty and resilience, and quantum communication and security.

These partnerships are not confined to academic circles. By collaborating with global industry leaders, the campus ensures that breakthroughs in AI and digital technologies are translated into practical applications that benefit businesses in Heilbronn and beyond. Local companies gain access to cutting-edge solutions, which strengthens their competitiveness in the global market.

The research initiatives spearheaded by TUM Campus Heilbronn directly contribute to the economic development of the Heilbronn-Franken region. For instance, AI solutions developed on campus have been piloted in industries such as manufacturing, logistics, and healthcare, demonstrating tangible benefits like efficiency gains, cost reduction, and improved decision-making.

A cornerstone of TUM's research efforts in Heilbronn, the Data Science Institute fosters an interdisciplinary approach to solving real-world problems. By uniting experts in management and computer science, the institute acts as a catalyst for innovative AI applications, facilitating collaborations that address societal and business challenges.

Designing Study Programmes for Innovation Ecosystems

As part of its mission to foster a robust innovation ecosystem in the Heilbronn region, TUM Campus Heilbronn has developed a thoughtfully curated portfolio of study programmes. These programmes are designed to address the multifaceted demands of a technology-driven economy, equipping graduates with the skills and knowledge required to excel in fields such as AI, digital transformation, and entrepreneurship. By combining technical expertise, management skills, and a global perspective, TUM Campus Heilbronn ensures its graduates are prepared to lead innovation and drive industry transformation both regionally and globally.

The foundation for this academic excellence was laid in 2018 when the TUM School of Management began its operations in Heilbronn by introducing two flagship programmes: the Master in Management and Master in Management and Innovation. Both programmes are taught entirely in English, establishing an international culture on campus from the outset and attracting a diverse pool of talent from around the world. The Master in Management caters to students with a bachelor's degree in engineering or natural sciences, offering them essential management knowledge and preparing them to bridge the gap between technical expertise and business acumen. On the other hand, the Master in Management and Innovation adopts a broader focus, targeting professionals interested in becoming managers of change by integrating innovation and entrepreneurship into their skillset. Together, these programmes have created a pipeline of international talent, strengthening Heilbronn's position as a hub for digital transformation and AI-driven solutions.

In 2019, the TUM School of Management expanded its offerings in Heilbronn by launching the Bachelor in Management and Technology, which was later redesigned and rebranded as the Bachelor in Management and Data Science. This programme reflects the increasing role of data-driven innovation in shaping industries and society. By combining a solid foundation in management with expertise in data science, the programme equips students with a versatile toolkit to analyse, interpret, and utilize data for strategic decision-making. The curriculum integrates emerging technologies such as AI and the Internet of Things, preparing graduates to lead initiatives that merge technical insights with business strategy.

The academic portfolio of TUM Campus Heilbronn further evolved with the arrival of the TUM School of Computation, Information, and Technology, which introduced the Bachelor and Master in Information Engineering. These programmes collectively provide a comprehensive pathway for students interested in mastering digital technologies and AI systems. The bachelor's programme emphasizes foundational knowledge in software engineering, data science, and system design, while the master's programme builds on this base by offering advanced insights into AI applications, big data analytics, and holistic IT systems. Students learn to design end-to-end solutions, from sensor integration to creating innovative business models, positioning them to lead transformative projects in industries such as automotive, manufacturing, and healthcare.

Recognizing the growing need for professionals who can bridge the gap between digital technology and business management, TUM Campus Heilbronn recently introduced the Master in Management and Digital Technology. This programme equips students with advanced management expertise while offering specialized knowledge in cutting-edge digital technologies such as blockchain, cybersecurity, and AI systems. Graduates of this programme are uniquely prepared to navigate the challenges and opportunities of an increasingly digitalized world, playing pivotal roles in implementing disruptive technologies and leading organizational change.

All these programmes are designed with key features that enable them to contribute actively to the innovation ecosystem in Heilbronn. A significant emphasis is placed on interdisciplinary collaboration, encouraging students to work across disciplines and fostering a culture of innovation and problem-solving. For instance, joint projects between management and technical students often result in practical, market-ready solutions for AI and digital transformation. Industry integration is another cornerstone of these programmes, which include internships, real-world case studies, and collaborative research projects with local companies. This ensures that students gain practical experience and are ready to meet the needs of the modern workforce. Additionally, entrepreneurial development is strongly supported through initiatives such as the Campus Founders programme and the TUM Venture Lab Heilbronn, which empower students to transform innovative ideas into successful startups. Many of these ventures focus on AI-driven solutions, contributing to the region's entrepreneurial ecosystem and advancing its role as a European leader in AI innovation.

The global perspective of these programmes further enhances their impact. By attracting international students and fostering partnerships with universities and industries worldwide, TUM Campus Heilbronn ensures that its graduates are equipped to navigate the global innovation landscape. These partnerships not only enrich the learning experience but also create opportunities for student exchange, international outreach, and cross-border collaborations.

The study programmes at TUM Campus Heilbronn are more than academic offerings—they are essential building blocks of a thriving innovation ecosystem. By combining technical excellence, management expertise, and entrepreneurial spirit, these programmes prepare graduates to tackle the challenges of AI, digital transformation, and sustainability. Together, they form the backbone of the campus's contribution to the Heilbronn innovation ecosystem, nurturing talent that drives both regional growth and global impact.

THE ROLE OF INDUSTRY COLLABORATION IN BUILDING AN AI ECOSYSTEM

TUM Campus Heilbronn serves as a linchpin in the development of an AI ecosystem in the Heilbronn region by actively fostering collaboration between academia, industry, and startups. This partnership-driven approach ensures that cutting-edge research in artificial intelligence is effectively translated into practical applications, offering immediate value to industries while maintaining a pipeline for innovation. The campus acts as a bridge between theoretical advancements and real-world needs, making AI accessible and implementable for regional and nationwide businesses in different industries.

The automotive industry as one important example is one of the cornerstones of Germany's economy, and AI technologies—particularly in the context of digital factories—represent a transformative opportunity. TUM Campus Heilbronn works closely with local automotive companies such as Audi to develop AI-driven solutions for predictive maintenance, supply chain optimization, and automation of production processes.

AI research conducted on campus focuses on applications such as real-time quality control using computer vision, robotic process automation, and digital twins. These innovations enable manufacturers to achieve higher efficiency, reduced waste, and enhanced customization in production. Joint projects between TUM and hidden champions such as ebm-papst are tailored to address industry-specific challenges, ensuring that new technologies are both scalable and impactful.

Partnerships with local businesses enable the rapid commercialization of AI technologies, ensuring that innovations are brought to market efficiently. This approach not only strengthens the competitiveness of regional industries but also helps create a feedback loop where industry needs shape academic research.

A key element of this process is the Heilbronn Data Science Institute, which provides a collaborative platform for data scientists, engineers, and managers to work directly with industry partners on applied AI projects.

Nurturing Startups and Entrepreneurship

Startups are vital to the dynamism of any innovation ecosystem, serving as agile agents of change capable of rapidly bringing disruptive technologies to market. Recognizing this, TUM Campus Heilbronn and the Dieter Schwarz Foundation have implemented a range of initiatives aimed at cultivating entrepreneurship and ensuring that the Heilbronn region becomes a hub for AI-driven startups.

The Campus Founders programme, initiated by the Dieter Schwarz Foundation, serves as a comprehensive support system for aspiring entrepreneurs. Entrepreneurs gain access to seasoned mentors, including successful founders, investors, and industry leaders. The programme also connects startups with venture capitalists and angel investors, providing the financial backing needed to scale innovations. Participants receive practical training in areas such as business planning, technology commercialization, and go-to-market strategies. One of the programmes specifically designed for startups in the field of AI is called AI Founders. It is a 12-week, early-stage AI accelerator programme that assists aspiring founders with new startup ideas in launching successful AI businesses. First success stories include the startup trail, which offers a way to operationalize AI governance, empowering developers and businesses to create trustworthy AI solutions.

The TUM Venture Lab in Heilbronn is a dedicated initiative designed to support startups and spin-offs in fields like AI, data science, and software development. The lab offers access to state-of-the-art computing infrastructure and prototyping resources, enabling startups to refine and test their technologies. By bringing together researchers and practitioners from diverse fields, the lab fosters innovative solutions that transcend traditional industry boundaries.

The TUM Venture Labs are specialized incubators established through a collaboration between the Technical University of Munich (TUM) and UnternehmerTUM, Europe's largest entrepreneurship centre. These labs are designed to support deep tech and life science startups throughout their early development stages, from idea generation to securing seed capital for business launch.

One of the key features of the TUM Venture Labs is that they offer domain-specific support: each Venture Lab focuses on a specific technological or scientific domain, such as robotics/AI, mobility, healthcare, and food/agro/biotech. This specialization allows for tailored support, leveraging deep domain expertise to address the unique challenges and opportunities within each field.

Another feature of the TUM Venture Labs is that they provide access to state-of-the-art infrastructure, mentoring from experienced professionals, and connections to a vast ecosystem of industry experts, investors, and academic researchers. This holistic approach ensures that startups have the necessary tools and guidance to develop and scale their innovations effectively.

They also foster close collaboration between TUM's academic community and industry partners, the Venture Labs facilitate the rapid translation of cutting-edge research into market-ready applications. This integration accelerates the commercialization of scientific breakthroughs, contributing to economic growth and technological advancement.

Finally, the TUM Venture Labs actively encourage students and researchers to pursue entrepreneurship as a viable career path, providing programmes and support systems that nurture innovative ideas and transform them into successful business ventures.

With this vibrant startup culture TUM Campus Heilbronn is drawing talented individuals to the region, creating a virtuous cycle of innovation and entrepreneurship.

HOW INTERNATIONALIZATION ENABLES INNOVATION

Internationalization has been a cornerstone of TUM Campus Heilbronn's strategy for driving innovation and fostering a dynamic AI ecosystem in the Heilbronn region. By integrating talent, ideas, and resources from across the globe, the campus has created an environment that not only supports groundbreaking research but also transforms innovations into practical applications. This global focus ensures that Heilbronn is not merely a regional hub for AI but a globally connected centre of excellence. Below, we explore the ways in which internationalization drives the success of this ecosystem.

TUM Campus Heilbronn thrives on its diversity of perspectives, made possible by its international students, researchers, and faculty. Hosting individuals from over 70 countries, the campus serves as a melting pot of cultures and expertise. This diversity fosters a cross-pollination of ideas, enabling teams to approach problems from multiple cultural and disciplinary viewpoints. For instance, an AI project on predictive analytics for healthcare might bring together a data scientist from India, a management expert from Germany, and a software engineer from Brazil. Each participant contributes unique insights, leading to creative and holistic solutions that push boundaries.

Interdisciplinary collaboration is actively encouraged at TUM Campus Heilbronn, particularly between management, data science, and engineering. Students and researchers frequently work on projects that require combining technical knowledge, business acumen, and cultural insights. A team tackling the challenge of optimizing logistics with AI, for example, might develop a real-time decision-making system that not only improves efficiency but also considers the cultural nuances of supply chain management in global markets. Such innovations, often born from diverse and interdisciplinary teams, are applied in fields ranging from autonomous systems to smart manufacturing and personalized healthcare.

By fostering a global mindset, TUM Campus Heilbronn empowers its students and researchers to address challenges that extend beyond regional boundaries. Whether tackling climate change through sustainable energy solutions or addressing ethical concerns in AI development, the campus prepares its community to make a meaningful impact on global issues.

Access to global expertise is another pillar of TUM Campus Heilbronn's success. Partnerships with leading universities and research institutions worldwide ensure that students and faculty remain at the forefront of AI innovation. Collaborations with institutions in North America, Asia, and Europe enable the exchange of groundbreaking research in areas such as machine learning, computer vision, and natural language processing.

Industry partnerships further amplify the impact of internationalization. By collaborating with global organizations, TUM Campus Heilbronn provides local companies with access to cutting-edge AI tools and solutions developed internationally. These partnerships ensure that industries in Heilbronn, especially in automotive, manufacturing, and logistics, remain competitive in the global AI landscape.

Beyond attracting talent, TUM Campus Heilbronn emphasizes the importance of global knowledge sharing. Faculty and researchers regularly collaborate with their counterparts worldwide, ensuring that Heilbronn is both a contributor to and a beneficiary of the global flow of knowledge.

The campus also serves as a hub for international conferences and workshops, where experts from around the world discuss emerging trends in AI and share practical insights. These events, such as a recent Supply Chain Finance Hub, foster connections between academia and industry, facilitating knowledge transfer that benefits the local innovation ecosystem. Moreover, collaborations with global research teams have led to significant advancements in AI applications, including autonomous systems, smart logistics, and personalized healthcare solutions. These innovations are now being adopted by companies in the region, reinforcing Heilbronn's reputation as a leader in applied AI.

Through its commitment to internationalization, TUM Campus Heilbronn has not only enriched its ecosystem but also positions the Heilbronn region as a global hub for AI innovation. Technologies and ideas developed on campus are shared with partners worldwide, amplifying the region's influence in the AI domain. For instance, the campus's international reputation has drawn world-class researchers and students, fostering a cosmopolitan atmosphere that enhances Heilbronn's appeal as a destination for academic and professional talent.

By importing best practices and facilitating global partnerships, the campus strengthens local industries, enabling them to compete on a global scale. The automotive sector, for example, has benefited from collaborations that integrate AI-driven quality control systems, while logistics companies in the region have adopted AI tools to optimize operations.

Internationalization has been instrumental in transforming TUM Campus Heilbronn into a global innovation hub. By leveraging a diversity of perspectives, accessing global expertise, and fostering cross-border knowledge sharing, the campus has established a thriving AI ecosystem that drives both regional development and international collaboration. Through partnerships with global research leaders, TUM Campus Heilbronn continues to elevate Heilbronn's status as a centre for AI excellence, deeply interconnected with the broader global innovation landscape.

THE ROLE OF THE INNOVATION PARK ARTIFICIAL INTELLIGENCE (IPAI)

The Innovation Park Artificial Intelligence (IPAI) stands as a transformative force within the Heilbronn innovation ecosystem, symbolizing the region's commitment to becoming a European leader in AI development and application. Emerging after the establishment of TUM Campus Heilbronn, the IPAI builds upon the campus's solid foundation of academic excellence, interdisciplinary collaboration, and global talent attraction. Acting as a natural extension of the campus's mission, the IPAI is designed to become the centrepiece of the region's innovation ecosystem, providing cutting-edge resources, advanced research facilities, and a robust network of industry partnerships.

The establishment of the IPAI was deeply influenced by the newly established presence of the TUM Campus Heilbronn. The campus's strong focus on AI research, its emphasis on digital technologies, and its success in drawing international talent created an environment ripe for the IPAI's development. Moreover, the region's hallmark collaboration between academia, industry, and government positioned Heilbronn as an ideal location for such a forward-thinking initiative. The IPAI was envisioned to complement and amplify the existing strengths of TUM Campus Heilbronn, enhancing the region's capacity to drive innovation and transform groundbreaking research into practical, real-world applications.

As the IPAI takes shape it is poised to become the epicentre of AI innovation in Europe, combining world-class research facilities, collaborative networks, and industry partnerships. The park is equipped with state-of-the-art computing infrastructure, AI-focused laboratories, and prototyping spaces, fostering an environment where interdisciplinary teams can work on transformative projects. Researchers specializing in areas such as robotics, data science, ethics, and business management collaborate to tackle some of the most pressing challenges in AI, bridging theoretical advancements with practical implementation.

IPAI goes beyond pure economic value creation. Based on recognizing the importance of sustainability and ethical responsibility in AI development, the IPAI platform promotes collaboration between research, AI development and established partners to ensure that AI technologies are used for the benefit of society. At the same time, IPAI aims at raising awareness of the topic of artificial intelligence among the general public and to provide access to education and discussions about AI for everyone.

A significant emphasis of the IPAI is on applied AI research, addressing industry-specific challenges across sectors. Projects within the IPAI include developing AI-driven automation systems for manufacturing, predictive analytics tools for optimizing supply chains, and smart healthcare systems for early diagnostics and personalized treatments. These projects not only reinforce the IPAI's role as a leader of applied AI but also directly contribute to the growth and competitiveness of regional industries.

The IPAI also plays a critical role in enhancing the innovation ecosystem in Heilbronn, creating a synergistic relationship with TUM Campus Heilbronn. Together, they form a comprehensive platform that supports the entire lifecycle of innovation, from education and research to commercialization. The IPAI's ability to attract global talent has significantly enriched the region's expertise in AI, drawing world-class researchers, engineers, and entrepreneurs. This influx of talent complements the diverse community at TUM Campus Heilbronn, fostering a dynamic exchange of ideas and perspectives that drives innovation.

International collaboration and knowledge exchange are key pillars of the IPAI's vision. By fostering partnerships with global AI hubs in North America, Asia, and Europe, the park positions Heilbronn as a critical node in the global AI network. These partnerships enable the exchange of knowledge, talent, and resources, ensuring that the region remains at the forefront of AI advancements. Additionally, the IPAI works closely with TUM researchers to address global challenges, such as climate change and healthcare accessibility, through AI-powered solutions.

Looking ahead, the IPAI aims to establish itself as Europe's largest AI ecosystem, setting standards for ethical AI development and interdisciplinary innovation. The relationship between TUM Campus Heilbronn and the IPAI is central to the success of the Heilbronn innovation ecosystem. Students from programmes such as the Master in Information Engineering and Master in Management and Digital Technology benefit from hands-on experience through collaborative projects at the IPAI, gaining exposure to cutting-edge AI applications. Joint initiatives, shared research goals, and entrepreneurial support ensure that the campus and the IPAI work seamlessly to drive innovation and prepare the next generation of leaders in AI and digital transformation.

The IPAI is more than just a platform—it is the cornerstone of Heilbronn's ambition to be a global hub for AI innovation. By complementing the academic and research activities of TUM Campus Heilbronn, the IPAI amplifies the region's ability to attract talent, foster interdisciplinary collaboration, and drive economic growth. Together, TUM Campus Heilbronn and the IPAI create a vibrant ecosystem where groundbreaking ideas are transformed into impactful solutions, solidifying Heilbronn's position as a leader in the global AI landscape.

COLLABORATION AS A CATALYST FOR INNOVATION: TUM AND REGIONAL PARTNERS

Collaboration lies at the heart of the success of the Heilbronn innovation ecosystem, where institutions with complementary expertise come together to amplify their collective impact. At the centre of this dynamic network is TUM Campus Heilbronn, which has established strong partnerships with key regional actors such as Hochschule Heilbronn, Duale Hochschule Baden-Württemberg (DHBW), the Fraunhofer Society, and the Ferdinand Steinbeis Institute. These collaborations create a thriving environment for interdisciplinary research, knowledge transfer, and the development of transformative solutions that benefit industries and society alike.

As one of the largest universities of applied sciences in the region, Hochschule Heilbronn brings a strong focus on practical, application-oriented education. Its expertise in areas such as mobility, engineering, and sustainable management complements TUM Campus Heilbronn's strengths in AI, data science, and digital transformation. The collaboration between the two institutions creates opportunities for students and researchers to engage in projects that combine theoretical insights with practical implementation.

For instance, students from both institutions attend joint classes such as the CEO Lecture Series, a class bringing high-calibre CEOs on the joint campus. Students from both institutions also collaborate on multidisciplinary projects, such as developing smart city solutions that address challenges in urban mobility and energy management. These joint efforts not only strengthen the innovation ecosystem but also prepare students to work seamlessly across disciplines.

The Duale Hochschule Baden-Württemberg (DHBW) plays a vital role in bridging academia and industry through its dual education model. By alternating between academic study and practical training in companies, DHBW students gain hands-on experience that aligns with industry needs. TUM's partnership with DHBW leverages this model to create opportunities for work-integrated learning in areas such as AI implementation, IoT applications, and smart manufacturing.

The Fraunhofer Society, renowned for its applied research, is a key partner in advancing the Heilbronn innovation ecosystem. Fraunhofer institutes bring cutting-edge expertise in fields such as cybersecurity, advanced manufacturing, and AI-powered systems, which align closely with the research priorities of TUM Campus Heilbronn.

The partnership with Fraunhofer creates opportunities for student involvement in applied research. TUM students participate in internships and thesis projects at Fraunhofer institutes, gaining invaluable experience in translating theoretical knowledge into practical applications. These experiences prepare graduates to contribute effectively to the rapidly evolving technological landscape.

The Ferdinand Steinbeis Institute, known for its focus on knowledge and technology transfer, plays a pivotal role in driving innovation at the intersection of academia and industry. Through its expertise in digitalization and innovation management, the institute complements TUM's research efforts in AI and digital technologies.

The collaboration between TUM Campus Heilbronn and these regional actors goes beyond individual projects, reflecting a shared vision for the development of a thriving innovation ecosystem. By pooling resources, expertise, and networks, these partnerships enhance the region's capacity to address complex challenges and seize emerging opportunities.

One of the most significant outcomes of these collaborations is the creation of interdisciplinary platforms where students, researchers, and industry professionals can interact and share ideas. Events such as hackathons, innovation workshops, and industry roundtables bring together diverse stakeholders, fostering a culture of co-creation that accelerates the development of innovative solutions. For instance, a recent innovation challenge organized jointly by Hochschule Heilbronn and Fraunhofer focused on developing AI-based solutions for sustainable development of cities, leading to prototypes that are now being further developed with industry partners.

The collaboration between TUM Campus Heilbronn and regional partners such as Hochschule Heilbronn, DHBW, Fraunhofer, and the Ferdinand Steinbeis Institute exemplifies the power of collective action in driving innovation. Together, these institutions create a vibrant ecosystem where academic research, practical expertise, and industry needs converge to produce impactful solutions. By working in synergy, they not only enhance the region's reputation as a hub for AI and digital transformation but also ensure that the benefits of innovation are felt across industries and communities. This unified approach positions Heilbronn as a model for how regional collaboration can foster global competitiveness in the age of digital transformation.

CONCLUSION

TUM Campus Heilbronn has demonstrated how the internationalization of a business school can drive the development of a strong innovation ecosystem. By attracting international talent, forging global partnerships, and working closely with local industry, the campus has helped transform Heilbronn into a hub for AI innovation.

The impact of TUM Campus Heilbronn goes far beyond the classroom. The campus has played a vital role in the region's economic development, fostering AI research, supporting entrepreneurship, and helping local businesses innovate. As a result, Heilbronn is quickly becoming recognized as a key player in the global AI landscape—a transformation enabled by the international reach and innovative spirit of TUM Campus Heilbronn.

As the campus continues to grow, particularly through initiatives like the Innovation Park Artificial Intelligence, its role in shaping the future of AI will only become more significant. The lessons learned from TUM Campus Heilbronn's success can serve as a blueprint for other regions looking to develop their innovation ecosystems, particularly in fast-moving fields like AI and digital transformation.

9

Business Schools and a New Global World

Will They Never Walk Alone?

STEFANO CASELLI

GLOBALIZATION OR SOMETHING ELSE?

There is a strong link between the evolution of the economic system and the higher education sector, represented at the highest level of excellence by business schools. The economic system and, more broadly, the social system express educational needs through individuals and organizations. Business schools not only meet these needs but also offer solutions and visions that aim to guide both the economic and social systems. Business schools do not walk alone but are interpreters and agents of the profound transformation of our systems and our way of being. The international growth path of business schools and the strategic options they embrace signify this mutual dependence established within the higher education system. Economically closed systems may settle for domestic schools focused on developing local culture. In contrast, strong economic interconnections, mutual dependence, cooperation, and expanded international relationships require and are stimulated by schools open and oriented towards international development.

These reflections take place in an extremely complex phase. The world emerging from the pandemic, which had already raised significant questions about the educational model and mobility, gave for a few months the illusion of extraordinary economic growth. However, this was soon challenged by issues that seemed to have disappeared: inflation, the rapid rise of interest rates, and the outbreak of conflicts questioning the status quo of widespread well-being and peace, leading to new uncertainties.

Stefano Caselli, *Business Schools and a New Global World*. In: *Management Education and the Rise of Uncertainty of Global Business*. Edited by: Eric Cornuel, Oxford University Press. © Oxford University Press (2025).
DOI: 10.1093/9780197794470.003.0010

The world of business schools cannot remain neutral or shield itself within its own comfort zone as it is a significant social actor. Post-pandemic instability and numerous questions cannot make us forget the pre-pandemic state of the world. Words like 'de-globalization' or 'slowbalization'[1] were already prevalent, signalling the end of a paradigm rooted in the 1980s, based on the progressive homogenization of consumption and production models and the reduction of regulatory and physical barriers through technological innovation.

A global world model with perfect mobility of human and physical resources is, in a certain sense, comforting for the fate of the world itself and represents perhaps the best of all possible worlds for business schools. They can offer their educational solutions and models on the widest possible scale. Today, this game plan is at least in part obsolete, or rather, it has been overtaken by a broader challenge. A challenge that means defining a new way of existing globally for politics, governments, and economic systems, with the hope that this new way constitutes a step forward for humanity in terms of GDP, employment, wealth distribution, democracy, and freedom. For business schools, this challenge means ensuring that the new way of being is directed towards a path that benefits humanity by contributing to the education of individuals and organizations, while also raising the bar of their own ambitions, balancing global values with local cultures and specifics.

A WORLD OF GREAT DIMENSIONS

What kind of industrial system and corporate structure does Europe need? This question is fundamental if we believe that the European Union can be a comprehensive and unique platform of rights, civilization, and development around which a stronger sense of community can be built. It can also express a model that could guide other geographical systems in their evolution. Much attention is paid to how countries finance themselves, but equally important is how corporate structures can create or fail to create wealth and employment. This issue naturally concerns Europe as a whole, as well as individual countries in their specificity and as part of a larger community.

The challenge of achieving a sustainable ratio between public debt and GDP is primarily played out on the denominator and the ability to grow it consistently. Large enterprises are central to this analysis because they are a fundamental engine of investment and innovation, a strong attractor of top talent, and the backbone of the ecosystem of smaller companies that grow alongside them. Furthermore, large enterprises are a crucial element of the competition between nations, which defines broader and more comprehensive balances. Industrial policy is an integral part of a nation's geopolitical strategy, which is why Europe and its countries must pay close attention and energy to this issue.

How does the map of Europe look in this context? If we look at 2023 data using the ranking of the top 500 global companies, the European Union as a whole has 90 companies, compared to 105 companies 10 years ago and 112 companies 20 years ago. There has been no progress; rather, there has been a slight decline, compounded by the loss of the United Kingdom as part of the common system. Within these 90 companies, there is a significant gap between different European countries. On one side, Germany and France, with 28 and 25 companies, respectively. On the other, the relevance of the Netherlands and Spain (with 11 and nine companies), followed by Italy, which has only six companies among the top 500, three of which are state-owned (Enel, ENI, and Poste Italiane) and three financial intermediaries (Generali, Intesa, and Unicredit). Ireland and Luxembourg are even further behind, sharing with the Netherlands a favourable tax regime but more known as financial hubs for holding companies, family offices, and funds rather than as platforms for attracting not only capital but also business systems as a whole. Unfortunately, the number of companies in the top 100 is also limited, ranging from the French group (Total, AXA, Crédit Agricole, and Electricité de France) to the German group (Volkswagen, Mercedes-Benz, Allianz, BMW, Deutsche Telekom, Deutsche Post), to the Italian (Generali and Enel), Dutch (Stellantis), and Finnish (Fortum) groups.

The analysis of these companies leads us to some considerations and the overcoming of certain prejudices. The first point is related to the fact that the state (directly or through entities similar to CDP or regions) is only partially present and, in rare cases (three in France and three in Germany, with Electricité de France, SNCF, La Poste, Deutsche Bahn, ZF, and Energie Baden-Württemberg), with a controlling position. The second point is that large companies are an essential part of the country's GDP and employment, without considering the induced effects of their presence in the economy. Data on the revenue-to-GDP ratio shows that large enterprises are critical components of their countries and offer a decisive contribution to GDP through their size and employment. The third point is the need to focus attention on the role of large enterprises and how their presence is central to Europe's development plan.

Much debate and attention are paid to the topic of SMEs and the need for adequate financial structures. Bruno Le Maire and Christian Lindner recently addressed the issue of closing the 'financial gap' in Europe in the *Financial Times*. This is even more relevant for Italy, which today has 188,000 SMEs playing a key role in the creation of GDP and employment. However, equal care must be dedicated to opening a debate on the role, characteristics, and ways of increasing the number of large enterprises by overcoming opposition and maturing a comprehensive design.

This issue leads to two fundamental reflections for our future. The first is related to the role of the state. In large companies, the state is present only occasionally, and there is no clear European identity of the 'entrepreneurial state'. The OECD, led by Carmine Di Noia, recently launched a survey to analyse in-depth the extent and effects of the state's presence in the shareholder structure of European companies, an issue that will require reflection based on robust empirical evidence (OECD 2023). The state's role must be more effectively oriented towards creating the conditions for Europe to have a higher number of global champions. This is true for the financial sector, where some cross-border M&A operations can scale up the European Union compared to American global champions, but it is also relevant for industrial sectors that face the corporate gigantism of the United States and China (today) and possibly other regions (India and the Gulf) in the immediate future. These topics are even more critical for Italy, which must open a serious discussion on how to expand its industrial presence, transitioning from being a country of small champions to one that also adds a few large industrial and financial groups. This means discussing industrial policy, organizational models, and long-term incentives (for mergers rather than conglomerates), as well as creating a capital market that is agile and effective.

The second reflection is about how to make the three dimensions—small, medium, and large enterprises—complementary and symbiotic. A vibrant and healthy industrial system continuously fosters opportunities for growth, from startups to medium-sized companies, and eventually into larger firms, or allows medium-sized companies to consolidate. The debate on how to close the 'financial gap' in Europe should primarily focus on this. Similarly, the educational models of European universities and business schools must guide young talents and entrepreneurs to embrace this paradigm.

If this challenge is not addressed and it does not become a central issue for the next European Commission and national governments, the risk is the continuation of the slow decline in the number of top 500 companies in Europe, with the emergence of models driven either by the state or the development of financial hubs that opportunistically attract capital. The European Union can do much more, just as a deeply entrepreneurial country like Italy can. Mario Draghi clearly raised this point in the report left to the new European Commission (2024).

Continue in its mission, now more than ever: this could be the only response to uncertainty and a world where the dream of globalization has brought both good and bad results, then slowed down, and now must be rethought. Daniel Susskind's book *Growth* (2024) captures this well, emphasizing that growth and globalization are fundamental forces that today need to be entirely rethought and directed towards new challenges. Therefore, it is necessary to rebuild a new dream with greater awareness, recognizing past mistakes and illusions.

Continuing the mission is essential, starting by preserving and strengthening the ability to attract talent from all over the world to offer content that speaks to the entire world. However, to achieve this, new elements are needed. The novelty lies in a few key areas.

The first is to step out of the comfort zone. The comfort zone is represented by the vertical silos of the various academic domains that form the core and DNA of business schools. But alongside these silos, new ones must be added, and then they must communicate until they become integrated. Data Science, AI, and geopolitics are skills that did not belong to the world of business schools but are more necessary than ever today to address participants and companies that face the challenge of combining traditional disciplines with emerging fields. Today, companies and managers face the challenge of integrating AI into decision-making processes, as well as the urgency of understanding geopolitics to build their strategies. The new disciplines are the common cognitive elements and languages that drive the evolution of business and growth. It is no coincidence that in 2023, the *Financial Times* highlighted that 'every big business needs its own Chief Political Officer'. As a result, the traditional boundaries between schools of government, engineering schools, and business schools will progressively dissolve in a scenario that is difficult to map today.

The second is knowing how to address larger companies. As we have seen earlier, large companies are becoming even larger and are part of a globalization process defined by country-based blocks that compete with each other. These large global companies attract talent and set the pace for investments and innovation. If business schools lack the ability to speak to large companies, their impact diminishes. Speaking to large companies means working with the best talents, confronting the frontiers of innovation, and contributing to decisions that lead to a fairer world. However, this also has a crucial feedback effect: engaging with large companies increases the ability to share best practices with smaller companies, helping them not only to grow but also to gain access to topics and knowledge that would otherwise exclude them.

The third is to decisively enhance the role of applied research. Business schools are the bridge between academia and the outside world. Applied research becomes the method that must attract significant questions and substantial resources, both human and financial. If this capacity is lacking, it means that the questions being asked are not significant enough. Business schools must, therefore, pose the right, big questions and then attract talents and resources to work on possible answers. And through these answers, training activities evolve progressively, increasing their ability to make an impact.

If these three directions are pursued with determination, every business school becomes (or continues to be) an international reference point, an organization that is international by definition, beyond its objectives and strategies. In the face of the risks of closure and domestic solutions, the only possible response is to work on shared values. Starting with the role of education, which must above all be a means of liberation and growth, as stated by the president of the Stockholm School of Economics (SSE) and the Global Alliance in Management Education (CEMS), Lars Strannegard, during the CEMS Annual Event in London at the end of 2023. CEMS is an extraordinary form of cooperation between management schools worldwide.

BUSINESS SCHOOLS AND IMPACT IN A WORLD WITH VAST FINANCIAL RESOURCES

The ways in which money is invested can no longer be considered a purely technical and therefore neutral choice. This assertion stems not only from the challenges (or trends) imposed by the new environmental, social, and governance (ESG) paradigm but from a more general observation of the numbers and the stakes involved. If we start with the numbers, the news appears more than good. Global GDP reached $110 trillion in 2022, compared to $66 trillion in 2010. But the growth in wealth, particularly financial wealth, has been even more significant. If financial assets (stocks and bonds) were worth $386 trillion in 2010, by 2022, they had grown to $870 trillion. The same can be said, though to a lesser extent, for real estate assets, which increased from $220 trillion in 2010 to $420 trillion in 2022. Financial wealth is now 7.9 times the value of global GDP, with $190 trillion in liquid assets, meaning that these assets can be invested at any time.

However, it's less comforting to note that this wealth is concentrated in the hands of a few, with 1% of the population holding 45% of the total, while half of the world's population holds only 1% of the wealth. This presents a significant and real problem of sustainability, not only in terms of human dignity.

What message can we derive from the surprising strength of these figures? The common denominator is undoubtedly the word 'responsibility'. Since liquidity is almost double global GDP, every investment choice, even of a single euro, can create or destroy value in any company, project, or activity. We've seen this in recent years, with cryptocurrency experiencing euphoric moments, driven by an excess of liquidity and an irresponsible desire to experiment with new paths. The availability of liquidity and financial wealth represents a great opportunity that must be harnessed with determination and responsibility to generate impact, creating new and better development and employment opportunities. As Mark Carney emphasizes in his book *Value(s)* (2021), the greatest challenge is to connect value with values. In other words, connecting financial returns with broader social returns.

What are the ways in which this can happen? Three key concepts come into play:

1. **Long-term investments:** If we want to link available savings to the real economy and ensure returns for investors while also having an impact on growth, the solution lies in allocating resources to initiatives that create long-term value. Physical and digital infrastructure projects, investments in research and innovation, and support for public-private initiatives are examples of how the strength of liquidity and financial assets can be put to work to generate returns while also creating a positive impact on the surrounding system.
2. **Risk capital investment:** Only equity investment allows companies to face the major challenges of today, including internal growth and acquisitions to gain more critical mass in a world increasingly characterized by large companies; the birth and growth of startups; innovation; and attracting talent. There is no development without these conditions. A shift towards equity requires both entrepreneurs' willingness to open their capital and pressure from investors to provide more equity and less debt.
3. **ESG finance:** This field arises not so much from trends or imposed rules but from a fundamental observation we must not forget: global trends are putting our ecosystem's existence in question. Food and water scarcity, pollution, war, poor corporate and institutional governance, poverty, lack of democracy, and climate change are issues that create gaps, progressively affecting the sustainability of our way of life.

> ESG principles in corporate decisions are an organic response to these gaps, aiming to progressively reverse course through individual and then collective behaviours and strategies that not only counter these issues but move in the opposite direction. This is the strongest and most decisive way to connect value with values.

Is it enough to direct wealth towards these three paths to ensure returns and impact the world's destiny? While the reasons for optimism suggest yes, there are clearly risks that need to be understood and addressed. Consider the cost of ESG compliance, especially in Europe; the possible prioritization of GDP and employment over sustainability; the use of ESG themes as ideological talking points or, worse, as political tools in upcoming elections, particularly in the US; or the presence of a war on Europe's doorstep. These are all factors that could challenge the scope of the ESG movement and reduce its relevance. We cannot afford that because this issue is not ideological but factual, and the stakes involve the long-term sustainability of our way of life.

Therefore, the role of public institutions, financial intermediaries, and universities becomes crucial. Public authorities and governments must not only design the rules but also create incentives to push companies towards a world that involves more risk capital and uses ESG factors as a competitive element. The often-ideologically debated tax lever could be a simple and powerful tool not only for convenience but also educationally, to help companies become more capitalized and better aligned with the three letters: E, S, and G. Financial intermediaries are responsible for managing and directing the enormous amount of available financial wealth, interacting with investors and companies. The responsibility for guiding these choices is immense, and the social role of the financial system should always be remembered. Universities and business schools have the vital role of producing high-quality research, disseminating it to explain broadly why reconciling financial returns with impact is both possible and necessary, and of creating the human capital of the future, revising their programmes and educational offerings through the lens of sustainability principles. Education builds the mindset and values of society.

Will we succeed? Yes, if we recognize that every single euro invested is not a separate issue or one that concerns only a few, but rather the main intersection where collective well-being is reinvested—both to provide financial returns (essential for paying our pensions and sustaining our welfare system) and to counter the many forces challenging our ecosystem. Connecting value with values becomes not only ethically responsible but also simply pragmatic.

THE SEARCH FOR STRATEGIC MODELS

The international development models of business schools share a common denominator: mobility and the attraction of resources. This applies to students, client organizations, faculty, and staff. A higher level of internationalization means, first of all, having classes populated by students from various nationalities. However, this requires having a faculty that reflects diverse backgrounds, while the staff must be able to provide services and management aligned with a broader spectrum of students. Diversity in origins also applies to clients, who now interact by purchasing custom programmes or sending their management, coming from different cultures and backgrounds. These forces and values are measured and stimulated by the main rankings, which, all other things being equal, reward a better position for greater international diversity in students, faculty, staff, and clients.

But beyond rankings, which undeniably carry weight, international development also brings the benefit of a more effective pedagogical model and a stronger network, which becomes important both for placement and fundraising purposes, as well as for generating greater impact within the community.

The methods for increasing the international reach of a business school have historically developed, and continue to evolve, through different but clearly recognizable options in the market.

First Option: Strong Centre of Gravity

In this model, the business school aims to attract resources to its home base by leveraging the reputation of its brand, but especially by capitalizing on the economic power, job market, and commercial relationships of its location. Business schools located on the East and West Coasts of the United States exhibit these characteristics, as do those in cities like London or Singapore. The stronger the value of per capita GDP and the more attractive the job market, the greater the possibilities for a business school to pursue this strategy. Business schools do not operate in isolation, so changes in the job market—such as post-Brexit labour market restrictions or, conversely, the talent attraction policies seen in Canada—can shift the context quickly. While traditional globalization allowed the strongest players to follow this strategy, the slowing of globalization makes this path less dogmatic and more uncertain, even for the best schools.

Second Option: Exchange Networks

A second option is to create an exchange network with other business schools, offering mobility to students and welcoming students from partner schools. The goal is not to expand the revenue base directly but to 'exchange' human capital with the aim of:

1. Making the school's offerings more attractive to prospective students who benefit from an overseas experience in another country or prestigious business school; and
2. Increasing the school's visibility among incoming students, who can promote it through their networks and word-of-mouth.

This strategy is effective not only for post-graduate programmes but also for pre-experience students. It was the foundation for the success of the oldest business school network, Partnership in International Management (PIM), founded by NYU Stern in 1974 and now including 67 business schools worldwide. A similar strategy, albeit in a more sophisticated form, is partially employed by the more recent Global Network for Advanced Management (GNAM), founded by Yale School of Management in 2014, which now includes 39 schools globally.

Third Option: Double Degree Programmes

A third option, which is not an alternative but rather an upgrade to the exchange model, involves creating double-degree agreements with partner schools. While the goal is similar to that of exchange programmes, the double-degree model strengthens not only the appeal of the programmes for students—who receive not only an exchange experience but also a second degree—but also signals the connection between the brands of two business schools.

Fourth Option: Joint and Standalone Double Degrees

A fourth option involves joint and standalone double-degree programmes. While the technical aspect still involves awarding two separate or joint diplomas, the strategy is much more robust because the programme is designed and managed jointly. Many Executive MBA (EMBA) programmes ranked highly in global rankings use this model, sometimes involving three partner schools, as in the well-known TRIUM programme. Compared to the second and third options, the emphasis on strategic alliances is clearly stronger, as is the coordination and brand alignment. For this reason, this choice can apply not only to master's programmes but also to open market executive programmes or custom executive programmes. A unique case in the pre-experience field involving both business schools and universities is the CEMS network's Master in International Management programme, which celebrated its 35th edition in 2023 and now includes 34 partner schools.

Fifth Option: Overseas Campuses

The fifth option is opening a branch or an actual campus (or a network of campuses, like ESCP, EDHEC, or IESE) overseas. This is a bold move and, compared to the corporate world, much less frequent. According to statistics of C-Bert, there is evidence of only 373 overseas campuses globally. Despite the visibility of some prestigious business schools, the phenomenon remains relatively limited, cautiously developed, and mostly undertaken by schools positioned higher in the rankings. Except for a few networked cases, opening an overseas campus seems to be characterized by a mix of overlapping and alternative factors:

1. The need (or ambition?) to demonstrate strength by playing the most complex card of international development;
2. The desire to test a market to understand its potential;
3. The opportunity to benefit from a strategic decision, often supported by subsidies from both the home and host countries; and
4. The structural decision to expand the school's reach, modifying processes and governance within the organization.

The Gulf region, Singapore, and to some extent China have been recurring destinations for such choices, while we await to see the effects of India's new law that opens its market to this type of decision for international business schools.

What does the future hold for these models in the post-pandemic, post-globalization world of uncertainty and poly-crises? On one hand, the element of 'business as usual' will certainly continue, not out of conservatism but due to the proven effectiveness of choices like exchange agreements and double degrees in their various forms. On the other hand, new scenarios could emerge.

The first involves unprecedented strengthening of networks, with the creation of broader exchange spaces or modular solutions that involve multiple schools in an extended form. Networks like CEMS and GNAM could take this leap, with expansive modular passporting solutions in executive education, both physically and virtually. The GNAM small network online courses (SNOCs) experiment is an interesting example of this. Similarly, within each of the European Universities created in 2019, intriguing solutions for executive education could develop.

The second is the emergence of disruptive solutions that borrow logic and dynamics from the corporate world but address the needs of business schools. It is hard to provide definitive answers today, but one certainty is that if business schools want to keep pace with the evolution of the global economic system, they will need to grow their intellectual capital, make investments, and become larger to engage with larger companies. Will fundraising suffice, or will business schools need to consider aggregation solutions and eventually raising financial resources through private equity or IPOs? How will this reconcile with the independence and intellectual freedom of research? These are questions that will need to be addressed without prejudice, with wisdom and a long-term vision.

FROM BUSINESS SCHOOLS TO MANAGEMENT SCHOOLS IN A BETTER WORLD

The future of business schools and their model of international development revolves around two concluding questions. The first is value-based: What is the challenge for business schools in their domestic or international arena, in post-experience training, and in applied research? The concept of 'value and values', as highlighted by Mark Carney, captures this idea and serves as a sort of manifesto. Value means growth. Every individual and every organization has its own metrics of value and growth, whether it be publicly traded companies, SMEs, public administrations, or non-profit organizations. Without growth and value, nothing is possible. But the more complex task is to guide value and align it with values, which are the necessary tools to bridge the multitude of gaps surrounding our world: from water and food scarcity to pollution, from the lack of democracy and good governance to war. Can we simply adopt a 'mind-the-gap' approach in the face of trends that challenge our way of existence? Or is the task of citizens and organizations to 'fill-the-gap'? The answer is clearly the latter.

The second question is definitional: business school or school of management? 'School' and 'management' are two extraordinary words, concepts that go far beyond the simple definition of a business school. A school is a community, and a community consists of stakeholders (students, faculty, staff, participants, companies, alumni, donors, etc.) who together build the educational process, with the transformative power of research at its core. Without research, education becomes repetition and formalism. Without interaction with the outside world, research loses its direction. The combination of these elements defines the essence of a school. It clarifies that education is not a mere act of consumption that ends with the use of something.

Management means responsibility—the responsibility to lead women, men, and organizations of all kinds. Faced with the complexity of the external world, the need for responsibility and management is more present than ever. This is why management schools must work with all types of organizations, from companies to financial institutions and public administrations. This is why they must enrich their skillset with all the necessary disciplinary fields, from artificial intelligence to geopolitics, economics, and business law. If a School of Management wants to have an impact, it must provide and offer all the disciplinary fields the market demands today. If this happens, international impact and development towards a fairer world will continue.

NOTE

1. On 24 January 2019 *The Economist* chose to publish an article and the cover of its printed edition to 'slowbalization', a neologism coined in 2015 by Dutch trend watcher Adjiedj Bakas.

REFERENCES

Carney, M. (2021). *Value(s): Building a Better World for All.* PublicAffairs.
Draghi, M. (2024). 'The Future of European Competitiveness'. European Commission.
Organisation for Economic Co-Operation and Development (OECD) (2023). 'Education at a Glance'.
Susskind, D. (2024). *Growth: A Reckoning.* Penguin.

10

A Peregrination in China Europe Business Education

Revisiting Internationalization and Management at CEIBS

FRANK BOURNOIS AND HONG WANG

INTRODUCTION

The evolution of business schools has been a journey deeply intertwined with their local and national origins, initially established to cultivate leaders for local industries. This is evident in the names of institutions such as London Business School, Rotterdam Business School, and ESCP Business School, which carry the legacy of their geographical and cultural roots. However, the narrative of business education has transcended these local boundaries, especially with the advent of globalization in the 1970s and 1990s. In response to the globalizing world economy, business schools have extended their reach by engaging with international associations and developing global programmes, marking a significant shift towards a more interconnected world of business education.

The emergence of consortia like CEMS (Global Alliance in Management Education) and the rise of globally integrated business schools, such as ESCP and China Europe International Business School (CEIBS), with campuses spread across different continents, signifies a new era of collaboration and integration. These institutions have become emblematic of the journey that business schools have undertaken, moving from local to global, and from national to international.

We opted for 'peregrination' in the title of this chapter to capture the essence of our voyage into the realm of business school internationalization. The phrase 'to travel in foreign lands' aptly represents our exploration.

Frank Bournois and Hong Wang, *A Peregrination in China Europe Business Education*. In: *Management Education and the Rise of Uncertainty of Global Business*. Edited by: Eric Cornuel, Oxford University Press. © Oxford University Press (2025). DOI: 10.1093/9780197794470.003.0011

Internationalization has always been associated with travelling, meeting and sailing with different cultures. In Greek/Roman mythology this is placed in the realm and powers of God Hermes (Greek), or Mercury (Roman). Hermes was held as the protector of travellers, merchants and orators. In a sense, all business schools can be considered as operating in the jurisdiction of Hermes. The name itself derives from 'Herma', referring to the Greek term 'a heap of stones', signalling physical boundaries and borders. These cairns played the role of standards showing travellers where to go and whence they came. In this chapter, our cairns for studying business school internationalization will be the 10 EQUIS standards that the European Foundation for Management and Development (EFMD) has developed.

Today, the global landscape presents a more complex tapestry of challenges and opportunities for business schools. Despite current economic fragility and geopolitical tensions, the need for internationalization in business education remains paramount. This necessity stems from both external global dynamics and internal imperatives for educational excellence.

Utilizing the EQUIS standards as our analytical framework, we will examine the internationalization journey of business schools, focusing on policies and practices that foster an inclusive, globally competitive environment conducive to sustainable educational excellence.

This chapter delves into the intricate cogs of a highly integrated model of business schools. We consider business schools as organizations subject to the principles they teach and research. This examination encompasses standards, culture, systems, personnel, and environment—key components that constitute the institutional framework, including coordination and standardization.

CEIBS, a joint venture between Europe and China, serves as our case study, illustrating the practical application of EQUIS standards. This unique partnership between the two continents acts as a miniature reflection of the broader peregrination that business schools have undertaken, encapsulating global management practices and their continuous integration within local contexts.

EQUIS STANDARDS: A HOLISTIC APPROACH TO INTERNATIONAL BUSINESS EDUCATION

Today, business schools turn to prestigious international accrediting bodies (EQUIS or the Association to Advance Collegiate Schools of Business, or AACSB) in their quest for legitimacy, improved status and reputation (Sohlo & Nätti, 2020). EQUIS was established by EFMD in 1997 to assess, improve, and accredit higher education institutions in management and business administration. It was designed to cater to the needs of business schools aiming for international impact, filling a gap in the market at the time (Kit, 2024).

Unlike AACSB, the value of EQUIS lies in its ability to assess schools against high international standards and its focus on strategic development (Teixeira & Maccari, 2018). Over the years, EQUIS standards have evolved to reflect the changing landscape of business education, putting more emphasis on internationalization, ethical practices, sustainability, and the integration of academic excellence with practical relevance.

In this chapter, we employ these benchmarks as our analytical framework to examine business schools' dedication to quality and their competitiveness on the international stage. Before we delve into the specifics of our case study, a synopsis of the dynamics between the 10 EQUIS standards will shed light on how business schools' internal mechanisms can be harnessed. These standards are not merely reactive solutions to specific problems, but can also be used to strategically steer business schools' internationalization initiatives.

Context, Governance, and Strategy (EQUIS Standard #1)

Business schools are expected to articulate a strategy that reflects their understanding of business and management practice. The common purpose of most business schools is to prepare future leaders for both private and public organizations. The EQUIS approach invites business schools to formulate their strategy based on intellectual rigor, practical insights, and a commitment to engaging with commercial and social stakeholders in a mutually beneficial manner.

Programmes (EQUIS Standard #2)

Business school programmes are pivotal in shaping future leaders, imparting essential knowledge and skills through a well-designed curriculum. Associate deans should design programmes with strategic foresight to prepare students for the evolving workplace (Barling, 2023). Programmes shall accommodate, on the one hand, the proliferation of novel learning technologies and methodologies, and on the other, the demand for fast-paced digestion of real-world learning needs (Joshi et al., 2022).[1] Focuses on enriching the student experience, aligning with learning outcomes, and fostering international perspectives with ethical conduct and sustainability are highly appreciated.

Students (EQUIS Standard #3)

Students are unanimously considered as the lifeblood of any educational institution. Business schools' focus extends beyond academic achievement to include students' personal and professional development, fostering managerial skills, ethical leadership, and intercultural sensitivity. The significance of international exposure and digital literacy, preparing students to thrive in a global and technologically advanced business environment are particularly emphasized (Le et al., 2018). The school's support systems, including career placement and alumni relations, are crucial for students' long-term success.

Faculty (EQUIS Standard #4)

Faculty members are the pillars of business schools, providing the intellectual and pedagogical foundation for student learning and development. The EQUIS standard mandates a minimal core faculty strength, emphasizing qualifications, expertise, and diversity, which are crucial for a well-rounded educational experience. Faculty not only deliver curriculum content but also contribute to research, innovation, and the strategic leadership of the school.

Faculty are expected to be actively involved in real-world business practices, international exposures, ethics, responsibility, and sustainability initiatives, ensuring that students receive an education that is globally relevant and ethically grounded.

Research and Development (EQUIS Standard #5)

Over the past three decades, research has become increasingly pivotal to the advancement of management knowledge. Business schools have the obligation to produce original research that is aligned with their strategic objectives, encompassing scholarly publications, practice-orientated activities, and pedagogic innovation. EQUIS emphasizes the integration of international features in research, pushing schools to engage with global issues, partner with institutions abroad, and produce work with a worldwide impact. In all cases, however, 'schools should be committed to knowledge creation as the foundation of quality in higher education' (EFMD Global, 2024, Chapter 5).

Executive Education (EQUIS Standard #6)

Executive education has always been a critical component of business schools, offering non-degree programmes tailored for continuous professional development. It addresses the evolving needs of working professionals and organizations. The EQUIS Standard for executive education underscores its importance by assessing strategic positioning, programme quality, and impact, including international dimensions that cater to a global audience. International executive education is difficult to achieve as it requires cross-cultural competencies, international networks, and in-depth understandings of global business challenges. As such, EQUIS advocates for assessing 'the proportion of core faculty capable of engaging with an international audience' (EFMD Global, 2024, Chapter 6). In summary, executive education is tasked with integrating digital platforms and streamlining the participant management process to ensure robust lifelong learning opportunities for a diverse audience.

Resources and Administration (EQUIS Standard #7)

Resources and administration are the bedrock of business schools' operational excellence. This EQUIS Standard emphasizes the necessity of financial viability, institutional continuity, and high-quality facilities to support the learning environment. Financial management and risk assessment also extend to international operations, ensuring the school's global initiatives are financially sustainable and strategically sound. In addition, EQUIS focuses on 'the overall sufficiency and quality of the school's administrative services and staff', including its ability to market and deliver its activities effectively (EFMD Global, 2024, Chapter 7). These areas are crucial to ensure that business schools can thrive in the global educational landscape.

Ethics, Responsibility, and Sustainability (EQUIS Standard #9)

Most business schools have developed as globally responsible citizens and highlighted the integration of ethics, responsibility, and sustainability across all facets of their operations. In demonstrating this integration, from admission criteria to curricular content, business schools shall showcase a holistic approach to preparing ethically aware graduates. This implies that 'leadership, faculty, staff and students are encouraged and supported to participate in these activities as an integral part of their professional engagement' (EFMD Global, 2024, Chapter 9).

Connections with Practices (EQUIS Standard #10)

Engaging with diverse stakeholders like entrepreneurs, governments, and corporations facilitates the exchange of knowledge and practical insights, enriches academic activities and ensures curricula remain relevant to real-world business challenges. Business schools need to raise the bar in terms of balancing academic excellence and managerial applicability, ultimately shaping future business leaders who are well-prepared for the dynamic global market.

All the above-mentioned accreditation standards, and the EQUIS standards in particular, represent a strong commitment to excellence in business education. These standards must not just be seen as guidelines but as a global benchmark for ensuring that business schools provide individual and collective efforts seeking to solve the complexities of international business (Cornuel & Thomas, 2024).

Internationalization (EQUIS Standard #8)

Let us now single out the EQUIS Standard of Internationalization, as it is the core of our analysis framework and shapes the global competitiveness and reputation of business schools. More importantly, it provides a roadmap for integrating international strategies effectively.

Emphasizing five key aspects, the implementation of internationalization is multifaceted.

1. **Diverse recruitment**: Essential for attracting a varied student body and faculty, fostering an intercultural learning environment.
2. **Curriculum design**: Enriched by global perspectives, international case studies, and English as the primary language of instruction, with a push for multilingualism.
3. **Digital innovation**: Utilizes technology for virtual exchanges, online projects, and seminars, simulating global interactions and offering flexible, technology-mediated learning.
4. **Faculty qualifications**: Internationally qualified and cross-culturally experienced faculty are crucial for teaching diverse students and preparing them to navigate cultural diversity in business.

5. **Global partnerships**: Form connections with the business community providing internships and research opportunities, and exposing students to various business practices for recruitment readiness.

REVISITING INTERNATIONALIZATION AND MANAGEMENT AT CEIBS

Upon a thorough review of the EQUIS standards, it becomes evident that integrating them into a business school's strategic planning and daily operations can significantly bolster its internationalization initiatives and improve the overall educational quality (Sohlo & Nätti, 2020).

In the subsequent analysis, we will examine how EQUIS standards have guided the internationalization and management practices at CEIBS. CEIBS' mission is to cultivate leaders who are not just globally competent but also ethically aware, and capable of navigating an interconnected world with conscientiousness and innovation. In an era characterized by volatility, uncertainty, complexity, and ambiguity, CEIBS' strategic thinking revolves around embracing change and pioneering innovative approaches in business education. Over the past 30 years, CEIBS has charted a course and paved the way, embodying 'global breadth' and reflecting a deep understanding of China. Consistent with this approach, CEIBS has formulated eight strategic initiatives, which can be categorized into three major areas.

Guided By the Imperative of Internationalization in Business Education

Since its inception in 1994, CEIBS has been actively introducing Western management theories and practices into China. For more than two decades, internationalization centred on introducing global management theories to China and working closely with individuals and firms wishing to do business in China.

Today's global landscape is in a state of flux, with new trends in globalization and technological revolutions necessitating a new breed of business leaders (Ding, 2024). In the midst of it, CEIBS recognizes that a more accurate understanding and sound judgements of global changes are necessary for an international business school (Lejeune et al., 2019). The school has responded to these challenges in the following ways, discussed in the sections below.

Reinforcing Its Position

CEIBS has consistently been ranked among the top business schools in Asia by the *Financial Times*. Unswervingly adhering to the positioning of internationalization, strengthening international exchanges, and enhancing the understanding and mutual trust between China and other cultures have been imperative for CEIBS to stabilize its top-notch position. CEIBS bolsters its international outreach with overseas learning programmes and alliances with Chinese firms going global.

Nurturing World-Class Faculty

In the past, faculty development has been used synonymously with the enhancement of teaching. At CEIBS, the school has been ensuring ample resources to support faculty throughout their academic career in teaching, research and gaining international exposure. A systematic, transparent, and flexible approach has been employed to configure faculty development programmes to best meet the school's mission. Currently, CEIBS boasts a permanent faculty of more than 80 professors with expertise in both Eastern and Western pedagogy and knowledge, and 98% of them come from overseas business schools in 20 countries.

Creating Signature Research

CEIBS furthers its internationalization by establishing interdisciplinary research centres and producing influential case studies that contribute to global business knowledge. In addition to traditional disciplines, CEIBS has established a '2+4+X' interdisciplinary research framework.[2] CEIBS has emphasized that 'to cultivate talent versed in both industrial transformation and economic management, business schools should further optimize their existing disciplines and remove barriers to interdisciplinary research'.[3] Moreover, nearly 3,000 high-quality cases have been collected, with China-themed cases developed by CEIBS being included in global case databases such as the Harvard Case Bank, Ivy Case Bank, and European Case Exchange Centre, constructing a platform for economic and cultural exchanges between China and the world.

Striving for the Thought Leadership

Thanks to its international genes, CEIBS has been striving for thought leadership in the business communities.

Committed to Sino-European Exchanges

CEIBS recognizes that China and Europe, as indispensable players on the world stage, must collaborate to address global challenges, promote multilateralism and technological innovation, and enhance the recovery and sustainable development of the global economy. Based on its campuses in Europe and Africa, CEIBS actively promotes economic and trade exchanges between China and Europe. Since 2012, CEIBS initiated and has organized the Europe Forum, successfully holding it nearly 30 times over the past decade in cities such as Paris, London, Zurich, and Frankfurt, spanning seven European countries and regions. The forum has established strategic partnerships with numerous European chambers of commerce, associations, and think tanks.

CEIBS Serves Regional Strategies

CEIBS includes campuses in China that contribute to the integration of the Yangtze River Delta from its Shanghai campus, the synergistic development of the Beijing-Tianjin-Hebei region from its Beijing campus, and the construction of the Guangdong-Hong Kong-Macao Greater Bay Area from its Shenzhen campus. The school also extends its reach to second and third-tier cities and underdeveloped regions, engaging with regional entrepreneurs and contributing to local economic transformation and development.

Empowerment of Alumni

Empowerment of alumni is a key focus, with CEIBS boasting over 30,000 alumni across more than 90 countries and regions. Alumni hold leadership positions in 142 Fortune 500 companies and 447 listed companies. CEIBS is creating an ecosystem that fosters lifelong learning and connects alumni with the school's academic and research activities.

Embracing the Future with Conscientiousness, Innovation, and Excellence

CEIBS actively expands enrolment and improves the degree programme curriculum. The school offers a Doctor of Business Administration (DBA) and five master's degree programmes, namely the full-time MBA (in English), MBA in Finance, Executive MBA, Global EMBA (in English), and Hospitality EMBA (co-organized with EHL Hospitality Management Business School in Switzerland). In 2025, CEIBS and ESCP Business also launched a

Master in Management. It is a double degree where students rotate on four CEIBS and ESCP campuses. Real situation learning courses, created in 2017, are embedded in both degree and Executive Education programmes, offering students firsthand knowledge from business leaders across various industries.

CEIBS recognizes the pivotal role of technology in reshaping business education. The integration of artificial intelligence, digitalization, and other emerging technologies is a fundamental aspect of the school's strategic vision. For instance, the CEIBS Research Centre for AI and Management Innovation aligns its research and teaching with China's AI development strategy, focusing on AI's impact on business management. The centre aims to build an AI collaboration platform and think tank with business school characteristics.

Sustainability

Amid changes in the global economic growth model and the steady advancement of the 'dual-carbon' strategy (aiming for carbon peak and carbon neutrality), environmental, social, and governance (ESG) concepts are increasingly gaining attention. Balancing between business and social value is essential for enterprises and entrepreneurs. As a pioneer in promoting corporate social responsibility (CSR) in China, CEIBS has embedded the CSR/ESG concept into its academic research, curriculum development, and campus operations. CEIBS ESG White Paper 2024 analyses global trends and China's practice in value creation of ESG by presenting ESG cases, student projects, faculty research outputs (e.g. Research on ESG Report of Chinese A-share Listed Companies).

In summary, the EQUIS standards have profoundly shaped CEIBS by offering a strategic planning framework that highlights internationalization, ethical leadership, and innovation. These standards have directed CEIBS in creating diverse, globally recognized programmes, recruiting esteemed international faculty, and promoting interdisciplinary research, which in turn has bolstered its standing as a premier international business school in Asia. Moreover, CEIBS has embedded EQUIS principles into its daily operations, including sustainability and technology integration, to cultivate a genuinely international learning environment for both students and alumni.

SUCCESS AND DERAILMENT FACTORS FOR BUSINESS SCHOOL INTERNATIONALIZATION

Managing a business school at a national level is a challenging task that few academics are willing to undertake. This reluctance is largely due to the fact that academics, who are experts and researchers, are not accustomed to dealing with multiple stakeholders (such as government, policymakers, education authorities, and trade unions), arbitrating budgetary decisions, and managing their peers. Leading an international school adds cultural complexity, and leading an international multi-campus school with international governance requires specific experience and skills.

Discussions and confidences shared by other deans and presidents have led to the identification of four key success factors and main derailment scenarios respectively that can make the international journey very tedious and strenuous.

Strong Governance and Executive Decision-Making Structures

Robust non-executive governance and strong executive decision-making structures are essential for supporting international strategic objectives and accommodating potential conflicting views in their agendas.

- **Non-executive governance**: Non-executive members play a crucial oversight and supervisory role, validating business orientations and driving strategy. Successful business schools benefit from dedicated members on their board and/or sub-committees (usually strategy, audit, appointment and remuneration, and ethics committees). For instance, at CEIBS, there is parity between the Chinese and European sides. Board members are independent high-profile individuals (e.g. Vice Chairman of the Standing Committee of the National People's Congress Junqi Yan; Former Prime Minister and President of the EU Romano Prodi; and former French Prime Minister Jean-Pierre Raffarin). These directors nurture the school with their international backgrounds and contribute ideas about preparing long-term future business leaders.
- **Executive decision-making**: Effective executive structures facilitate rapid strategic implementation across financial, academic, personnel, and ESG areas, among others. At CEIBS, this is handled by the eight-member Management Committee, co-led by a Chinese and a European President. The Committee includes members of various nationalities (Chinese, Swiss, French, Malaysian, and American), ensuring a diverse perspective. Consensus and quality of operational delivery are achieved and ensured through regular meetings with Chinese/English simultaneous interpretation. Sustainability and AI concerns are consistently prioritized for the benefit of students, faculty, and alumni.

Clear and Coherent Strategy

A well-defined and cohesive strategy is essential for aligning the school's mission with the demands of the job market. The mission to 'educate responsible leaders' is more than a mere slogan; it is CEIBS' commitment. With the guidance of its 40-member Corporate Advisory Board, CEIBS customizes activities and programmes to support Chinese companies expanding globally and international companies entering the Chinese market. Moreover, the regular issuance of a Quarterly Strategic Implementation Report ensures the school community meets deadlines, shares progress, and actively participates in subsequent strategy phases.

Diverse and Internationally Recognized Faculty

A diverse and internationally recognized faculty that excels in both research and teaching is crucial. Academic departments are responsible for recruitment, selecting candidates with significant research achievements and proven teaching skills for international audiences. Faculty members, once hired, provide teaching sessions to programme directors, which heightens their awareness of managing their employability. This is further emphasized by regular teaching evaluations, with career advancement primarily based on research and high-impact publications. At CEIBS, faculty are incentivized with personalized rewards, and salaries are within the top 10% of AACSB's faculty salary database. After retirement, a notable percentage (30%) of emeriti professors with international passports continue to serve the school as long as programmes express the demands for their teaching. This enables the school to flexibly adjust to fluctuations in demand and supply.

Innovative Programme Offerings

Innovative programme offerings that evolve in response to the international business landscape are vital at CEIBS.

- **Executive education programmes**: A comprehensive Executive Education programme suite is essential for meeting corporate demands. Faculty dedicate significant time to tailoring their instruction and collaborating with clients on content development.

- **Case studies**: Faculty members produce a large number of case studies with Chinese companies expanding globally and international firms penetrating the Chinese market.
- **International corporate advisory board**: This 40-member Board has been a key catalyst for refreshing teaching materials.
- **Faculty engagement**: Faculty are encouraged to serve as non-executive directors on corporate boards, offering companies their expertise and gaining deeper insights into managerial challenges. Moreover, approximately 20 endowed chairs enhance and intensify faculty-industry connections.

Potential Derailment Factors

Business school leaders must pay special attention to derailment factors that may diminish the level of internationalization. We would like to highlight four aspects that are recurrent in conversations between deans.

Geopolitical Uncertainties

Geopolitical uncertainties and reductions in global trade impact international student mobility, as seen during the 2020–2022 pandemic. As advocates for the benefits of globalization, schools must engage in active cooperation with other schools, companies, and embassies to maintain high levels of student mobility. Scholarship policies may be used to attract foreign students if necessary. Language can sometimes be a barrier to student mobility. Schools must redouble efforts to offer programmes in English and local languages. Striking a balance between English-taught and local language sessions is crucial for maintaining international standards.

Faculty Recruitment and Retention

In a highly competitive global market, it is imperative for schools to attract and retain top-tier international faculty. In addition to a compelling reward system, schools require robust recruitment strategies that account for growth, turnover, and retirement (Altman & Bournois, 2004). This is essential for delivering high-quality services to clients and students. Schools must have clear procedures to separate from underperforming faculty. A frequent risk is a disconnect between the quality of their teaching and their research output. Annual in-depth performance interviews with faculty help mitigate this risk.

Financial Issues

Whilst financial mismanagement is not expected in any business, economic fluctuations and revenue variations can occur. It is vital that schools retain a reservoir of solutions for growth, such as creating new programmes, adopting innovative teaching technologies, and offering new services. A sound financial situation safeguards the capacity to invest in more international initiatives and develop global operations in remote campuses.

Quality of Administrative Staff

The calibre of administrative staff is often referred to as a derailment factor or a weak link in a school's ecosystem (Barling, 2023). Superior performance is contingent upon robust collaboration between frontline (faculty) and back-office personnel. Classroom equipment, for instance, requires both IT support and subtle logistical assistance. The school's culture and core values significantly influence the mindset of employees. Well-defined procedures and policies empower staff to operate more swiftly and efficiently, under the guidance of meticulously chosen middle managers.

CONCLUSION

First and foremost, internationalization is a human activity because men and women enjoy travel and trade. There will always be business. It is the duty of business schools to help students and future leaders manage their activities inside and across their borders.

To compare and evaluate what and how business schools do, the 10 EQUIS standards serve as beacons of reference towards which and between which business schools can navigate. Every business school has its unique sea chart with its own heading and wayfaring to its international beacon/standard and to its international aim.

Looking back with hindsight on CEIBS' peregrination between China, Europe, and the world, our strategic plan was designed and is being implemented with EQUIS internationalization in mind.

In particular, we are striving to deliver on its initiatives, such as expanding CEIBS' world-class faculty, diversifying CEIBS' programme portfolio, bridging China and Europe, and exemplifying ESG education (Wang, 2024).

Our experience shows the necessity for business school leadership to permanently be aware of their success and derailment factors. Amongst these our strong belief is that specific and careful attention

Table 10.1. SUCCESS AND DERAILMENT FACTORS FOR INTERNATIONAL BUSINESS SCHOOLS

Success Factors		Related EQUIS Standards	Derailment Factors		Related EQUIS Standards
3.1.1	Strong governance	#1, #7, #8	3.2.1	Geopolitical uncertainties	#1, #2, #3, #8, #10
3.1.2	Clear and coherent strategy	#1, #8, #9, #10	3.2.2	Faculty recruitment and retention	#1, #4, #5, #8
3.1.3	Diverse and international recognized faculty	#4, #5, #8, #10	3.2.3	Financial issues	#1, #7, #8
3.1.4	Innovative Programme offerings	#2, #3, #6, #7, #8, #10	3.2.4	Quality of administration staff	#7, #8

has to be paid to (1) geopolitical uncertainties, (2) faculty recruitment and retention, (3) financial issues, and (4) quality of administration staff.

Greek God Hermes was the protector of trade, wealth and travel. What is less known is that he also symbolizes luck. Let's hope that in times of so many geopolitical uncertainties, business schools find luck-bringing God Hermes on their way to pursue their international peregrination.

NOTES

1. According to Joshi, Rastogi, and Klein, in the post-pandemic era, the future of work is evolving into an environment of continuous learning.
2. According to the CEIBS 5-Year Plan, '2+4+X' means two think tank platforms (CEIBS Case Center, CEIBS Lujiazui International Institute of Finance); four interdisciplinary research areas (China and the world, ESG, AI powered enterprise and management, service excellence); and X research institutes and centres (e.g. CEIBS Centre for Family Heritage, CEIBS Centre for Wealth Management, CEIBS Healthcare Sector Research Centre).
3. As expressed by Wang Hong as president of CEIBS (Wang 2024).

REFERENCES

Altman, Y., & Bournois, F. (2004). 'The "Coconut Tree" Model of Careers: The Case of French Academia'. *Journal of Vocational Behavior*, 64/2, 320–328.

Barling, J. (2023). *Brave New Workplace: Designing Productive, Healthy, and Safe Organizations*. Oxford University Press.

Cornuel, E., & Thomas, H. (2024). 'EFMD and Societal Impact'. In E. Cornuel, ed., *Business School Research: Excellence, Academic Quality and Positive Impact*. EFMD Global Focus, 12–15.

Ding, J. (2024). 'The Rise and Fall of Technological Leadership: General-purpose Technology Diffusion and Economic Power Transitions'. *International Studies Quarterly*, supplementary appendix.

EFMD Global. (2024). *EQUIS Standards and Criteria 2024*. https://www.efmdglobal.org/accreditations-assessments/business-schools/equis/equis-guides-documents/.

Joshi, M., Rastogi, G., & Klein, J. R. (2022). *Global Business in the Age of Destruction and Distraction*. Oxford University Press.

Kit, A. (2024). 'The Role of International Accreditation Agencies in Business School Practices' Institutionalization Processes'. *Management International*, 28/2, 76–91.

Le, Q., Ling, T., & Yau, J. (2018). 'Do International Cocurricular Activities Have an Impact on Cultivating a Global Mindset in Business School Students?' *Journal of Teaching in International Business*, 29/1, 62–75.

Lejeune, C., Starkey, K., Kalika, M., & Tempest, S. (2019). 'The Impact of Business Schools: Increasing the Range of Strategic Choices'. *Management International*, 23/2, 88–98.

Sohlo, S., & Nätti, S. (2020). 'International Business Accreditation as a Trigger for Business School Development'. *Journal of Economic and Administrative Sciences*, 36/1, 64–81.

Teixeira, G., & Maccari, E. A. (2018). 'The Institutional Role of Business Cahool Accreditation Agencies: A Systematic Literature Review'. *Revista de Gestao*, 25/3, 274–290.

Wang, Hong. (2024). 'The Future of Global Business Education in a New Landscape'. *EFMD Global Focus*, 17/2, 94–100.

11

Overcoming Particularism

Universalistic Management Education and the Rise of Uncertainty

PIERRE KLETZ

Marx argued that while crises can cause major disruptions and difficulties within the capitalist system, they have the function of brutally resolving the system's contradictions and imbalances. Crises were, in his view, an inherent part of the functioning of capitalism, with its ability to 'recycle' crises, even though the consequences of such crises can be severe for workers and society in general.

This pattern has often been developed beyond the economic sphere to analyse any increase in uncertainty. Gramsci, for example, considered that the 'organic' crisis, which he so-called because it is not limited to the economic sphere but may also encompass aspects of culture, politics and education, is characterized by the increase of uncertainties and essentially generates opportunities (Gramsci, 2011).

While the ideas of Marx and Gramsci were critical of capitalism, liberal analyses have even more strongly adopted approaches that maintain that in a competitive system the rise of uncertainty creates dangers, but above all opportunities. Thus, the dominant view of capitalism is often characterized by an unshakeable optimism that every crisis and even every uncertainty, beyond the difficulties it creates, is a source of progress and new opportunities.

MANAGEMENT EDUCATION AND TRAINING TO FACE UNCERTAINTY

Business schools, which by their very nature develop their activities in tandem with the business world, have tended to adopt the same optimistic

Pierre Kletz, *Overcoming Particularism.* In: *Management Education and the Rise of Uncertainty of Global Business.* Edited by: Eric Cornuel, Oxford University Press.
DOI: 10.1093/9780197794470.003.0012

attitude towards their activities in the face of the uncertainties and new challenges presented by the business world. This has had a profound impact on the approaches and practices in the world of management education, above all leading to major advances within the institutions in this field.

Consequently, a comprehensive review of the existing literature on the communication of management education institutions, an examination of the literature specifically devoted to this area, consultation of specialist websites, and in-depth interviews with business school deans seem to indicate a consensus among experts in the field. It is generally acknowledged that the rise of uncertainty in the global economy has created challenges for management education institutions, but that these have been effectively addressed, resulting in increased resilience.

In the field of business education, there is broad agreement among academic institutions on the optimal approach to addressing the challenges posed by increasing uncertainty. This consensus is encapsulated in the term 'three points', which is often cited in business schools to describe the pedagogical approach to these challenges:

- the presentation and teaching of the general and technical knowledge required to address a problem;
- enabling students to formulate an attitude and a personal stance in the face of social or business challenges (often by providing a broader education in the context of the problem and by introducing philosophical and ethical components); and
- ensuring that students can act autonomously and contribute to their projects, even in a context of uncertainty, thanks to the fact that they have benefited from a process of reflection and assimilation of knowledge.

These three phases, which can take place successively or simultaneously, appear to be remarkably beneficial not only from a pedagogical perspective, but also from the point of view of the civic orientation of management education institutions. The essence of these phases lies in the cultivation of autonomy and independent thinking among students, equipping them with the ability to form their own opinions and act in accordance with their principles, while making a positive contribution to the objectives of their respective organizations. This approach emphasizes adaptability and the ability to implement original and relevant behaviours, thus preparing students to thrive in dynamic and uncertain business environments.

The dominant perspective asserts that business schools are capable of formulating and implementing responses to the challenges posed by the uncertainties of globalization, thereby empowering themselves and aligning with the needs and expectations of their students. This fortification, according to this perspective, involves ensuring that students or graduates are able to formulate personal responses tailored to the needs of the company.

The subsequent discussion will use a number of examples to illustrate both the challenges posed by the uncertainties of globalization and the ways in which schools have developed an appropriate response.

AN EDUCATION THAT DEVELOPS GENERAL CULTURE AND BUSINESS CULTURE TO RESPOND TO THE RISE OF UNCERTAINTIES

The contemporary business environment is characterized by a need for professionals who can operate in a dynamic and uncertain global context. In response to these challenges, educational institutions have adapted their curricula to encompass both general culture and business culture, thereby equipping students with the skills and knowledge necessary to navigate these complexities.

In the last three decades, companies have expanded their operations in a progressively globalized environment, resulting in heightened competition and the emergence of novel business modalities. This shift has prompted business schools to recalibrate their approach to leadership training, encompassing not only management techniques but also an understanding of economic and geopolitical trends on a global scale, complemented by the study of local dynamics. Consequently, business schools have been compelled to cultivate professionals who possess the capacity to function in a context that integrates both the local and the global, while demonstrating adaptability to international market conditions. This shift has been accompanied by increased instability, manifesting not only at the micro level but also at the macro level (e.g. economic crises, trade tensions between major powers, rapid changes in international regulations). In general, business schools must prepare their students to function in contexts characterized by perpetual uncertainty.

This paradigm shift has prompted business schools to rethink their approach to education, moving away from a focus on training students to be high-level management technicians. Instead, there has been an emphasis on developing general culture and business culture courses, empowering students to contextualize their practices within a broader global framework. In response to these challenges, business schools have adopted strategies to enhance the internationalization of their programmes. These strategies encompass the establishment of international partnerships among institutions, the facilitation of international student exchanges, and the introduction of double degrees. Concurrently, there has been an expansion in the curriculum of business schools to include modules on emerging markets, international business and intercultural management. This development has been accompanied by an increase in general culture courses, including philosophy, ethics, sociology, and psychology, as well as business culture.

The objective of this initiative was not to cultivate 'super technicians' for the purpose of globalization; rather, it was to nurture leaders who possess the capacity to function effectively in a range of dynamic contexts, with a particular emphasis on multicultural environments. This adaptation was not confined to general culture courses but also encompassed management courses with a direct relevance to globalization (such as intercultural management, international negotiations, and managing change in a global context).

The internationalization of the student body in business schools can also be interpreted as an attempt by these schools to familiarize their students with global contexts by developing hybrid or flexible programmes to meet diversified needs that are often marked by internationalization. It is evident that the adaptability of these models also offers flexibility in the face of global uncertainty.

EDUCATION FOR AUTONOMY AND THE RAPID EVOLUTION OF SKILLS AND PROFESSIONS

In the contemporary business school educational paradigm there has been an evolution beyond the mere mastery of management techniques; there is now an emphasis on cultivating the ability of graduates to analyse and proactively respond to the challenges they encounter. The last two decades have witnessed the emergence of global challenges, and management education has incorporated the study of these challenges, under the assumption that such study would enhance the autonomy of graduates in their professional pursuits and ensure the relevance of their actions.

It is imperative to examine the upheavals that have affected global business and society at large, and the manner in which business schools have adapted their programmes and curricula in response. The business realm necessitates skills that are in a state of perpetual evolution, a consequence of the incessant emergence of novel technologies (e.g. big data, artificial intelligence, blockchain). These technologies, while promising immense opportunities, concomitantly contribute to the escalating uncertainties that characterize global business. The ability of management education institutions to anticipate these changes and integrate them into their curricula is a major challenge.

One of the key issues in these developments is the ability of management education institutions to meet the growing demand for technological skills. Many business schools now include courses on emerging digital transformations and innovation management. There has been an increase in collaborative efforts between technology companies and business schools, facilitating the integration of young, innovative professionals who possess the ability to challenge conventional thinking. This collaboration also offers educational institutions the chance to provide students with hands-on experience. Most significantly, educational institutions have come to acknowledge that technological advancements, such as globalization, signify perpetual changes that will influence students' future working environments. Consequently, educational institutions are tasked with cultivating students' adaptability, equipping them with the capacity to adjust their skill sets and behaviour to novel circumstances on a continual basis. Notably, educational institutions are expected to cultivate students' ability to adapt their contributions to diverse business scenarios. Management education has a long-standing tradition of responding to these challenges through experiential learning methodologies. Indeed, case studies have played a prominent role in business school pedagogy for nearly half a century. In recent years, this approach has been complemented by projects with multinational companies and management simulations. This experiential approach fosters students' development of decision-making skills within complex global contexts. The profound impact of global business expansion on the environment, the exacerbation of development disparities, the disruption of labour standards in developing countries, and the rural exodus these nations are experiencing have been extensively studied. Notwithstanding the significance of these factors to society and business, the issue of sustainability and social responsibility has undoubtedly exerted the most profound influence on the life and curricula of business schools. The subsequent discussion will address the implications of this pervasive and dynamic proliferation. It is noteworthy to mention the context of the expansion of these issues, which stem from the increasing expectation that companies must operate in a sustainable manner and assume social responsibility, both in terms of the consequences of their activities and a civic approach to their role in the communities to which they may belong and in society in general. This novel paradigm shift has profound ramifications for contemporary approaches across a wide spectrum of disciplines, including but not limited to leadership, sustainability, ethics and governance. It is evident that this paradigm shift has substantial implications for current methodologies, programmes and activities in business schools. Specifically, curricula have been substantially enriched with courses on green finance, the circular economy, social entrepreneurship and related subjects.

RESPONDING TO CHANGING STUDENT EXPECTATIONS

All of the above examples are characterized by a proactive response on the part of management education to societal or business change in a context of increasing uncertainty. This has led business schools to modify their approaches, curricula, and programmes. Schools are diversifying their offerings and developing a proactive attitude in response to fundamental change, the effect of which should be to strengthen these institutions.

A far more complex challenge—potentially more destabilizing or, on the contrary, more conducive to positive change—arises when it is the demand that changes; that is, when the factors that previously determined students' choice of school or their expectations during their studies, change. For example, there is much evidence of a profound change in students' expectations, both in the institutions in which they wish to study and in the content of what is taught.

In sharp contrast to the attitudes prevalent in the 1980s and 1990s, a period (elaborately depicted in cinema; see Zidi [1987]) characterized by more stable growth and less ambiguity about the future, numerous studies and articles reveal that students today place significant emphasis on aligning the values of institutions with their own beliefs (Haski-Leventhal et al., 2022; Petrick & Scherer, 2005). This shift is particularly pronounced among business school students, who, in the past, appeared to relinquish moral values in favour of pursuing solely technical skills deemed essential for a lucrative career. This shift is particularly pronounced in the context of mounting uncertainty, where the pursuit of personalized content and answers to life's fundamental questions has emerged as a pivotal aspect of the educational experience, often eclipsing the traditional focus on learning management techniques (Hodge, 2024). Moreover, business schools, through their management and faculty, have long recognized a transformation in the expectations of teaching content. The integration of experiential components such as local presence, interaction with leading professionals, and practical international experience (e.g. internships, missions, concrete projects) into traditional courses has become imperative, complementing the traditional lecture-based curriculum.

In light of the prevailing uncertainties, recent business school graduates have been emphasizing the necessity for business studies to impart not only technical expertise but also a structured way of thinking. Furthermore, certain issues that were virtually non-existent 15 years ago have now become pivotal to both curricula and students' expectations. Notably, issues such as sustainability, ethics, social engagement, and social responsibility are highly valued by students, both in their choice of courses and in their interest in their programmes and the projects they include. Perhaps most significantly, these same issues are at the forefront of students' expectations regarding the take-away message, representing the most important aspect of their business school experience (Wylie, 2023).

The GMAC Prospective Students Survey 2024, which examines trends in the applicant pool, programme preferences, mobility considerations, and career goals, also highlights a significant increase in demand from applicants for equity and inclusion, sustainability, and health and well-being in their academic experience. The survey shows that almost three-quarters of prospective students consider equity and inclusion, sustainability, and health and well-being to be important or very important to their academic experience. This emergent trend was a key motivator behind the inclusion of these questions in the survey. The findings also underscore a shift in student preferences, indicating a shift from management techniques towards methods, rigour, and analysis. Programmes that emphasize strategy and business analysis are particularly sought-after, while problem-solving and data analysis and interpretation emerge as the primary skills students aspire to master after completing their management studies.

Concurrently, educational institutions have acknowledged this emerging trend and have reported a response to these expectations, often highlighting their provision of programmes, certificates, and specializations that tackle long-term issues such as sustainable development and social entrepreneurship, which have garnered significant interest from applicants and a high level of satisfaction among students. This phenomenon is further substantiated by prominent educational institutions, including North American schools such as MIT's Sloan sustainability certification, Stern's MBA programme at New York University, and Rotman's MBA programme in Toronto, widely regarded as a Canadian benchmark in sustainability studies. These institutions offer a diverse array of sustainable development specializations within their MBA programmes, including specializations in sustainable development and courses such as sustainable finance, which provides two Master of Science degrees with a focus on sustainable development. European institutions exemplify this commitment, evidenced by specializations such as sustainable and disruptive innovation at HEC Paris or the 1+1 programme at Said Oxford, which allows students to pursue a BA and an MSc in sustainability concurrently. Student engagement is further demonstrated by the substantial participation in sustainability competitions such as the Hult Prize, founded on the conviction that business possesses the capacity and responsibility to enhance lives. The Hult Prize is a global student competition that challenges university teams to solve the world's most pressing problems with viable business ideas. Similarly, UNESCO Institute for Information Technologies in Education (IITE) and Nisai Group are jointly organizing the exclusive sustainable development goal

(SDG) competition 'Bridging Green Education: Uniting Sustainable Communities' to support student initiatives in green education to achieve the SDGs.

This convergence of elements demonstrates both the growing public interest in sustainability and long-term issues, and the impact this has on student demand. The importance of accreditation for schools is well known, and rankings such as Corporate Knights' Better World MBA Ranking, an annual ranking of the world's most sustainable MBA programmes, are growing and involving more schools each year. The EFMD has also included sustainability criteria in all its accreditations.[1]

Finally, international bodies have shown a growing interest in sustainable programmes. Programmes recognized by organizations such as the United Nations or development banks for their sustainability and social impact often attract international students seeking an education that will enable them to contribute to global development goals. For example, partnerships between business schools and the United Nations Global Compact are often used to attract students who are increasingly aware of these issues.

RESPONDING TO STUDENT DEMAND, RATHER THAN CONFRONTING THEM WITH AN OFFER DESIGNED INDEPENDENTLY OF THEM

In response to the expressed needs and demands of students, educational institutions have modified their approach, shifting from a one-dimensional, top-down curriculum design to a more collaborative, student-centred model.

This shift in pedagogical approach may engender a sense of optimism with respect to the issue of management education in the context of mounting uncertainty in global business.

Indeed, it has been posited that in the face of an unstable environment and social and business changes that are challenging to anticipate, the domain of business schools has exhibited a capacity to adapt its pedagogical approach, thereby ensuring that its students are well-equipped to make a substantial contribution to the organizations they join and to cultivate a career that meets their personal aspirations and professional requirements.

Management education institutions have demonstrated their capacity to equip students with the necessary skills to effectively navigate the two predominant types of consequences arising from the rise in uncertainty in global business. These include the 'technical' challenges posed by rising uncertainty (for example, rising interest rates after a period when they had been historically low, inflation and its consequences for business demand, the rise of protectionism and the constraints it creates on markets, and the spread of teleworking and its consequences for the internationalization of managerial and skilled work). Another salient factor is the emergence of novel social commitments for companies (such as sustainable development, and corporate social responsibility, environmental resilience).

Management education institutions have demonstrated an unquestionable capacity to address these challenges, with business schools exemplifying their ability to equip students with the necessary competencies to navigate and prepare for these external pressures. However, a comprehensive analysis reveals a common thread among these challenges, which is the external nature of these pressures.

Consequently, an overly optimistic approach runs the risk of undermining the most important challenge that the rise in uncertainty entails for schools, particularly in the context of global business: namely, the necessity to address the heightened expectations of students. Confronted with mounting ambiguity, students are articulating a range of demands that are becoming increasingly distinct; we are observing an escalation in the particularities of these demands.

While the validity of these arguments is acknowledged, it is important to recognize that the tendency to equate students with clients of business schools may have obscured this reality. Moreover, equating students with customers is incongruent with several fundamental principles of education, primarily because students, by definition, do not possess complete knowledge of their learning needs and requirements—which, in contrast, is a knowledge domain that is held by the institution providing the education. Furthermore, while acknowledging the significant financial investment often required of business school attendance, equating an educational relationship with a purely commercial one is clearly inadequate.

TRAINING FOR THE SPECIFIC THROUGH THE SPECIFIC, RATHER THAN THROUGH THE GENERAL

In order to facilitate training in specific topics, there has been a shift in management education towards a more specialized approach, as opposed to a more general one.

In response to specific expectations and needs, whether real or perceived, on the part of both students and the market, business schools have developed a wide range of specialized programmes. While this type of programme has existed for a considerable period, it was once considered a minority choice. However, this paradigm is currently undergoing a significant transformation and becoming the prevailing norm.

The rationale provided by these institutions for this transition signifies a transformation in their pedagogical approach.

Indeed, traditional generalist MBAs aim to impart a comprehensive understanding of both general culture and the intricacies of business, empowering students to apply these insights to their chosen career sectors.

Historically, generalist MBAs have served as the prevailing paradigm; however, during the 1970s, there was a paradigm shift towards specializations and concentrations, typically incorporated into the latter stages of the programme, with the objective of facilitating student access to sectors and companies aligned with their interests.

Contemporary trends, however, reveal an apparent paradigm shift in the rationale of these institutions. The evolution of MBA programmes has resulted in the development of specialized curricula with a predominant focus on facilitating students' placement within structures and organizations that are closely aligned with their chosen specializations. It is evident that educational institutions are not deviating from the notion that students can pursue careers in diverse sectors or alternative domains. Instead, there is a growing recognition that the training imparted within a specialized programme is sufficiently comprehensive to equip students with the adaptability to adjust their competencies to the demands of a particular sector or environment, which might differ from the one for which they were initially prepared.

The prevailing logic, which initially operated from the general to the particular, is now being reoriented to a more specific approach, moving from the particular to the particular.

A STRONG EMERGENCE OF SPECIALIZED PROGRAMMES

The specialization offered by educational institutions to their students is based on various logics.

Specialized Master of Business Administration (MBA) and master's programmes are offered by educational institutions to target expanding professions and sectors where the world of management education has identified a need for management skills. Examples of this include:

- MBA or MSc programmes specializing in luxury management or, more generally, in the management of creative industries.
- MBA or MSc programmes focusing on tourism and hospitality. Some institutions may choose to offer even more specialized master's programmes, such as those dedicated exclusively to the world of wine (e.g.

Kedge Business School, Neoma Business School, University of Bologna, Trieste School of Management, Sonoma State University).

- Health management programmes have expanded spectacularly. A particularly significant development in this regard is the establishment of the first Business School for Health by UCL (University College London) in September 2022. This represents an evolution in the trend for business schools to train their students for a specific sector, transcending the mere launch of a programme and opting for a business school specialized in a single sector. A relevant example of a business school specializing in health while maintaining a generalist status is the Carey Business School at Johns Hopkins University.

The development of specialized master's programmes is not merely about training for a specific profession or the challenges of a particular sector; business schools are also seeking to offer programmes that provide skills that are not based on the technicalities of a profession or sector but are driven by social change. The numerous MBA programmes specializing in information technology management issues provide an example of such a trend. A similar rationale underpins all MBA programmes that focus on sustainability, with the shared objective being to equip students with the specific skills required to respond to social evolution.

This specialization encompasses the subject of this book, with relevant examples of specialized programmes including MBAs in global management, which are largely focused on the rise of uncertainties in global business (e.g. MBA in Global Business, University of Wisconsin-Parkside; Master of Global Management, Thunderbird School, MBA in Global Business at NYU Stern). These programmes address uncertainties related to issues with global supply chains, trade risk management, country risk management, and multinational trade agreements.

This phenomenon can be interpreted as a response on the part of management schools to the rise of particularism in student demand and expectations, by diversifying their programmes and areas of interest. The review of curricula reveals a reduction in the proportion of core courses. The presence of common core components in the curricula has significantly diminished, and what appears to be a common core increasingly differs from one institution to another, or even from one programme to another, for both MBAs and master's programmes in management. Additionally, specialization can impede versatility among graduates, as it reduces their adaptability. A programme that is excessively specialized may hinder an individual's capacity to transition to more generalist roles. Ensuring a balance between specialization and general education is imperative to ensure long-term employability, particularly in the context of global business uncertainty. Moreover, this specialization could potentially lead to significant future challenges for goal compatibility in organizations.

Ultimately, this evolution necessitates a fundamental re-examination of the universality of teaching and the universalism of educational institutions and educators themselves.

THE CHALLENGE POSED BY THE WEAKENING CONSENSUS IN BUSINESS SCHOOLS

Apart from the fact that common sense tells us that the universality of teaching is inherent in the act of teaching itself (Socrates demonstrated in his time that even the teaching of relativism must be universal if it is to defend the cause it claims to represent[2]), the dislocation of common core curricula, and more generally the diffusion and divergence of curricula and programmes, cannot simply be interpreted as a sign that management education is undergoing vibrant development and that initiatives are multiplying. It is undoubtedly a symptom of a problem for management education: a minimal consensus on what should be taught, and therefore what is important, is disappearing.

In addition, the proliferation of programmes or specialization options in management education has taken place around issues for which there is a social consensus on their importance and how they should be addressed; the issues that have been most frequently the subject of programme creation (sustainability, corporate social responsibility, the environment, the relationship between management and technology, etc.) are the subject of a broad social consensus. For a management school, taking a stance on the issues that the creation of programmes necessarily entails does not represent a real intellectual and social risk of opposition or challenge to the subjects chosen or the direction of teaching.

However, the proliferation of student interests and the increasing absence of values on which there is consensus among students are not sufficiently taken into account if we confine ourselves to creating programmes whose central theme enjoys broad social acceptance.

The argument that there have always been differences of opinion and values within business schools fails to recognize the extent of the changes that have taken place. For example, to say that in recent decades at every election students at major business schools have been divided between those who voted liberal, those who voted conservative, and those who voted social democratic in its various forms should not obscure the fact that everyone identified with adherence to the values of liberal democracy; one was conservative, liberal, or social democratic within the framework of adherence to liberal democracy.

A major change has taken place in business schools in Europe, America and Asia, including some of the most prestigious: the 'illiberal' commitments of students have been widely expressed, as the recent European elections have shown. The French legislative elections were even more revealing, as the creation of groups and associations in business schools supporting political tendencies with a problematic relationship with liberal democracy, such as the Rassemblement National or La France Insoumise, became widespread. Until now, these institutions have rarely openly supported such political groups or the parties from which they emerged. Similarly, the strong emergence of the 'woke' movement within business schools is a completely new phenomenon that should be seen alongside the deep-rooted nature of 'illiberal' movements.

The attacks of 7 October 2023 and the subsequent war in Gaza can be seen as events that revealed the extent of the gap between the worldviews and the values and commitments of business school students. The most radical pro-Hamas movements have largely been structured around the most convinced adherents of wokism and illiberalism, and this proximity is now widely underlined well beyond academic publications: 'Since October 2023, universities have seen the Middle East conflict hijack the anti-racist discourse in vogue on American campuses and turn it into anti-Semitism and an apology for Hamas' (Jaulmes, 2024).

Harvard Business School Dean Srikant Datar's 'Statement on Attack Against Israel', published on 10 October 2023, is an authentic and enlightened commitment, but it underlines the depth of disagreement that runs through even a school as prestigious and recognized as Harvard Business School. While the dean of HBS issues statements, speeches and letters two or three times a year, the one on Gaza is revealing in that it refers to the divisions that run through the campus and calls for unity: 'At this very difficult time, I urge you to reach out and support one another, to listen to those who are hurting, and to be generous to one another and kind to yourselves' (Datar, 2023). It is interesting to note that beyond this observation of the depth of the differences in values and opinions that run across campuses, business schools have not taken a position or developed proactive activities.

It could be argued that the examples given above belong to the political sphere, which is not that of business schools. However, it seems that the innovations and projects developed by management education in response to increasing uncertainty are always aimed at promoting important issues on which there is consensus because they are considered urgent and essential for the successful development of society (sustainability is an excellent example of such an issue).

On the other hand, they shy away from issues that are open or that are the result of debates between two opposing camps: for example, the exploitation of shale gas and oil, which pollutes and produces greenhouse gases, but which supports growth by reducing business costs and helping to control energy costs. Many other issues are addressed in one way or another, even though they are open options (cryptocurrencies are not only objects of exchange but also of speculation; or the question of pensions in France).

CONCLUSION

Business schools have traditionally functioned as institutions that facilitate debate, where there has been a high degree of consensus on certain ethical values, on a conception of economic development and the role of business, and more generally on the business themes that structure curricula and programmes. The rise of social and global uncertainty has shattered many of these consensuses, and in particular has led to the emergence of a dispersion of student expectations and needs in terms of subject matter and teaching methods.

In response, the management education sector has adopted a strategy of specialization in curricula and programmes, which is arguably appropriate in the short term. However, this shift towards greater programme specialization may have unintended long-term consequences for the versatility and employability of managers within organizations, potentially leading to a decline in organizational goal compatibility and exacerbating anomic tendencies in society.

Consequently, there is a need for a return to—and a strengthening of—common core curricula, informed by consultation with both business and students. The aim is not only to equip students with the ability to tackle a wide range of managerial challenges, but to instil in them a mindset that precludes consideration of issues within the confines of the manager's immediate environment.

In a context of global business uncertainty, this requires the adoption of universalism as the standard for management education.

NOTES

1. For example, EQUIS has introduced criteria dealing with ethics, responsibility, and sustainability at each chapter of the self-assessment process.

2. Each is the measure of truth, which is therefore relative to each one. In the Protagoras, Socrates refutes this option by showing that if my truth is that 'there is a single truth', then the relativist, who thinks 'everyone has his own truth', must recognize this truth as true . . . Even if he defends the contrary (Plato 2006).

REFERENCES

Datar, S. (2023). 'Statement on Attack Against Israel'. *Harvard Business Review*, 10 October. https://www.hbs.edu/about/leadership/statements-and-speeches/attacks-against-israel.

Graduate Management Admission Council (GMAC). (2024). *Prospective Students Survey 2024 Report*. chrome-extension://efaidnbmnnnibpcajpcglclefindmkaj/https://www.gmac.com/-/media/files/gmac/research/prospective-student-data/2024-pss-research-report_final_digital-2.pdf.

Gramsci, A. (2011). *Prison Notebooks*. Trans. J. A. Buttigieg II. Columbia University Press.

Haski-Leventhal, D., Pournader, M., & Leigh, J. S. A. (2022). 'Responsible Management Education as Socialization: Business Students' Values, Attitudes and Intentions'. *Journal of Business Ethics*, 176, 17–35.

Hodge, K. (2024). 'What I Learnt on My EMBA: Students Share Their Experiences and What the Course Meant for Their Careers'. *Financial Times*, 13 October.

Jaulmes, A. (2024). 'Il faudra un effort de longue haleine pour purger les universités et les institutions': aux États-Unis, le crépuscule du wokisme' *Le Figaro*, 16 December. https://www.lefigaro.fr/international/aux-etats-unis-le-crepuscule-du-wokisme. Translated by author

Petrick, J. A., & Scherer, R. F. (2005). 'Management Educators' Expectations for Professional Ethics Development.' *Journal of Business Ethics*, 61, 301–314.

Plato. (2006). *Protagoras and Meno*. Trans. Adam Beresford. Intr. Lesley Brown. Penguin.

Stone, O., dir. (1987). *Wall Street*. Twentieth Century Fox.

Wylie, I. (2023). 'Big Hitters: Executive MBA Projects Target Social Impact'. *Financial Times*, 15 October.

Zidi, C., dir. (1987). *Associations de Malfaiteurs*. Films 7 co.

12

Inclusive Internationalization

Discovering the New World of Management Education

IAN FENWICK

THE TECTONIC PLATES UNDERPINNING MANAGEMENT EDUCATION ARE IN MOTION

The management education landscape, once dominated by Western (usually American) business schools exporting their models of education to the rest of the world, is transforming into a vibrant, interconnected, global, multicultural network of diversity, inclusion, and learning.

Today, business schools are not merely creators and purveyors of knowledge; they are hubs of cultural exchange, innovation, and adaptation, prized for their convening powers. In a return to their traditional melting-pot role, universities are places to *amalgamate* the varied strands of human experience and outlook. They are places above the hurly-burly of transitory politics, where diversity of opinion is valued for its own sake, and of the creativity of its constructive criticism.

Internationalization is at the heart of this terraforming. Once a euphemism for the expanding reach of Western educational models, today's internationalization is truer to its word. It is the integration of diverse perspectives; the embracing of local contexts and of local ideas; and the creation of a body of knowledge—a world outlook—that vastly exceeds the sum of its parts. This international outlook is becoming a key component in the creation of leaders able to navigate the complexities of tomorrow's world. We believe tomorrow's world will be one where physical distances have been largely conquered: whether by inexpensive rapid travel or by digital interactions. In tomorrow's world it will be the cultural distances that remain to be spanned, navigated, and negotiated.

Ian Fenwick, *Inclusive Internationalization.* In: *Management Education and the Rise of Uncertainty of Global Business.* Edited by: Eric Cornuel, Oxford University Press.
DOI: 10.1093/9780197794470.003.0013

This chapter delves into the internationalization journey of management education, exploring how its development from a simplistic export of ideas to a more nuanced, inclusive approach that breeds ideas for the future.

HISTORICAL CONTEXT: THE ROOTS (ROUTES?) OF INTERNATIONALIZATION

In the aftermath of World War II, the United States emerged as a global economic powerhouse. Naturally, its business schools—Harvard, Wharton, Kellogg—became the gold standard for management education,[1] despite the earliest business schools coming from Europe. If you were a business school outside the US, the name of the game was imitation. Curricula, teaching methods, the case study approach—and even the case studies themselves—were imported wholesale with little thought to local context. Never have so many B-school students around the world known so much about Southwest Airlines (Frei & Hajim, 2001) without ever having been on a Southwest flight!

This was a one-size-fits-all model. Western (read: American) business practices were *obviously* universally applicable. Our school, Sasin School of Management, was a perfect example of that concept. During our first decade, Sasin's curriculum, admissions policies, and visiting professor model were entirely reliant on our Western partners, Kellogg and Wharton. The school, and the model of wholesale mimicry, was incredibly successful.

The belief was that the principles of management were universal and that American practices could be transplanted to any cultural or economic context: classroom imperialism for sure. And it worked—for a while.

This approach had several implications:

1. **Standardization:** Business schools worldwide adopted a standardized curriculum that prioritized Western theories and practices. Accreditation procedures initially reinforced this standardization.
2. **Lack of contextualization:** The unique cultural and economic contexts of different regions were often overlooked, leading to a mismatch between what was taught and what was relevant locally.
3. **English as the lingua franca:** English became the primary language of instruction—as it had become the primary language of business—reinforcing the dominance of Anglo-American business concepts.

But Reality Has a Funny Way of Shaking Things Up

As business schools proliferated across Europe, Asia, and beyond, it became clear that this America First approach didn't always work. What got results in Boston didn't necessarily lead to business excellence in Bangkok or Buenos Aires. The assumption that American business models were inherently superior often led to a disconnect between what was taught and what was needed on the ground. Students were the first to notice. Questions such as 'How does this apply to my business?' became more strident. Faculty started to reflect on this, and the universality of the management education model started to crumble.

It was time for a change.

THE SHIFT TOWARDS INCLUSIVITY: ADAPTING, NOT ADOPTING

As the early internationalization model ran out of steam, business schools began to recognize that different parts of the world contained their own unique challenges, opportunities, and business mores. The competitive landscape, customer preferences, tastes and habits, and resource costs all varied across the world. Of course they did. There was—and is—no way at all that one size fits all.

This recognition marked the beginning of a shift from imitation to adaptation.

Recognizing Diverse Business Environments

No longer was it enough to simply import Western business practices. Business schools needed to understand their local context and integrate unique local challenges into their models and into their curricula.

Most obviously, this meant incorporating local case studies, understanding regional business practices, and valuing diverse perspectives. Underlying this was the realization that students need *both* an international and a local grounding. Leaders of tomorrow must flourish locally and globally. As a result, the curricula they study must be globally grounded, but very definitely locally applied.

The word 'glocal' reared its head, an ugly and ungainly—but effective—child.

Moving Beyond Western Mimicry

We also saw a growing appreciation for the diversity of business practices around the world. It seemed that some regional ideas and practices were not only different than those of the West but might in fact be superior.

Schools in Asia, for example, began integrating Buddhist and Confucian principles into their management teachings. In Africa, business schools started focusing on social entrepreneurship and development economics, areas of relevance to their local contexts. European schools, meanwhile, emphasized cross-cultural competence and the importance of understanding different business cultures.

BEYOND TOKENISM: THE REALITIES OF INCLUSIVE INTERNATIONALIZATION

While the shift towards a more inclusive approach to internationalization is a positive development, it is not without its challenges. There is a risk of falling into what we might call 'woke-washing' akin to 'greenwashing' in the environmental, social, and governance world: adopting superficial inclusivity without truly engaging with the complexities of diverse business environments. Some schools play up their international and inclusive credentials—exchange programmes, research partners—without really learning or integrating that learning into their curricula or benefiting from the creativity that empowered diversity brings.

Achieving Genuine Inclusivity

Inclusive internationalization requires more than just celebrating cultural holidays, making sure that exam dates avoid the holidays of leading religions, and including a few non-local case studies. This is the window dressing: the *woke-washing*. The education of tomorrow's leaders must go well beyond that to a fundamental shift in delivery of business education. This includes rethinking curricula, investing in faculty development, and creating a genuinely inclusive environment for all students.

Business schools need to focus on deep engagement with diverse perspectives. This means moving beyond tokenism and creating a curriculum that genuinely reflects the diversity of the global business world. It also means fostering an environment where all students feel valued and included, and where diverse voices are not just heard, but actively sought out.

Strategies for Deep Engagement and Authentic Inclusivity

1. **Curriculum design:** Develop a curriculum that integrates diverse perspectives throughout, not just in specific courses or modules.
2. **Faculty development:** Invest in recruiting, training, and developing faculty who are equipped to teach from a global perspective. There can be no better route than faculty who are themselves—by education, experience, and outlook—truly global.
3. **Student support:** Create support systems for international students to help them navigate the challenges of studying in a foreign country and ensure that local students are integrated into the international student milieu.

LEARNING FROM THE WORLD: CASE STUDIES OF SUCCESSFUL INTERNATIONALIZATION

Internationalization in management education takes many forms, from strategic partnerships to immersive action-learning experiences. However, not all global programmes are created equal.

While some schools focus on traditional exchange programmes, others have pioneered innovative approaches merging global exposure with real-world application. The following two case studies—one from Sasin School of Management and another from INSEAD—illustrate how institutions can cultivate meaningful international learning experiences to prepare students for leadership in an interconnected world.

Sasin's International Action Learning Labs: Bridging Global and Regional Expertise

Sasin School of Management has redefined internationalization through our international Action Learning Labs, an initiative developed in collaboration with MIT Sloan School of Management, Fudan School of Management, and Tsinghua University School of Economics. Unlike conventional exchange programmes, with their primary focus on classroom learning, Sasin's Action Learning Labs immerse students in real-world business challenges across multiple countries.

These labs bring together students from partner institutions to work directly with businesses in diverse economic and cultural contexts. Over the course of the programme, teams collaborate with companies in sectors ranging from technology startups to multinational corporations, tackling strategic issues such as market expansion, digital transformation, and sustainability initiatives. The experience is highly immersive, requiring students to apply business theories in practice, navigate cross-cultural team dynamics, and develop actionable solutions for real clients.

What sets Sasin's approach apart is its focus on bridging global business practices with regional expertise. Through hands-on projects in the Association of Southeast Asian Nations markets and China, students gain firsthand exposure to emerging economies, regulatory complexities, and local consumer behaviours, making them uniquely equipped to operate in both developed and emerging markets. By forcing students to confront the agility and adaptability required in Asian business environments, Sasin's Action Learning Labs equip students with skills that go beyond textbook knowledge—preparing them for leadership in an unpredictable, fast-changing global economy.

INSEAD's Multi-Campus Model: 'The Business School for the World'

While many business schools offer exchange programmes, INSEAD has taken internationalization a step further by creating a fully integrated multi-campus model. With campuses in France, Singapore, Abu Dhabi, and San Francisco, INSEAD allows students to study across multiple continents without needing a separate exchange agreement.

This model ensures that INSEAD students experience the regional economic and cultural nuances of different business environments while maintaining a cohesive learning journey. The Global Executive MBA (GEMBA) programme,[2] for instance, requires students to take modules across multiple campuses, exposing them to the unique challenges and opportunities of European, Asian, Middle Eastern, and North American markets. This approach encourages students to develop a global mindset while also understanding regional business practices in depth.

Another defining feature of INSEAD's internationalization strategy is its Global Strategy Lab (INSEAD, 2023), where students tackle complex business problems across different geographic markets. Working in diverse teams, they conduct comparative analyses of industries, regulatory frameworks, and consumer behaviours in different regions, providing them with a practical understanding of international strategy and leadership.

By integrating mobility into its core structure rather than treating it as an optional exchange programme, INSEAD ensures that its students graduate with a deep, embedded understanding of global business—not just theoretical knowledge but practical, lived experience in different economic and cultural contexts.

Key Takeaways from Sasin and INSEAD's Approaches

These two case studies highlight different but complementary approaches to internationalizing management education:

1. Sasin's International Action Learning Labs emphasize real-world, cross-border problem-solving by integrating students into live business projects in emerging markets, ensuring they develop practical expertise in navigating global business challenges in high-growth regions.
2. INSEAD's multi-campus model embeds international mobility into its curriculum, enabling students to immerse themselves in diverse economic and cultural contexts without needing separate exchange agreements.

Both models go beyond passive learning and encourage active engagement with global business environments, preparing students to lead in an increasingly interconnected and complex world.

THE ROLE OF TECHNOLOGY: BREAKING BARRIERS AND BUILDING BRIDGES

Technology has played a critical role in facilitating the internationalization of management education. From online learning platforms to exchange programmes, technology has made it easier than ever for students to access a global education.

Digital Tools and Platforms in International Education

The rise of digital technology has revolutionized the way education is delivered and the way it is experienced. The recent pandemic vastly accelerated this management education revolution (Smith, 2020), breaking down geographical barriers and creating new international collaboration and learning opportunities (El Garah, et al., 2023). Online platforms like Coursera, edX, and university-specific learning management systems have made access to courses from top business schools possible for students anywhere in the world. We believe this will be a key seed of next level internationalization.

Virtual classrooms will allow students from different countries to participate seamlessly in discussions, group projects, and case studies in real time from around the globe. This global interaction will develop a truly global mindset and cross-cultural competences.

Perhaps this will be the global business school of the future.

Digital platforms also enable the sharing of resources and knowledge across borders, making it easier for schools to incorporate diverse perspectives into their curricula.

Virtual Exchange Programmes and Global Classrooms

One of the most innovative uses of technology in international education is the concept of virtual exchange programmes.[3] These programmes pair students from different countries in joint projects, often supported by digital collaboration tools. For instance, a business strategy class might involve students from a university in the US working together with students from a school in Brazil to analyse a case study on a multinational corporation operating in both regions. Such experiences provide students with practical insights into global business practices and the challenges of cross-cultural collaboration.

Global classrooms,[4] where students from multiple countries attend the same online class, further enhance this experience. These classrooms are designed to leverage the diverse experiences and perspectives of the participants, often featuring guest speakers from various industries and regions. This format not only enriches the learning experience but also prepares students to work in increasingly diverse and dispersed teams.

How Technology Facilitates Global Collaboration and Learning

Technology has also enabled new forms of collaboration between institutions. Business schools can now co-design and co-deliver courses, bringing together faculty and students from different countries in ways that were previously not possible. For example, a course on international marketing could be co-taught by professors from a US business school and a Japanese university, with students participating in joint projects and discussions.

The use of data analytics and artificial intelligence in education is opening new possibilities for personalized learning experiences. These technologies can help identify individual learning needs and preferences, providing tailored resources and support to students. For international students, this can be particularly beneficial in overcoming language barriers and adapting to different educational styles.

THE POWER OF DIVERSITY AND INCLUSION IN MANAGEMENT EDUCATION

Diversity and inclusion are not just buzzwords in the context of management education—they are fundamental to the mission of preparing future business leaders. A diverse classroom mirrors the complexities of the global business environment, providing students with the opportunity to engage with different perspectives, challenge their own assumptions, and develop a more nuanced understanding of the world (Drexel University, n.d.).

The Business Case for Diversity in the Classroom

Research has consistently shown that diverse teams perform better, make more innovative decisions, and are more effective at problem-solving (Rock & Grant, 2016). In a business school setting, diversity in the classroom can lead to richer discussions, more creative solutions, and a broader understanding of global business challenges.

For instance, a case study on market entry strategies will be analysed very differently by students from different cultural and professional backgrounds. A student from India may focus on regulatory challenges, while a student from Germany might prioritize operational efficiency. This diversity of thought enriches the learning experience and prepares students for the complexities of global business.

Creating a Diverse and Inclusive Curriculum

To truly leverage the benefits of diversity, business schools must go beyond simply admitting students from different backgrounds. They need to create a curriculum that reflects diverse perspectives and addresses issues of equity and inclusion in business. This might involve incorporating case studies from a variety of cultural and economic contexts, featuring diverse protagonists, and addressing global challenges such as inequality, sustainability, and ethical business practices.

Furthermore, courses on intercultural communication, inclusive leadership, and global business ethics should be integrated into the core curriculum. These courses can help students develop the skills and attitudes needed to lead in a diverse and interconnected world.

Impact on Student Learning Outcomes and Career Success

A commitment to diversity and inclusion in management education has a tangible impact on student outcomes. Studies have shown that students who engage with diverse perspectives during their studies are more likely to succeed in their careers (Holoien, 2013). They are better prepared to navigate complex, multicultural environments, more adept at managing diverse teams, and more innovative in their thinking.

For international students, an inclusive environment can also help them feel more welcome and supported, leading to better academic and personal outcomes. Support services such as mentorship programmes, language assistance, and cultural integration activities are essential for creating a truly inclusive learning environment.

NAVIGATING THE FUTURE: ADAPTABILITY AND LIFELONG LEARNING

The business world is changing at a faster pace than ever before, driven by rapid technological advancements, shifting economic landscapes, and evolving societal expectations. In this context, the ability to adapt and continuously learn is not just a 'nice-to-have' but a critical skill for business leaders.

The Changing Demands of the Business World

The traditional career path of entering a company after graduation and climbing the corporate ladder is becoming less common. Today, professionals are more likely to change jobs, industries, and even career paths multiple times throughout their lives. This requires a new set of skills, including adaptability, resilience, and a commitment to lifelong learning.

Business schools are responding to these changes by redesigning their programmes to be more flexible and relevant. This includes offering modular programmes that allow students to build their own learning paths, integrating short courses and certifications that address specific skills, and emphasizing experiential learning opportunities.

Preparing Students for Continuous Learning and Adaptability

We know that management education must go beyond imparting knowledge and skills and instil a mindset of continuous learning and adaptability. This means encouraging students to be curious, open to new ideas, and willing to step out of their comfort zones. It also means providing them with the tools and resources to continue their education long after they graduate.

Programmes that emphasize problem-based learning, real-world projects, and internships are particularly effective in this regard. They help students develop the practical skills and adaptive thinking they need to thrive in a rapidly changing business environment. And partnerships with industry can provide valuable insights into emerging trends and skills in demand, ensuring that the curriculum remains relevant.

How Business Schools Are Evolving Their Programmes to Meet Future Needs

Many business schools are already leading the way in reimagining management education for the twenty-first century. For example:

1. **Flexible learning options:** Many institutions are now offering modular programmes that allow students to customize their learning experience. This includes online courses, short-term certificates, and stackable credits that can be applied towards a degree.
2. **Emphasis on soft skills:** With the increasing complexity of the business world, soft skills such as emotional intelligence, cross-cultural communication, and ethical leadership are becoming more important. Business schools are integrating these skills into their core curricula to better prepare students for leadership roles.
3. **Focus on sustainability and social responsibility:** As businesses are increasingly held accountable for their impact on society and the environment, management education is also shifting towards a greater emphasis on sustainability and social responsibility. Schools are incorporating these topics into their programmes to prepare students to lead in a more responsible and ethical manner.

CONCLUSION: RETHINKING INTERNATIONALIZATION IN MANAGEMENT EDUCATION

The evolution of internationalization in management education is no longer about expanding the geographic reach of Western business schools; it is about creating truly global learning environments that prepare students to lead across cultures, industries, and socio-economic contexts. The shift from a one-size-fits-all model to an adaptive, inclusive approach has forced business schools to reconsider their role in shaping leaders who can navigate complex and interconnected markets.

The most successful management programmes today are those that integrate local relevance with global competency. As seen in Sasin School of Management's partnership model, meaningful internationalization is not about replicating existing business models but about creating educational experiences that expose students to different ways of thinking, problem-solving, and leading. Similarly, Sasin's emphasis on sustainability and social impact demonstrates that the internationalization of business education must not only foster economic success but also encourage responsible and ethical leadership in a rapidly changing world.

The Future of Internationalization: Moving Beyond Borders

The future of internationalization in management education is not about increasing the number of exchange programmes or adding more foreign faculty members—it is about creating immersive and contextually rich learning experiences. Schools that focus on experiential learning, digital collaboration, and cross-disciplinary approaches will produce graduates who are not just well-travelled but well-prepared to lead across diverse cultural and economic landscapes.

A key lesson from the examples discussed in this chapter is that internationalization should not be passive. It is not enough to simply expose students to different cultures; schools must engage students in real-world problem-solving, whether through cross-border business consulting projects, partnerships with companies operating in emerging markets, or collaborative research initiatives on sustainability and global business ethics. This kind of engagement ensures that internationalization is not just about mobility but about learning how to think, collaborate, and lead globally (Mullins, 2021).

The Challenge Ahead: Authenticity Over Symbolism in a Politically Shifting Landscape

A major challenge that business schools must address is avoiding performative internationalization. As institutions seek to market themselves as 'global', there is a risk of reducing internationalization to a set of metrics—the number of foreign students enrolled, the number of partnerships signed, or the percentage of international faculty members. While these numbers may look impressive, they do not necessarily translate into meaningful learning experiences.

Recent political shifts in key economic regions, particularly in the United States, have created an additional obstacle to internationalization efforts. Growing pushback against diversity, equity, and inclusion (DEI) initiatives and internationalization efforts has led to legislative challenges that directly affect business education. In some states, funding for DEI-related programmes has been cut and policies discouraging international partnerships have emerged, limiting opportunities for cross-cultural collaboration. Visa restrictions for international students and faculty have also made it harder for global talent to participate in American business schools, reducing the diversity of perspectives in classrooms and weakening institutional ties with global business networks.

These developments risk isolating US business schools from the global academic community, potentially making their graduates less prepared for an interconnected world where cross-cultural collaboration is essential. Schools outside the US that once looked to American institutions for leadership in management education are now diversifying their partnerships, forming stronger ties with European, Asian, and Latin American schools instead. The challenge for US business schools will be to navigate these political headwinds while maintaining their relevance in an increasingly globalized business environment.

In response, some institutions will have to start developing alternative strategies, such as partnering with international institutions through online platforms, expanding global campuses, and embedding international case studies within their curricula. These adaptive approaches ensure that even if physical mobility is restricted, students still gain exposure to global business challenges. However, in the long run, institutions must advocate for policies that reinforce the importance of international collaboration in business education, ensuring that political changes do not hinder the development of globally competent business leaders.

A Call to Action: Rethinking the Role of Business Schools in a Globalized World

As management education continues to evolve, business schools must redefine what it means to be 'global'. Rather than simply providing opportunities for travel, they should focus on embedding internationalization into every aspect of the learning experience—from curriculum design to faculty development to student engagement.

The future of business leadership does not belong to those who can recite best practices from Western corporations but to those who can adapt, collaborate, and innovate across cultural and economic boundaries. Schools that integrate cultural intelligence, sustainability, and ethical decision-making into their internationalization strategies will not only produce more employable graduates but will also contribute to the development of more responsible, globally minded business leaders.

Ultimately, true internationalization is not about how many countries a school has partnerships with, but about how deeply those partnerships impact the way students think, learn, and lead. For business schools looking to remain relevant in the twenty-first century, the challenge is clear: move beyond symbolic gestures and embrace a model of internationalization that is immersive, integrated, and truly transformative.

NOTES

1. See the ESCP Business School website at https://escp.eu/history.
2. See the programme information page at https://www.insead.edu/master-programmes/global-executive-mba.
3. Such as those at the University of Applied Sciences and Arts, Northwestern Switzerland; see https://www.fhnw.ch/en/degree-programmes/business/virtual-exchange.
4. See examples of global classrooms at Drexel University at https://drexel.edu/global/student-programs/global-classrooms/.

REFERENCES

Drexel University. (n.d.). 'The Importance of Diversity & Multicultural Awareness in Education'. School of Education. https://drexel.edu/soe/resources/student-teaching/advice/importance-of-cultural-diversity-in-classroom/#:~:text=Students0Better%20Prepared%20for%20a%20Diverse,%20them%20up%20to%20flourish%20in%20the%20workforce.

Frei, F. X., & Hajim, C. (2001). 'Rapid Rewards at Southwest Airlines'. Harvard Business School. https://hbsp.harvard.edu/product/602065-PDF-ENG?Ntt=southwest%20airlines.

El Garah, W., Naudé, P., & Osbaldeston, M. (2023). 'An Emerging Market Perspective on the Internationalisation of Business Schools'. *Global Focus: The EFMD Business*

Magazine, 16 January. https://globalfocusmagazine.com/an-emerging-market-perspective-on-the-internationalisation-of-business-schools/.
Holoien, D. S. (2013). 'Do Differences Make a Difference? The Effects of Diversity on Learning, Intergroup Outcomes, and Civic Engagement'. Princeton University. chrome-extension://efaidnbmnnnibpcajpcglclefindmkaj/https://inclusive.princeton.edu/sites/g/files/toruqf7151/files/pu-report-diversity-outcomes.pdf.
INSEAD. (2023). 'Global Strategy'. Course syllabus. chrome-extension://efaidnbmnnnibpcajpcglclefindmkaj/https://www.insead.edu/system/files/2023-11/2420-P5-MBA_Course%20outline%20Global%20Strategy_Nov2023.pdf?aad=BAhJIkR7InR5cGUiOiJpc3N1ZXIiLCJ1cmwiOiJodHRwczovL3d3dy5pbnNlYWQuZWR1LyIsImlkIjozNzA5MDMyOH0GOgZFVA%3D%3D%E2%80%94038eba244eb6653736ab3b581d5a63faced1c888.
Mullins, S. (2021). 'It's Important for Business Schools to Have International Links No Matter Where They Call Home'. *EFMD Global Blog*, 18 August. https://blog.efmdglobal.org/2021/08/18/its-important-for-business-schools-to-have-international-links-no-matter-where-they-call-home/.
Rock, D., & Grant, H. (2016). 'Why Diverse Teams Are Smarter'. *Harvard Business Review*, 4 November. https://hbr.org/2016/11/why-diverse-teams-are-smarter.
Smith, R. (2020). 'A Business School Disrupted: A View from Singapore'. *Global Focus: The EFMD Business Magazine*, 2 June. https://globalfocusmagazine.com/a-business-school-disrupted-a-view-from-singapore/.

13

Academic Institutions and Peacebuilding

ELOÏC-ANIL PEYRACHE

Nearly a decade ago, Steve Schwarzman, in explaining his substantial investment to establish the Schwarzman College at Tsinghua University, articulated a profound vision: he anticipated rising tensions between the West and China and sought to mitigate these challenges through education. By bringing talented individuals from around the globe to study at Tsinghua University, he aimed to foster enduring relationships with future leaders in China. His hope was that in times of escalating conflict these connections would serve as bridges for dialogue and understanding, contributing to global peace. This initiative underscores one dimension of the transformative role that higher educational institutions can play in peacebuilding—nurturing networks of mutual trust and collaboration across cultures and borders.

This kind of reflection naturally finds its place in a book devoted to the rise of uncertainty in global business. Indeed, since John Maynard Keynes' seminal work in 1919, numerous studies have demonstrated that the rise of uncertainty in business is frequently synonymous with social tensions and possibly war. This is due to the fact that it places actors in economic and social contexts that they are unable to control, that are anxiety-provoking for them, and that lead them to behave aggressively in ways that support their states' warmongering.

In light of these findings, management education holds particular pertinence in two distinct domains. Firstly, management education can provide players with the necessary tools to understand and navigate the complexities of the world. This in turn can reduce their anxiety levels and, consequently, mitigate aggressive behaviours. Furthermore, management

Eloïc-Anil Peyrache, *Academic Institutions and Peacebuilding.* In: *Management Education and the Rise of Uncertainty of Global Business.* Edited by: Eric Cornuel, Oxford University Press. © Oxford University Press (2025).
DOI: 10.1093/9780197794470.003.0014

education empowers individuals to make informed decisions and implement effective actions to mitigate uncertainty, thereby fostering an environment conducive to peacebuilding. Moreover, by integrating peacebuilding into their curricula, business schools can train leaders capable of anticipating conflict, fostering constructive dialogue, and building sustainable economic ecosystems.

In a world where uncertainty is becoming the norm, peacebuilding transcends its traditional role to become a cornerstone of effective and ethical management, consolidating the role of business schools as catalysts for share prosperity, stability, and innovation in the global landscape. The question of academic institutions and peacebuilding is thus consubstantial with that of management education in the face of rising uncertainty.

The relationship between education and conflict is not a new concept. However, as Millican (2017) observes, much of the existing research has focused on primary and secondary education (Smith & Vaux, 2003; McGlynn et al., 2009) or the broader societal role of universities (Stoecker & Beckman, 2010). Some work has been done on the responsibility of higher education in insecure environments. For instance, Milton (2013) explored how universities could play a significant role in peacebuilding and reconstruction in Iraq and Libya, noting that 'higher education has been the neglected pillar of recovery'. However, these studies often focus on conflict zones, leaving underexplored the broader potential of academic institutions in fostering peace both locally and globally.

THE DUALITY OF BUSINESS AND SOCIETY

If society is on fire, there is no business and if there is no business then society will be on fire. Societal unrest, whether driven by war or inequality, poses a direct threat to the viability of business operations. In regions plagued by conflict, businesses face disrupted supply chains, diminished consumer confidence, and volatile markets. Prolonged conflicts in Syria have devastated local economies, forcing businesses to shut down and discouraging foreign investment. Similarly, social unrest, as witnessed in South Africa during episodes of widespread protests, can lead to property destruction, loss of revenue, and heightened uncertainty.

Environmental crises provide another stark example. The devastating floods in Pakistan in 2022 displaced millions and destroyed infrastructure, significantly impacting local businesses. Supply chains were disrupted, and consumer markets shrank as affected populations prioritized survival over consumption. This underscores the vulnerability of business operations to broader societal instability.

Political instability also creates significant challenges. In countries such as Myanmar, ongoing political upheaval has resulted in sanctions, capital flight, and the withdrawal of foreign companies, further exacerbating economic hardship. These examples illustrate that businesses cannot thrive in environments marked by systemic instability.

The ripple effects of societal instability extend beyond immediate disruptions. Political and social upheaval often erode institutional trust, weaken governance, and dismantle the rule of law—all foundational elements for business operations. Without these, markets cannot function effectively, and economic growth stagnates. As inequality rises globally and fragmentation intensifies, risks of escalating conflicts and social riots increase. The conflict in Ukraine and the Yellow Vests movement in France exemplify this trend. For businesses, fostering societal stability becomes not just a moral imperative but a strategic necessity for survival and growth.

If There Is No Business, Society Will Be on Fire

Conversely, businesses are essential for maintaining societal stability and promoting peacebuilding (see Nelson 2000; Fort & Schipani 2007). By creating jobs, generating wealth, and fostering innovation, they provide the economic backbone that supports social order. Economic activity offers individuals livelihoods, purpose, and a sense of belonging, which are critical for preventing unrest. When businesses fail or economies collapse, the resulting unemployment, inequality, and disenfranchisement can ignite social tensions and lead to conflict. Historical examples illustrate this dynamic vividly. During the Great Depression, widespread unemployment and economic hardship fuelled social and political unrest across the globe, creating fertile ground for extremist ideologies. Similarly, the 2008 global financial crisis demonstrated how economic downturns can lead to widespread discontent. The Occupy Wall Street movement in the United States and anti-austerity protests in Europe highlighted the deep frustrations of societies grappling with unemployment and inequality. In contemporary settings, the collapse of major industries in Detroit in the US resulted in economic decline and urban decay, with significant social consequences, including increased crime rates and population outflow. On the other hand, initiatives like Germany's Mittelstand, a network of small and medium-sized enterprises, have demonstrated how robust business ecosystems can sustain social cohesion by creating stable jobs and fostering community resilience.

As analysed by Joseph et al. (2022), there are multiple domains of interactions between organizations and its environment. Business interact with institutions and inclusive institutions are central to peacebuilding (see Acemoglu & Robinson, 2012). Companies can advocate for trade policies between countries and regions that foster economic interdependence among conflicting groups, thereby promoting the inclusion of previously marginalised communities in economic activities (Golan-Nadir & Cohen, 2017; Hayward & Magennis, 2014).

In addition to their economic contributions, businesses play a cultural and symbolic role in uniting communities. By championing inclusive practices, fostering innovation, and supporting initiatives that address shared challenges, businesses can build bridges across divides. For instance, multinational corporations operating in post-conflict regions often invest in local capacity-building and cross-community collaboration, helping to rebuild trust and promote reconciliation. Businesses can supply essential goods, services and technologies as part of their normal operations in order to alleviate the effects of conflict on communities (Alger, 2007; Martin, 2011, Boyle & Boguslaw, 2007). Business operations encompass a network of stakeholders collaborating in profit-driven activities, creating opportunities for businesses to foster inclusive economic partnerships that reduce inequality and strengthen intergroup cohesion (Ghimire & Upreti, 2012; Joseph & Van Buren, 2022; Ganson et al., 2022).

THE ROLE OF ACADEMIC INSTITUTIONS IN ADDRESSING THE DUALITY

Watson (2007) outlined three overarching theories regarding the purpose of higher education. First, higher education institutions aim to foster social mobility and drive societal improvement for the greater good. Second, they are viewed as hubs for professional development, equipping individuals with expertise and vocational identities to cultivate the next generation of informed citizens and skilled professionals. Finally, higher education functions as research engines aligned with regional and national economic ambitions, contributing to business growth and serving as a source of national pride. If Bourner (2008) also identifies the same central roles of higher education, his critique highlights that historically, one of these roles often dominates at the expense of the others. He stresses the need for balance among these three roles, as overemphasizing one can marginalize the others. He advocates for an integrated approach where teaching, research, and societal service mutually reinforce each other, ensuring that universities remain relevant and impactful across all dimensions of their mission.

The dual dependency between business and societal stability places a significant responsibility on business schools and higher education as a whole. This chapter aims to highlight the various dimensions within these central roles that contribute to a more peaceful environment, addressing both local societal cohesion and global peacebuilding efforts.

Academic Research: A Foundation for Social and Global Peace

In a world increasingly marked by conflict, inequality, and environmental crises, the role of academic research in fostering social and global peace cannot be overstated. However, recent trends have highlighted challenges that must be addressed to fully realize the potential of academic research as a force for good. During COVID-19 pandemic, Algan et al. (2021) examined how trust levels influenced public support across 12 countries. They found that trust in scientists was a critical determinant of societies' resilience in combating the pandemic. The study also highlighted that in countries where trust in government was low, the independence of scientists and scientific institutions became essential to secure public support for health measures. This underscores the importance of maintaining and fostering trust in scientific communities, especially during health crises, to ensure effective public health responses. This erosion of trust is compounded by perceptions that knowledge serves as a tool of domination by one social class over another, further alienating sections of society from the one who have selective academic degrees (see Sandel, 2020).

Additionally, the rise of social media has created a landscape of overwhelming information and widespread distortion of facts and truths. Studies on social media, for instance, have highlighted its dual potential to both exacerbate conflicts through the spread of misinformation and promote dialogue by connecting diverse communities (Howard & Hussain, 2013). Research into the impact of digital technologies has illuminated how misinformation undermines public trust and fosters division. In such an environment there is an urgent need for reliable, evidence-based insights to counter misinformation and guide informed decision-making. Academic research, with its commitment to rigor and objectivity, is uniquely positioned to address these challenges and contribute meaningfully to the promotion of peace.

This section explores several critical dimensions through which academic research promotes peace, including understanding societal issues, providing evidence-based data, developing implementable solutions, and influencing decision-makers.

Understanding the Challenges and Moving Beyond Intuition

One of the most fundamental contributions of academic research is its capacity to deepen our understanding of the underlying causes and dynamics of social and global tensions. It is distinguished by its reliance on rigorous methodologies to produce reliable and actionable data. One of the pressing challenges in contemporary research is the sheer volume of unstructured data now available, particularly from digital platforms and social media. Decision-makers often lack the tools or expertise to manage and interpret these data sets effectively. Researchers play a pivotal role in cleaning, organizing, and analysing these unstructured data to uncover patterns and trends that are otherwise hidden.

For instance, studies have explored the psychological and sociological roots of anger and fear that lead to societal unrest, revealing how economic insecurity, political polarization, and cultural alienation create conditions ripe for conflict (see Fisher, 2020). Algan and Renault (2024) suggests that emotions, especially anger, play a substantial role in shaping public opinion and political preferences in France. The rise of the 'emotional voter' underscores the importance of understanding the emotional underpinnings of political engagement and the potential implications for democratic processes. Finally, research into historical events such as the Arab Spring highlights how a combination of economic hardship, lack of political freedom, and social media-fuelled anger sparked widespread uprisings (Howard & Hussain, 2013).

Similarly, research on historical patterns of violence and reconciliation provides critical insights. Johan Galtung's framework of structural violence demonstrates how inequalities embedded within societal systems, such as education and healthcare access, perpetuate long-term conflict (Galtung, 1996). Alesina and Perotti (1996) demonstrated that inequality significantly increases the likelihood of social unrest and political instability by undermining social cohesion. Quantitative studies on income inequality and its links to crime rates have also demonstrated the significant role of economic disparities in fuelling social tensions (Wilkinson & Pickett, 2010). Research on gender inequality has shown that empowering women leads to more stable and peaceful societies, underscoring the importance of addressing these interconnected issues (Hudson et al., 2012).

Economic research has also shed light on the connections between global trade, environment and peace. The *capitalist peace theory* (Gartzke, 2007) suggests that economic interdependence through trade reduces the likelihood of war, as countries with strong economic ties have more to lose in a conflict. Martin, Mayer, and Thoenig (2008) empirically validated this theory by showing that trade relationships between countries decrease the probability of interstate conflicts, emphasizing the importance of fostering global economic cooperation. Homer-Dixon (1994) have demonstrated how climate change exacerbates resource scarcity, leading to disputes over water, arable land, and other essentials. Such conflicts are particularly evident in regions like the Sahel in Africa, where desertification has intensified competition among communities.

These insights challenge oversimplified narratives and promote policies grounded in empirical evidence, fostering sustainable peacebuilding efforts. This ability to bring clarity and insight to overwhelming amounts of information underscores the indispensable role of academic research in making sense of complex global challenges. Understanding these underlying conditions enables academics and policymakers to preemptively address triggers of violence, fostering environments more conducive to peace.

Developing Implementable Solutions and Influencing Decision-Makers

One of the key challenges faced by universities, particularly business schools, is ensuring that the insights and innovations produced through academic research extend beyond the confines of academia and influence broader society. While the primary focus of many institutions has historically been on publishing in academic journals, there is a growing recognition of the need to valorize research in ways that make it accessible and actionable for policymakers, practitioners, and the public.

Business schools, in particular, have demonstrated the transformative potential of research in addressing societal challenges. Michael E. Porter's framework on shared value has been adopted by major corporations. Similarly, Richard Thaler's research on behavioural economics, particularly his work on nudge theory, has had a profound impact on public policy and Schwab's advocacy for balancing the interests of shareholders with those of employees, customers, and society has significantly influenced global business agendas, pushing companies towards more sustainable and inclusive practices. Beyond these seminal examples, a growing body of work has explored the economic underpinnings of conflict and the role of corporations in fostering peace. For example, studies on supply chain resilience in conflict zones have highlighted how businesses can mitigate risks while promoting stability (see Tang, 2006). Research conducted by the United Nations Global Compact and academic institutions has examined how corporate social responsibility initiatives in post-conflict regions, such as Rwanda, have supported reconciliation and economic recovery. Similarly, research on microfinance in conflict-affected areas, such as Afghanistan, demonstrates how access to capital can empower marginalised communities, reduce economic grievances, and foster long-term peace.

More generally, academic research has played a pivotal role in the development of restorative justice frameworks, which have been shown to reduce recidivism and promote reconciliation in deeply divided societies (Braithwaite, 2002). Restorative justice practices have been implemented successfully in post-apartheid South Africa, where community-driven reconciliation programmes were instrumental in addressing the legacy of racial segregation and violence. In public health, studies on conflict-sensitive healthcare delivery models demonstrate how equitable access to services can de-escalate tensions in post-conflict zones (MacQueen et al., 2001). Another notable example is research into urban planning as a tool for peacebuilding. Studies have shown that inclusive urban designs that prioritize shared public spaces and equitable housing policies can reduce segregation and foster community cohesion. In Colombia, initiatives based on such research have transformed conflict-ridden neighbourhoods into vibrant communities by improving infrastructure and creating opportunities for economic development (Moser & McIlwaine, 2014). Additionally, academic research has informed programmes addressing the reintegration of former combatants into civilian life. Studies on disarmament, demobilization, and reintegration processes have provided actionable insights into how economic incentives, psychological support, and community involvement can facilitate successful transitions.

To maximize its impact, academic research must bridge the gap between knowledge production and policy implementation. A significant risk is that research output remains confined to academic circles, written in jargon and formats that are inaccessible to policymakers, practitioners, and the broader public. Consequently, research must extend beyond publication and researchers achieve this by engaging with policymakers, disseminating findings through accessible platforms, and participating in advisory roles. For instance, work on the economic benefits of investing in peace initiatives has influenced international funding priorities, such as those of the United Nations Peacebuilding Fund (UNPBF, 2016). Furthermore, collaborations between academia and organizations like the World Bank and the OECD have advanced policies that address structural inequalities, reduce corruption, and enhance governance (Collier, 2007). By framing their findings in ways that resonate with decision-makers, academics ensure that research informs actions at local, national, and global levels.

Academic research is indispensable in the quest for social and global peace. By deepening our understanding of societal challenges, providing hard data, developing implementable solutions, and influencing decision-makers, research serves as a powerful tool for addressing the root causes of conflict and fostering harmony.

Education: Promoter of Peace

Education is one of the most powerful tools for fostering social stability and global peace. Beyond its traditional role of knowledge dissemination, education shapes the mindset, skills, and values of future leaders, equipping them to navigate the complexities of societal stability and the interplay between business and peace. Institutions of higher education, especially business schools, have evolved into multicultural hubs, bringing together individuals from diverse nationalities and backgrounds. These environments play a critical role in building bridges, fostering mutual understanding, and preparing students to contribute positively to society. This section explores the multifaceted impact of education on peace, focusing on curriculum design, leadership development, and the unique role of universities as intercultural spaces.

Equipping Students with Knowledge and Tools

An essential aspect of education's role in promoting peace lies in the content of what students learn. Curricula that integrate studies on conflict resolution, ethics, and global citizenship prepare students to understand and address the root causes of societal instability. For example, business schools that incorporate modules on corporate social responsibility and sustainable development empower students to align profit motives with societal well-being (Moon, 2007). Similarly, interdisciplinary courses that combine political science, sociology, and environmental studies equip students to analyse and navigate complex global challenges, such as climate change and migration, which are often linked to conflict (Homer-Dixon, 1994). Numerous programmes on ethics and leadership in global contexts encourage students to reflect on the broader implications of their actions in business and governance. This awareness fosters a sense of responsibility, enabling students to make decisions that align with societal well-being.

A particularly significant development in recent years has been the growing emphasis on Business and Human Rights within academic curricula. Programmes such as those at the Geneva Academy of International Humanitarian Law and Human Rights or HEC Paris offer specialized courses equipping students with the knowledge to address issues like labour rights violations, environmental degradation, and community displacement caused by business operations (Ruggie, 2011). Through experiential projects, they immerse students in real-world cases of corporate malfeasance, teaching them to craft actionable solutions based on international norms.

Additionally, there is a growing focus on the purpose of business as a subject of academic inquiry, particularly at institutions like HEC Paris. By integrating discussions on the evolving role of business in society, courses encourage students to challenge traditional notions of profit maximisation and explore how companies can create value for multiple stakeholders. For example, case studies on purpose-driven companies like Patagonia and Danone are used to demonstrate how businesses can balance profitability with social and environmental impact, inspiring students to rethink the fundamental objectives of business and promote shared prosperity.

Further, experiential learning opportunities like the Model United Nations offer students a platform to engage directly with global governance issues, honing their negotiation and problem-solving skills. By combining practical exercises with theoretical learning, universities ensure that students are equipped not only with knowledge but also with the ability to apply it effectively in real-world contexts.

Developing Solutions-Oriented Mindset and Leadership Skills

Education is not just about imparting knowledge; it is also about shaping the mindset and leadership qualities of students. Universities play a pivotal role in cultivating values such as empathy, resilience, and ethical decision-making, which are essential for peacebuilding. Leadership programmes that emphasise collaborative problem-solving and cultural intelligence prepare students to lead diverse teams and mediate conflicts effectively.

For instance, the University for Peace, established by the United Nations, offers specialized programmes in peace education and conflict transformation, focusing on leadership development. These programmes foster a deep understanding of nonviolent communication and consensus-building, enabling graduates to mediate disputes and promote harmony in various contexts. Additionally, initiatives such as Harvard's Leadership for Sustainable Development Program encourage students to adopt a systems-thinking approach, equipping them to address the interconnected nature of modern challenges.

Similarly, Stanford University's Design for Extreme Affordability programme challenges students to create solutions for real-world problems in developing regions. By collaborating across disciplines, students learn to address complex issues with innovation and compassion, embodying the principles of leadership for social impact. These programmes highlight how education fosters a mindset that prioritizes collective well-being over individual gains, reinforcing the foundation of peace-oriented leadership.

Platforms for Intercultural Dialogue

One of the most unique contributions of business schools to peace is their role as intercultural spaces. Modern campuses often host students from over a hundred different nationalities, creating opportunities for dialogue and mutual understanding that transcend cultural and national boundaries. By bringing together individuals from diverse backgrounds, they foster environments where prejudices can be dismantled and collaborative relationships can flourish. A meta-analysis by Pettigrew and Tropp (2006) demonstrates that positive contact between diverse groups reduces prejudice and fosters harmonious relationships.

The impact of this cultural diversity extends beyond the classroom. Research has shown that exposure to diverse perspectives during higher education significantly enhances students' openness and tolerance (Chang, 1999). Erasmus+, one of the largest student exchange programmes in the world, exemplifies how international academic mobility can foster peace. According to a study conducted by the European Commission (2019), Erasmus+ participants report increased cultural awareness, empathy, and adaptability—qualities that are essential for fostering peaceful coexistence. Students who participate in such programmes are more likely to engage in intercultural dialogue and build long-term connections across borders. Bilateral partnerships and collaborations between universities in different countries also amplify the impact of intercultural dialogue. Joint degree programmes, such as those offered by Yale University and HEC Paris, integrate diverse perspectives into academic curricula, preparing students to navigate and lead in a globalized world. These initiatives underscore the critical role of universities in building bridges rather than dykes, fostering collaboration, and equipping students to address the complexities of a multicultural society.

Moreover, universities at large often act as microcosms of global society, where students experience the benefits and challenges of diversity. Interactions with peers from different cultures enable students to develop critical skills such as cross-cultural communication, conflict resolution, and global citizenship. In Oxford's Refugee Scholars Programme, students from conflict-affected regions collaborate with peers in research projects addressing global issues, promoting both academic enrichment and mutual understanding. The Imagine Fellows programme at HEC Paris offer scholarships to talents from war-torn countries and engage students from all over the world on peacebuilding initiatives. The Global Village initiative at Rotterdam School of Management invites students from around the world to share their cultural heritage through food, art, and storytelling, creating a celebratory atmosphere of diversity and inclusion. Such events provide a foundation for empathy and help dismantle stereotypes.

Academic Institutions: Platforms for Shared Prosperity

Universities have always been recognized as spaces for knowledge creation and transmission, but their role extends beyond these traditional functions. As active institutions embedded in society, universities influence social structures, drive innovation, and empower individuals and communities. This section explores the multifaceted ways in which business schools contribute to societal progress, including promoting social mobility, fostering entrepreneurship, and creating platforms for collaborative problem-solving.

Promoting Social Mobility

As countries become more economically divided, social mobility emerges as a cornerstone for sustaining social peace within nations. Beyond their educational mission, academic institutions have the ability to change destinies by promoting social mobility, fostering inclusion, and addressing systemic inequalities. They provide individuals from underprivileged backgrounds with the skills and qualifications necessary to access opportunities that might otherwise remain out of reach. Studies have consistently shown that higher education reduces income inequality and enhances upward social mobility (Chetty et al., 2017). For example, initiatives like the First-Generation College Program at the University of California, Berkeley or the Equal Opportunity Program from HEC Paris specifically target students from marginalized communities, providing them with financial aid, mentorship, and academic support to ensure their success.

By opening doors to opportunities that might otherwise remain inaccessible, they empower individuals to transcend socio-economic barriers, thereby contributing to a more equitable and harmonious society. By doing so, they play a pivotal role in enabling upward mobility by equipping students from diverse socio-economic backgrounds with the skills and networks needed to thrive in competitive markets. But beyond granting access to higher education, academic institutions play a crucial role in inspiring ambition among youth from underprivileged areas. By engaging directly with schools and communities, they can shift perceptions about what is achievable and help students realize their potential. Programmes like the Aim High initiative at King's College London work with secondary school students from underrepresented backgrounds to raise their aspirations. The Bridge to College programme at the University of Chicago partners with local high schools to offer preparatory courses, ensuring that students from disadvantaged neighbourhoods are equipped to succeed academically. These initiatives involve mentoring, campus visits, and tailored workshops that encourage students to envision themselves as future university graduates. All these programmes help young individuals understand that they are talented and capable of thriving in academic environments. They also create a supportive pathway that helps students navigate the application process and overcome systemic barriers.

Finally, scholarships and affirmative action policies further democratize access to education. Programmes like the Rhodes, Mastercard, or Laidlaw Scholarships have enabled talented students from low-income countries to study at prestigious institutions, equipping them to become leaders in their respective fields. These initiatives demonstrate how universities actively address systemic barriers, fostering greater inclusivity and equity in society.

Fostering Entrepreneurship for Social Impact

In addition to promoting traditional career paths, business schools are increasingly leveraging entrepreneurship as means to promote social mobility and foster peacebuilding. Entrepreneurship programmes provide individuals, particularly those from underprivileged regions, with the tools and resources to create their own opportunities. For instance, the Massachusetts Institute of Technology's Global Startup Labs empower students from emerging economies to develop business ideas and connect with investors, fostering economic development and innovation. The HEC StandUp Program for vulnerable Women aims to address systemic barriers faced by women in starting and scaling businesses by providing them with essential tools, resources, and support networks.

University incubators and accelerators also play a crucial role in this ecosystem. Initiatives like the Social Entrepreneurship Accelerator at Duke University support ventures aimed at addressing societal challenges, such as poverty alleviation and healthcare accessibility. These programmes not only provide funding and mentorship but also facilitate access to networks that are essential for scaling impact-driven businesses. By fostering entrepreneurial mindsets, business schools empower individuals to drive change in their communities and beyond.

Research underscores the transformative role of entrepreneurship in peacebuilding. A review by Joseph, Katsos, and Van Buren (2023) highlights several dimensions through which entrepreneurship contributes to peace. For instance, entrepreneurship can effectively reintegrate previously violent actors back into society, providing them with livelihoods that disincentivize violence (Gündüz et al., 2006). Programmes in post-conflict regions have successfully facilitated the reintegration of ex-combatants by equipping them with business skills and resources to start small enterprises. This approach not only promotes reconciliation but also builds shared identities among members of groups that were previously in conflict (Tobias et al., 2013). Entrepreneurship also fosters a sense of shared purpose and collaboration, particularly in regions with deep-seated divisions. Initiatives that bring together individuals from different backgrounds to co-create businesses not only produce economic benefits but also help dismantle prejudices and foster mutual respect. For instance, joint entrepreneurial ventures in Northern Ireland have been instrumental in bridging divides between Catholic and Protestant communities, illustrating the potential of business to unite historically conflicting groups (Joseph et al., 2023).

Organizing Controversial Discourses and Transmitting Democratic Values

A critical yet often understated role of universities is their capacity to serve as platforms for controversial discourse and the transmission of democratic values. Universities are among the few institutions that actively encourage the exchange of diverse viewpoints, even when these viewpoints challenge prevailing societal norms. This openness to debate and dissent is fundamental to democracy.

Academic freedom ensures that scholars and students can explore contentious issues without fear of censorship or retaliation. For instance, universities frequently organize debates and panel discussions on topics like climate change, systemic racism, and economic inequality, bringing together experts and stakeholders with opposing views. These events foster critical thinking, expose participants to multiple perspectives, and cultivate a culture of respectful dialogue.

Programmes like the Deliberative Democracy Lab at Stanford University exemplify how universities can actively engage communities in democratic processes. By organizing citizen assemblies and public forums, such initiatives empower individuals to deliberate on complex policy issues, fostering a sense of shared responsibility and civic engagement. Similarly, the Free Speech and Open Inquiry initiative at the University of Chicago underscores the importance of protecting freedom of expression while maintaining a respectful and inclusive academic environment.

The impact of these efforts extends beyond the university campus. Graduates who have been exposed to democratic values and practices often become advocates for justice and equity in their professional and personal lives. In this way, universities contribute to the cultivation of a more informed, engaged, and equitable society.

Creating Collaborative Ecosystems for Problem-Solving

Another significant contribution of universities is their role in creating ecosystems that bring together diverse stakeholders to tackle complex challenges. Academic institutions serve as platforms where academics, industry leaders, policymakers, and community members converge to co-create solutions. These collaborative efforts harness the complementary strengths of various actors, fostering innovation and driving progress.

There are several impactful initiatives that exemplify how universities can leverage their resources and academic expertise to address pressing social issues and serve as catalysts for peacebuilding within their communities. Stanford University's D School has become a hub for design thinking, facilitating interdisciplinary collaboration to address issues ranging from urban planning to public health. Similarly, the University of Cambridge's Global Challenges Initiative brings together experts from different fields to address pressing global issues such as climate change and food security. The Programme for a Peaceful City at the University of Bradford, established in response to Bradford's history of ethnic and social tensions, promotes dialogue, mutual understanding, and conflict resolution among its multicultural population. By creating forums for conversation and collaboration across religious, ethnic, and socio-economic divides, it has become a platform for fostering trust and building a peaceful urban environment. The Detroit Revitalization Initiative led by Wayne State University demonstrate how universities can catalyse economic renewal in struggling regions by fostering entrepreneurship, providing workforce training and supporting community projects.

CONCLUSION

This chapter has highlighted the transformative potential of academic institutions, particularly in the context of business education, to contribute to peacebuilding at both local and global levels. Education can serve as a powerful force for fostering societal cohesion and global understanding, equipping future leaders with the tools and awareness needed to address the complexities of our interconnected world. However, it is equally important to acknowledge that academic institutions can, under certain circumstances, exacerbate social tensions and conflicts. The literature provides examples where education has deepened divisions, particularly when access to education is uneven or when curricula reinforce biases and inequalities (see Smith & Vaux, 2003; McGlynn et al., 2009). These risks underscore the need for vigilance in ensuring that higher education serves as an agent of inclusion and reconciliation rather than division.

Moreover, the political context surrounding higher education can significantly influence its delivery and impact. As Plantan (2002) and Millican (2017) have observed, higher education institutions often operate within politically charged environments, where external pressures can compromise their autonomy and effectiveness. In some cases, political interference can distort the educational mission, favouring propaganda or exclusionary practices over critical inquiry and inclusivity. These challenges highlight the importance of safeguarding academic freedom and ensuring that universities maintain their commitment to universal values of equity, inclusion, and dialogue.

The framework proposed by Bourner (2008) remains particularly relevant in addressing these challenges. Bourner's identification of the three central roles of academic institutions—educating students, advancing knowledge through research, and serving broader society—underscores the need for balance. In a world marked by growing global fragmentation and local social tensions, these roles are not only complementary but essential for fostering a more peaceful environment. Universities must educate students to navigate cultural and societal complexities, produce research that addresses root causes of conflict, and engage with communities to promote equity and understanding.

Ultimately, higher education is both a reflection of and a contributor to societal dynamics. By fully embracing their potential as hubs for dialogue, innovation, and inclusion, academic institutions can play a pivotal role in shaping a more harmonious and sustainable future. However, this requires a conscious commitment to balancing their roles, resisting external pressures that threaten their mission, and continually striving to be catalysts for positive change in an increasingly divided world.

REFERENCES

Acemoglu, D., & Robinson, J. (2012). *Why Nations Fail: The Origins of Power, Prosperity and Poverty*. Crown.

Alesina, A., & Perotti, R. (1996). 'Income Distribution, Political Instability, and Investment'. *European Economic Review*, 40/6, 1203–1228.

Algan, Y., Cohen, D., Davoine, E., Foucault, M., & Stantcheva, S. (2021). 'Trust in Scientists in Times of Pandemic: Panel Evidence from 12 Countries'. *Proceedings of the National Academy of Sciences*, 118/40, 1–8.

Algan, Y., & Renault, T. (2024). La France sous nos tweets: portait d'une France en colère et de ses conséquences politiques. Notes de l'Observatoire du bien-être 2409, CEPREMAP.

Alger, C. F. (2007). 'There Are Peacebuilding Tasks for Everybody'. *International Studies Review*, 9, 534–554.

Bourner, T. (2008). 'The Fully Functioning University'. *Higher Education Review*, 40/2, 3–23.

Boyle, M. E., & Boguslaw, J. (2007). 'Business, Poverty and Corporate Citizenship: Naming the Issues and Framing Solutions'. *Journal of Corporate Citizenship*, 26, 101–120.

Braithwaite, J. (2002). *Restorative Justice and Responsive Regulation*. Oxford University Press.

Chang, M. J. (1999). 'Does Racial Diversity Matter? The Educational Impact of a Racially Diverse Undergraduate Population'. *Journal of College Student Development*, 40/4, 377–395.

Chetty, R., Friedman, J. N., Saez, E., Turner, N., & Yagan, D. (2017). 'Mobility Report Cards: The Role of Colleges in Intergenerational Mobility'. National Bureau of Economic Research.

Collier, P. (2007). *The Bottom Billion: Why the Poorest Countries Are Failing and What Can Be Done About It*. Oxford University Press.

Fisher, M. (2020). 'The Rise of Anger and Fear in Society: A Global Perspective'. *Journal of Social Psychology*, 12/4, 345–360.

Fort, T. L., & Schipani, C. (2007). 'An Action Plan for the Role of Business in Fostering Peace'. *American Business Law Journal*, 44/2, 359–377.

European Commission. (2019). *Erasmus+ Higher Education Impact Study*. https://op.europa.eu/en/publication-detail/-/publication/94d97f5c-7ae2-11e9-9f05-01aa75ed71a1/language-en.

Galtung, J. (1996). *Peace by Peaceful Means: Peace and Conflict, Development and Civilization*. Sage Publications.

Gartzke, E. (2007). 'The Capitalist Peace'. *American Journal of Political Science*, 51/1, 166–191.

Ganson, B., He, T. L., & Henisz, W. J. (2022). 'Business and Peace: The Impact of Firm–Stakeholder Relational Strategies on Conflict Risk'. *Academy of Management Review*, 47, 259–281.

Ghimire, S., & Upreti, B. R. (2012). 'Corporate Engagement for Conflict Transformation: Conceptualising the Business-Peace Interface'. *Journal of Conflict Transformation & Security*, 2, 77–100.

Golan-Nadir, N., & Cohen, N. (2017). 'The Role of Individual Agents in Promoting Peace Processes: Business People and Policy Entrepreneurship in the Israeli–Palestinian Conflict'. *Policy Studies*, 38, 21–38.

Gündüz, C., Killick, N., & Banfield, J. (2006). *Local Business, Local Peace: The Peacebuilding Potential of the Domestic Private Sector*. International Alert.

Hayward, K., & Magennis, E. (2014). 'The Business of Building Peace: Private Sector Cooperation Across the Irish Border'. *Irish Political Studies*, 29, 154–175.
Homer-Dixon, T. (1994). 'Environmental Scarcities and Violent Conflict: Evidence from Cases'. *International Security*, 19/1, 5–40.
Howard, P. N., & Hussain, M. M. (2013). *Democracy's Fourth Wave? Digital Media and the Arab Spring*. Oxford University Press.
Hudson, V. M., Ballif-Spanvill, B., Caprioli, M., & Emmett, C. F. (2012). *Sex and World Peace*. Columbia University Press.
Jay J., Maon F., Uribe-Jaramillo M. T., Katsos J. E., & Lindgreen A. (2024). 'Business, Conflict, and Peace: A Systematic Literature Review and Conceptual Framework'. *Journal of Management Studies*, 62/4, 1779–1810.
Joseph, J., Katsos, J. E., & Van Buren, H. J. (2022). 'Entrepreneurship and Peacebuilding: A Review and Synthesis'. *Business & Society*, 62, 322–362.
Joseph, J., & Van Buren, H. J. (2022). 'Entrepreneurship, Conflict, and Peace: The Role of Inclusion and Value Creation'. *Business & Society*, 61/6, 1558–1593.
MacQueen, G., Santa-Barbara, J., & Neufeld, V. (2001). 'Health and Human Security: The Medical Peace Work Approach'. *Medicine, Conflict, and Survival*, 17/4, 306–320.
Martin, M. (2011). 'Conflicted Corporates: Rethinking the Role of Business in Global Security'. *Global Policy*, 3, 35–45.
Martin, P., Mayer, T., & Thoenig, M. (2008). 'Make Trade Not War?' *Review of Economic Studies*, 75/3, 865–900.
McGlynn, C., Zembylas, M., Bekerman, Z., & Gallagher, T., eds. (2009). *Peace Education in Conflict and Post-Conflict Societies: Comparative Perspectives*. Palgrave MacMillan.
Millican, J. (2017). *Universities and Conflict: The Role of Higher Education in Peacebuilding and Resistance*. Routledge.
Milton, S. (2013). 'The Neglected Pillar of Recovery: A Study of Higher Education in Post-war Iraq and Libya'. PhD Thesis. University of York.
Moon, J. (2007). 'The Contribution of Corporate Social Responsibility to Sustainable Development'. *Sustainable Development Journal*, 15/5, 296–306.
Moser, C. N. O., & McIlwaine, C. (2014). 'New Frontiers in Twenty-First Century Urban Conflict and Violence'. *Environment and Urbanization*, 26/2, 331–344.
Nelson, J. (2000). *The Business of Peace: The Private Sector as a Partner in Conflict Prevention and Resolution*. Prince of Wales Business Leaders Forum.
Pettigrew, T. F., & Tropp, L. R. (2006). 'A Meta-Analytic Test of Intergroup Contact Theory'. *Journal of Personality and Social Psychology*, 90/5, 751–783.
Plantan, F. (2002). *Education in Ethics and Civics and Social Commitment in University Students*. Steering Committee for Higher Education and Research.
Ruggie, J. G. (2011). 'Guiding Principles on Business and Human Rights: Implementing the United Nations "Protect, Respect and Remedy" Framework'. UN Office of the High Commissioner for Human Rights.
Sandel, M. J. (2020). *The Tyranny of Merit: What's Become of the Common Good?* Farrar, Straus and Giroux.
Smith, A., & Vaux, T. (2003). *Education, Conflict and International Development*. Department for International Development.
Stoecker, R., & Beckman, M. (2010). 'Making Higher Education Civic Engagement Matter in the Community'. Retrieved from compact.org/news/making-higher-education-civic-engagement-matter-in-the-community/9748.

Tang, C. S. (2006). 'Perspectives in Supply Chain Risk Management'. *International Journal of Production Economics*, 103/2, 451–488.
Tobias, J. M., Mair, J., & Barbosa-Leiker, C. (2013). 'Peace Through Entrepreneurship: An Emergent Mechanism of Change'. *Academy of Management Perspectives*, 27/3, 241–252.
UNPBF (2016). *United Nations Peacebuilding Fund: Annual Report*. United Nations.
Watson, D. (2007). 'Does Higher Education Need a Hippocratic Oath?'. *Higher Education Quarterly*, 61/3, 362–374.
Wilkinson, R., & Pickett, K. (2010). *The Spirit Level: Why Greater Equality Makes Societies Stronger*. Bloomsbury Press.

INDEX

For the benefit of digital users, indexed terms that span two pages (e.g., 52–53) may, on occasion, appear on only one of those pages.

Tables and Figures are indicated by *t* or *f* following the page number.

AACSB *see* Association to Advance Collegiate Schools of Business (AACSB)
academic alliances, 64, 86–87, 123
academic consortia, 86, 149
academic institutions *see* higher education institutions (HEIs)
academic joint ventures, 86
academic labour market, 20–22, 25–29
academic networks *see* networks
academic research *see* research
accessibility, 45, 47–50, 104–105
accreditation of business schools, 26, 61, 150–151
ACE *see* American Council on Education (ACE)
adaptability of business schools, 182–183, 189–190
administration, 153, 162
AI *see* artificial intelligence (AI)
alliances, academic, 64, 86–87, 123
alumni empowerment, 157
American Council on Education (ACE), 84–85
  Model for Comprehensive Internationalization, 87
Aniagu, Ozioma, 76–77
applied research, 30, 141
artificial intelligence (AI), 53, 126–127, 130–132, 140
Asia-Pacific, 23–24, 28
Association to Advance Collegiate Schools of Business (AACSB), 26, 68, 91–93, 150–151
AUC *see* School of Business, American University Cairo (Egypt)
Australia, 23, 114–115, 116–117
automotive industry, 126–127
autonomy, education for, 168–169
awards, 68

Beelen, Jos, 43–46
Belgium, 58–60, 64
'belonging' concept, 78
BlackRock, 71–72
Brinkerhoff, Tad, 74, 76
B-schools *see* business schools
business
  culture courses, 167–168
  diversity in practice, 182–183
  duality with society, 196–209
  internationalization, 42
business schools
  adaptation and lifelong learning, 189–190
  evolution of, 149
  forces for and against change, 110–111
  and globalization, 20–21, 136–137
  internationalization *see* business schools internationalization
  isomorphism, 108–109, 112–114, 118
  legitimacy, 108–110, 113–118
  and local relevance, 59–61
  or management schools, 147–148
  markets, 30–33, 30*f*, 95
  platforms for shared prosperity, 206–209
  and uncertainty, 14–15, 140–141, 165–167

values, 147
business schools internationalization
case studies, 184–186
definition, 20–21, 84–86
and global approach, 191, 193
and globalization, 61–62, 149–150
historical context, 181–183
and local relevance, 58–59, 63–65
meaning of, 61, 180–181
pushback, 192
strategies *see* internationalization strategies

campuses abroad, 86, 146
Canada, 70, 115–116
capitalism, 165
capitalist peace theory, 200–201
career development
and faculty internationalization, 35–37
of MBA programme graduates, 68–70, 74
Caribbean, 45
Carnegie Mellon University, 69, 72–74
Accelerate Leadership Center (ALC), 77–79
Graduate Business Association, 79
MBA programmes, 71
Tepper School of Business *see* Tepper School of Business
Carney, Mark, 147
case studies, 160, 184–186
CEIBS *see* China Europe International Business School (CEIBS)
CEMS *see* Global Alliance in Management Education (CEMS)
China, 24, 155
China Europe International Business School (CEIBS), 150, 155–163
Europe Forum, 157
CIBERS (Centers for International Business Education and Research) programme, 42, 43–45*t*
classrooms
diversity, 188
global, 187
learning technologies, 49, 187
in US business schools, 68
climate change, 200–201
COIL *see* collaborative online learning (COIL)
collaboration
academic, 86
facilitated by technology, 187
global, 129–130
interdisciplinary, 129
and internationalization, 54
and problem-solving, 209
and regional partners, 132–134
and role of industry, 126–128, 129–130
collaborative online learning (COIL), 46, 96
community connections, 51, 59–60, 101–102, 198, 202
companies
large, 137–138, 140–141
top global, 138–139
complexity, 10–15
'comprehensive internationalization,' 84–85
conformity, 2–3, 109
consensus
lack of in business schools, 176–178
and uncertainty, 178
consortia, 86, 149
corporate influence market, 30, 32–33, 30*f*
Corporate Knights' Better World MBA Ranking, 172
corporate sponsorship, 74–75
COVID-19 pandemic
and academic labour market, 21–22
and digital learning, 63
impact on education, 41–42
impact on internationalization, 46–47, 48, 49–50, 83–84, 88–91, 104–105*f*
impact on society, 7
impact on urban planning, 8
lessons from, 102–106
and questioning of internationalization, 15
response to, 94–99
scholarly literature, 40
school strategies for dealing with, 99–102
crises, and capitalism, 165
cultural differences, 24–25*f*, 45–46, 77–78, 79–80, 167–168, 205–206

curricula
challenges posed by lack of consensus, 176–178
change in topics, 13
design, 154
and humanities, 10
and inclusivity, 184
and peacebuilding role, 203–204
UNESCO topics, 13, 110

Data Science Institute, TUM Campus Heilbronn, 122, 124, 127
decision-making
executive, 159
influencing with academic research, 201–203
response to COVID-19 pandemic, 98
and strategies, 99–100, 109
Delp, Lyenda, 71–72
deterministic approaches, 16–17
dialogic principle, 11–12
Dieter Schwarz Foundation, 121, 127
Campus Founders programme, 127
digital innovation
challenges of, 47
and internationalization, 15, 47, 52–53, 63, 154, 186–187
response to COVID-19 pandemic, 95–96
strategies in COVID-19 pandemic, 100–101
discourses, platforms for controversial, 208–209
distant modes, 96, 102
diversity *see also* cultural differences
in business practice, 182–183
in faculty, 160
in internationalization, 144
of international students, 78
and platforms for dialogue, 205–206
power of, 188–189
in recruitment, 154
diversity, equity, and inclusion (DEI), 192
diversity, equity, inclusion and belonging (DEIB), 78
double degree programmes, 145–146
Duale Hochschule Baden-Württemberg (DHBW), 133
dual schools, 86
Duke University, Social Entrepreneurship Accelerator, 207–208

EAESP *see* Escola de Administração de Empresas de São Paulo da Fundação Getulio Vargas (EAESP FGV) (Brazil)
ecological considerations of COVID-19 pandemic, 104
economics, 3–4
economic system, 136–137
EFMD *see* European Foundation for Management Development (EFMD)
EIASM *see* European Institute for Advanced Studies in Management (EIASM)
elite business schools/institutions, 28
'embeddedness,' 3
emerging markets, 15
'end of history,' 14
English language, 181
entrepreneurship, 76–77, 127–128, 207–208
environmental, social, and governance (ESG) concepts, 142–143, 158
environmental crises, 196
Erasmus+, 36, 205
Escola de Administração de Empresas de São Paulo da Fundação Getulio Vargas (EAESP FGV) (Brazil), 91–93*t*, 94–95, 96–98
ESG *see* environmental, social, and governance (ESG) concepts
ethics, 153–154
Europe
developments against faculty internationalization, 27–30
drivers of faculty internationalization, 22–27
faculty internationalization, 20–22, 37
faculty models, 30–33
increase in faculty internationalization, 23
MBA programmes, 70
European Foundation for Management Development (EFMD)
EQUIS standards, 26, 51–52, 61, 87–88, 109, 114, 150–154, 155–158, 162–163
mission, 2–3, 4–5
sustainability, 172

European Higher Education Area, 25
European Institute for Advanced Studies in Management (EIASM), 33–34
European Quality Improvement System (EQUIS) standards, 26, 51–52, 61, 87–88, 109, 114, 150–154, 155–158, 162–163
European Recovery Program, 60
European Tertiary Registration Register, 22–23
European Union
  faculty internationalization, 28–29
  'financial gap,' 138–139
  free movement of workers, 25
  SMEs, 138–139
  top global companies, 138–139
Europe Forum, 157
exchange networks, 145, 147, 157, 187
executive education, 153, 160
Executive MBA (EMBA) programmes, 145–146

faculty
  average share of national and international, 24–25*f*
  development, 154, 184
  developments against internationalization, 27–30
  diversity, 160
  drivers of internationalization, 22–27
  and EQUIS standards, 152, 156
  in European business schools, 20–22, 37
  markets, 30, 32–33, 30*f*
  recruitment, 33–34, 97, 161
  staff mobility, 46
  strategic implications in managing, 33–37
  support, 97–98
  values, 30–33
  well-being, 96, 101–102
failure, and complexity, 13
Ferdinand Steinbeis Institute, 133–134
financial intermediaries, 143
financial resources, 141–143, 153, 162
Financial Times
  Global MBA ranking, 26, 72, 85
  Master's in Management (MiM) ranking, 22–23–24*f*, 24–25*f*
  rankings of business schools, 61
financial wealth, global, 141–143
flexibility
  career development, 35–36
  learning options, 190
FOME alliance *see* Future of Management Education (FOME) alliance
forecast-planning-execution sequence, 13–14
Fortune 500 companies, 66
France, 24–25, 59–60, 138, 177
Fraunhofer Society, 133–134
Future of Management Education (FOME) alliance, 64

Gaza, war in, 177
GDP
  global, 141
  and public debt, 137–138
gender inequality, 200
general culture courses, 167–168
geopolitics, 103–104, 140, 161
Germany, 121–122, 138
Global Alliance in Management Education (CEMS), 141, 145–147, 149
global classrooms, 187
global companies, 138–139, 140–141
global financial wealth, 141–143
global GDP, 141
globalization
  of business, 14
  of business schools, 20–21, 61–62, 136–137, 140–141, 149–150
  and complexity, 13–14
Global Network for Advanced Management (GNAM), 145, 147
global networks, 86
'glocal,' 62, 65, 182
GMAC *see* Graduate Management Admission Council (GMAC)
GNAM *see* Global Network for Advanced Management (GNAM)
governance, 159
government sponsorship, 74–75
Graduate Management Admission Council (GMAC), 68–69, 171
Great Depression, 197
growth, pursuit of, 4
Gustavson School of Business *see* Peter B. Gustavson School of Business, University of Victoria (Canada)

Harvard Business School, 177
HEC Paris, 204
  Imagine Fellow, 205–206
  StandUp Program for vulnerable Women, 207
higher education institutions (HEIs)
  before COVID-19 pandemic, 42–47
  and duality between society and business, 198–209
  and faculty internationalization, 22–23
  impact of COVID-19 pandemic, 41–42
  lessons from COVID-19 pandemic, 104–106
  platforms for shared prosperity, 206–209
  potential for peacebuilding, 195–196, 210
  purpose, 198
  response to uncertainty, 140–141
  as source of revenue, 68
  and technology, 52
history
  'end of', 14
  of internationalization, 181–183
  meaning of, 6, 16–18
Hochschule Heilbronn, 133–134
Hult Prize, 171–172
humanities, 10
human rights, 203–204
hybrid education, 15, 96

IaH *see* internationalization at home (IaH)
IAU *see* International Association of Universities (IAU)
'illiberal' movements, 177
immigration, 66, 70, 115–117
Imperial College Business School (UK), 91–93*t*, 93, 96–98
inclusion
  development of through IaH, 53
  and internationalization, 47–50, 54, 183–184
  of international students, 78
  power of, 188–189
income inequality, 200, 206
India, 24
Indonesia, 74
Indonesia Endowment Fund for Education (LPDP), 74
industry
  collaboration, 126–128, 129–130
  policy, 137–138
  system, 139
innovation, 109–110, 128–130
innovation ecosystems
  in Germany, 121–122, 134–135
  role of industry, 126–128
  role of Innovation Park Artificial Intelligence (IPAI), 130–132
  role of TUM Campus Heilbronn, 122–126
Innovation Park Artificial Intelligence (IPAI), 130–132
INSEAD, 185–186
International Association of Universities (IAU), Global Surveys on Internationalization in Higher Education (3rd), 43–46
internationalization
  of business schools *see* business schools internationalization
  definition, 20–21
  framework for evaluating in higher education, 87–88
  future research, 54
  meaning of, 54
  potential derailment factors, 161–162
internationalization at home (IaH), 40–41, 43–46, 51–53, 86
internationalization strategies
  of business schools, 42–43–45*t*, 86, 114–118, 167–168
  competitive, 109
  definition, 109
  finding balance, 108–110
  and MBA programmes, 67, 75–80
  models in business schools, 144–147
  recruitment, 33–37
  response to COVID-19 pandemic, 94–99
  specialization, 171–172, 173–176, 178
  success and derailment factors, 158–159–162–163*t*
  successful case studies, 184–186
  as a trend, 15, 18
international students
  benefits, 72

cultural differences, 24–25*f*, 45–46, 77–78, 79–80, 167–168, 205–206
entrepreneurship, 76–77
growth of, 114–117
and inclusion, 78, 184, 189
international experiences, 79–80
MBA programmes, 66–67, 68–71, 80
recruitment, 75–76, 96–97, 122–123
well-being, 77
investments, 100–101, 142
Ireland, 138
isomorphism in business schools, 108–109, 112–113_P24, 118
Italy, 138–139

Japan, 74
joint degree programmes, 205
joint ventures, academic, 86

Kapadia, Kalpesh, 70–71
King's College London, Aim High initiative, 206–207
Korea, 74

labour market, in business schools, 20–22, 25–29
language, 34, 181
large companies, 137–138, 140–141
Latin America, 45, 49
leadership
programmes, 204–205
thought, 30, 30*f*, 156–157
legitimacy
challenges to business school, 108–110
definition, 111–112
and geopolitics, 114–118
organizational, 111–113, 114–115
lifelong learning, 189–190
LinkedIn, 69
local relevance
in business environments, 182
of business schools, 58–62, 65
and innovation, 130
through an international lens, 63–64
location, of business schools, 62, 144
long-term investments, 142
LPDP *see* Indonesia Endowment Fund for Education (LPDP)
Luxembourg, 138

Major, David L., 78
management, concept of, 148
management education *see* business schools
management schools, or business schools, 147–148
Marshall Plan, 60
Massachusetts Institute of Technology, Global Startup Labs, 207
Master of Business Administration (MBA) programmes *see also* study programmes
career development, 74
Carnegie Mellon University, 71
case study for internationalization, 75–80
challenges of online education, 47
emergence of specialized, 174–176
Executive MBA (EMBA) programmes, 145–146
Global MBA ranking, 26, 72, 85
reasons for internationalization, 71–75
salaries, 68–69
specialization, 174
in US, 66–71, 80
'meaning of history,' 6, 16–18
Memphis State University, 43
microfinance, 201–202
Mittelstand, 197
Morin, Edgar, 8, 10–12
multi-campus schools, 86, 185–186
Myanmar, 197

Netherlands, 28–29, 32–33, 58–59, 138
networks
academic, 34–35
exchange, 145, 147, 157, 187
global, 86
impact of COVID-19 pandemic, 47
New Zealand, 115
Nisai Group, 171–172
Nobel Prize, 68
non-executive governance, 159
Northern Ireland, 208

on-campus model, 63, 104
Onetto, Marc, 72–73
online education *see* digital innovation

organizational legitimacy, 111–113, 114–115
overseas campuses, 86, 146

Pakistan, 196
Partnership in International Management (PIM), 145
partnerships
academic, 86
global, 123–124, 154
lessons from COVID-19 pandemic, 103–104
reciprocal recruitment, 33–34
response to COVID-19 pandemic, 95
peacebuilding
and higher educational institutions, 195–196
potential for, 210
role of academic research, 199–203
role of entrepreneurship, 208
through education, 203–206
Peter B. Gustavson School of Business, University of Victoria (Canada), 91–93*t*, 93, 96–98
PhD programmes, 68
political context
and faculty internationalization, 29–30
instability, 197
and peacebuilding role, 210
risks of international students, 70
Portugal, 24–25
problem-solving, 209
public debt, 137–138
public health, 202
public institutions, 143

QUT Faculty of Business and Law, Queensland University of Technology (Australia), 91–93*t*, 94, 96–100

rankings
business schools, 144
Corporate Knights' Better World MBA Ranking, 172
Financial Times, 22–23–24*f*, 24–25*f*, 26, 61, 72, 85
IaH, 43–46
university, 72
real-world issues, 15
recruitment
diversity, 154
faculty, 33–34, 97, 161
international students, 75–76, 96–97, 122–123
partnerships, 33–34
regional partners, 132–134, 157
research
applied, 30, 141
and EQUIS standards, 152, 156
partnerships, 123–124
role in peacebuilding, 199–203
in US business schools, 68
resources, 153
responsibility, 153–154, 203–204
restorative justice frameworks, 202
retention, 36–37, 161
'rising uncertainty,' 7–10, 17, 172–173
risk capital investment, 142
Rotterdam School of Management, Global Village, 205–206
Russia, 48–49

salaries of MBA graduates, 68–69
Sasin School of Management, 181, 191
Action Learning Labs, 184–186
scholarly literature, 40–41
scholarships, 207
school, concept of, 147–148
School of Business, American University Cairo (Egypt), 91–93*t*, 95, 97–99
Schwarzman, Steve, 195
Schwarzman College, Tsinghua University, 195
scientific approach, 3, 8–9
Sino-European exchanges, 157
sister schools, 86
SKEMA Business School, France, 91–93*t*, 96–98
skills and professions, 169
SMEs, 138–139
social consensus, 176
social media, 199
social mobility, 206–207
society
duality with business, 196–198
duality with business and role of higher education institutions, 198–209
fostering entrepreneurship, 207–208
instability, 203–204
responsibility, 190
unrest, 196–197, 200

soft skills, 53, 190
solutions-oriented mindset, 204–205
Southern Illinois University, 43
Spain, 24–25, 138
specialization
  challenges posed by, 176–178
  emergence of programmes, 174–176
  shift to approach of, 173–174
  strategy of, 171–172, 173–176, 178
sponsorship, 74–75
stakeholders, 112, 154
standardization, 181
Stanford University
  Deliberative Democracy Lab, 209
  D School, 209
startups, 127–128
state control, 138–139
strategies *see* internationalization strategies
students
  accessibility, 45, 47–50, 104–105
  changing expectations, 170–172
  demand, 172–173
  and EQUIS standards, 152
  impact of COVID-19 pandemic, 41, 46, 48, 96, 101–102
  and inclusion, 184
  markets, 30, 32–33, 30*f*
  virtual student mobility (VSM), 47
  well-being, 96–97
study programmes *see also* Master of Business Administration (MBA) programmes
  culture courses, 167–168
  double degree programmes, 145–146
  and EQUIS standards, 151
  executive education, 160
  for innovation ecosystems, 124–126
  innovative offerings, 160
  joint degree programmes, 205
  lack of consensus, 176–178
  leadership, 204–205
  specialization, 174–176
  study abroad courses, 79–80
  virtual exchange, 187
support
  faculty, 97–98
  legislative and financial, 52–53
sustainability, 153–154, 158, 171–172, 190
Sveriges Riksbank Prize in Economic Sciences in Memory of Alfred Nobel 2015-2023, 68
Switzerland, 25
Syria, 196

Technical University of Munich (TUM), 121, 128
technology
  accessibility and inclusion, 50
  impact of COVID-19 pandemic, 41–42, 49
  and internationalization, 15, 52, 54
  meeting global challenges, 169
  role of, 186–188
Tepper School of Business, 68–69, 70–71, 75–80
  Business English and Cultural Immersion (BECI) Summer Program, 75–76
Terray, Lionel, *Les Conquérants de l'inutile (The Conquerors of the Useless)*, 1–2
thought leadership, 30–33, 30*f*, 156–157
trade connections, 200–201
transdisciplinary approach, 9–11, 14–15
trust, 199
Tsinghua University, 195
TUM Campus Heilbronn
  building global research partnerships, 123–124
  collaboration and regional partners, 132–134
  enabling innovation, 128–130
  establishment of, 121–122
  and innovation ecosystems, 122–126, 134–135
  nurturing startups and entrepreneurship, 127–128
  recruitment, 122–123
  role of artificial intelligence, 130–132
  role of industry collaboration, 126–128
  study programmes for innovation ecosystems, 124–126
TUM School of Computation, Information and Technology, 122, 125
TUM School of Management, 122, 124
TUM Venture Lab, 127–128

uncertainty
change brought about by global, 14–15
in geopolitics, 161
induced by institutional change, 4–5
and lack of consensus, 178
meeting the challenges of, 165–167
response of higher education, 140–141
response to COVID-19 pandemic, 140–141
response to in management education, 6
rising, 7–10, 17, 172–173
transdisciplinary approach, 9–11
UNESCO, 13, 47
Institute for Information Technologies, 171–172
United Kingdom, 24, 28, 86, 116
United Nations, University for Peace, 204
United States
business schools, 68, 181–182, 192
faculty internationalization, 23
impact of COVID-19 pandemic, 49
MBA programmes, 66–75, 80
PhD programmes, 68
political risks impact, 70
United States Department of State, EducationUSA network, 74
United States News and World Report, Best Business Schools, 72
universalism, 178
universities *see* business schools; higher education institutions (HEIs)
Universities Canada, international students, 115
University of Bradford, Programme for a Peaceful City, 209
University of Cambridge, Global Challenges Initiative, 209
University of Chicago
Bridge to College programme, 206–207
Free Speech and Open Inquiry initiative, 209
University of Oxford, Refugee Scholars Programme, 205–206
University of Victoria, 98
univocal approach, 3–4
UnternehmerTUM, 128
urban planning, 8, 202

values
connecting with, 142–143, 147
faculty, 30–33
transmitting democratic, 208–209
violence, 200
virtual learning
classrooms, 187
communities, 53
exchange programmes, 46, 187
guest speakers, 52
visiting scholars, 52
virtual student mobility (VSM), concept, 47
visiting scholars, virtual, 52
Vlerick, André, 60
Vlerick Business School, 60–61, 64

Wayne State University, Detroit Revitalization Initiative, 209
well-being
faculty, 96, 101–102
international students, 77
students, 96–97
Wharton-INSEAD alliance, 33–34